The Special Needs Child and Divorce

Second Edition

A PRACTICAL GUIDE TO HANDLING AND EVALUATING CASES

Margaret "Pegi" S. Price

ABA
AMERICAN BAR ASSOCIATION
Family Law Section

Cover design by Monica Alejo

Printed in the United States of America.

26 25 24 23 22   5 4 3 2 1

A catalog record for this book is available from the Library of Congress.

Contents

CHAPTER 14
Checklists 275

Samples, forms, and checklists are available for download at https://ambar.org/SpecNeeds2e

Author's Note

This book is not focused on autism. It deals with many types of special needs. If any particular special needs have not been specifically addressed, it was not intentional. There are so many special needs and our knowledge base is constantly expanding about special needs. This book attempts to address special needs generally, with emphasis on some of the more prevalent types, and types that are currently not being addressed well when families go through divorce, paternity actions, and modifications of family court orders.

About the Author

The author, Margaret "Pegi" S. Price, JD, is a professor and lawyer. Before going into full-time academia, her practice was limited exclusively to the practice of family law—divorce, paternity, child support, custody and visitation, guardianships, and adoptions. Pegi is a past chair of the Family Law Section of the Bar Association of Metropolitan St. Louis and was a member of AFCC, the Association of Family and Conciliation Courts, and of the National Council on Family Relations (NCFR). Pegi has written many legal articles on family law and other topics. She presented a paper and was a speaker at the 2006 World Autism Congress in Cape Town, South Africa, on the subject of divorce and families with autism. Pegi has also spoken on the subject of divorce and families with autism at the National Conference of the Autism Society of America and at regional legal community conferences and seminars for educators and professionals in the special needs community.

She is a past president of the Gateway (St. Louis) chapter of the Autism Society of America and has done extensive lobbying of state government on behalf of families with special needs. Pegi is very involved in the special needs community, works with many individuals and families who have special needs, and does public speaking on this subject to increase awareness of special needs and spread a message of hope to families.

Her son was diagnosed with autism at age three (1998) and underwent intensive early intervention and therapy. Three years later, Pegi went through a divorce and wrote her first parenting plan involving serious special needs. Two years after the divorce (March 2003), her son emerged from autism. His story aired on NBC in February 2005 as one of the first children in the United States to emerge from autism. He is called a pioneer in the field of autism. His story was the subject of a feature on CW11, which filmed him at school and while flying an airplane. He flew airplanes for four years, beginning when he was ten years old.

Her son was 14 years old when the first edition of this book was published. He is now 27, and has a BA in theater, film, and digital production with a concentration in writing for the performing arts; an MFA in professional screenwriting; and is beginning his teaching career at a local college. Pegi hopes that sharing his story inspires attorneys, judges, and families to believe in what these children can do if we meet their special needs when their families go through divorce.

Although the author's experience has been primarily with autism, her experience spans many types of special needs. Her younger sister is disabled and required hours of daily physical therapy throughout childhood. Pegi has done a great deal of work with special needs children and adults, including working with cognitively challenged persons and teaching fine art to children and adults with vision loss.

Acknowledgments

In the years since the publication of the first edition, attorneys and families from all over the United States have reached out to me for guidance in their family law cases involving children with special needs. The legal profession has become more aware of the issues these cases involve, and judges are more willing to do what these families need rather than routinely using cookie-cutter charts and visitation schedules. I would like to acknowledge the families who never give up on their children, the lawyers who fight relentlessly for their clients, and the judges who have the courage to be a part of the progress this field needs. I have great optimism that the treasured members of our society who face life with greater challenges than some others have the possibility of a better future.

This book could not have been written without the help of many people. I consulted with more than 30 family court judges, 200 lawyers who specialize in family law, and 120 professionals who work with families going through divorce or with people who have special needs. Many of these people offered extremely helpful suggestions that helped shape this book. To list all of you would take pages, so thank you all. I deeply appreciate your help. In addition, particular individuals who should be acknowledged and thanked are Mickey LaFerla, Stuart Goldenberg, the Honorable Debra H. Lehrmann, Gail D. Baker, Linda Ravdin, Julie Roscoe, Joe Burcke, and everyone in my office. Thanks also to Elizabeth Diehl, MD, and Garrett Burris, MD; the Judevine Center for Autism; Kieran Coyne, who coauthored with me the parenting plan and separation agreement that were adapted for this book; and the focus group from the Juvenile and Family Court of St. Louis County, Missouri, consisting of Brian Seltzer, JD, MSW; Joyce Guleff, MS, LCSW; Mario Dollschnieder, PhD, LMFT; Robin Murray, JD; Kim Bay, BA, DJO; and Toni Bernotas, PhD, MBA.

Saving the best for last, thank you Sam, my son, the inspiration for this book.

Introduction

President John F. Kennedy said:

> When written in Chinese, the word crisis is composed of two characters. One represents danger and the other represents opportunity.[1]

The court system is overwhelmed when it comes to dealing with all the divorces, paternity cases, modifications, child custody, child visitation, and child support issues.[2] Despite the knowledge and experience of the judges and courthouse staff, the sheer volume and complexity of family law cases are beyond the level at which the current Family Court system is designed to function.[3] Approximately half of all marriages end in divorce.[4] Divorce affects more than one million children each year in the United States.[5] The current system is not set up to adequately address the unique needs inherent in cases involving children with special needs. The number of special needs children in the United States and throughout the world is skyrocketing.[6] When you add the burgeoning numbers of special needs cases to an already overwhelmed legal system, the situation approaches the level of crisis.

Fortunately, there are at least two ways to look at every situation. As John F. Kennedy stated, one is danger and one is opportunity. The danger is obvious. Families with special needs children have much higher divorce rates and much greater needs than those of families with typical children. As more and more children are diagnosed with special needs every year, this group is quickly growing. If their unique needs are not met when they go through the divorce process, a rapidly increasing segment of our society will be in crisis.

Another way to look at this situation is to see the opportunity to rework the existing system to better meet the needs of these unique members of society. This book attempts to do just that by looking at what special needs are, how they are relevant in the arena of divorce, and how we can make the system work better for these children and their families.

---

1. Speech, John F. Kennedy, April 12, 1959.
2. Schepard, A. (2002). Law schools and family court reform. *Family Court Review, 40*(4), 460–472.
3. Katz, S. (1994). Historical perspective and current trends in the legal process of divorce. *The Future of Children—Children and Divorce, 4*(1), 44–62.
4. Riley, G. (1997). *Divorce: An American tradition.* Lincoln, NE: University of Nebraska Press; Coates, B. (2004). *Divorce with decency: The complete how-to guide and survivor's guide to the legal, emotional, economic, and social issues.* Honolulu, HI: University of Hawaii Press.
5. Leslie, L., Rappo, P., Abelson, H., Jenkins, R., Sewall, S., & Chesney, R., et al. (2000). Final report of the FOPE II Pediatric Generalists of the Future Workgroup. *Pediatrics, 106*(5 Supp), 1199–1223.
6. Saposnek, D., Perryman, H., Berkow, J., & Ellsworth, S. (2005). Special needs children in family court cases. *Family Court Review, 43*(4), 566–581.

CHAPTER 1

What Are Special Needs?

Sometimes it seems as though everyone has a diagnosis of some sort. If you cannot claim something that has an acronym as your label, you are not in the club. The perceived overuse of labels and diagnoses can cause us to become desensitized to the importance of some diagnoses when it comes to divorce cases. When do these things rise to the level of affecting divorce and other family law cases?

In 1998 the Maternal and Child Health Bureau published a new definition of children with special health care needs (CSHCN) as those "children who have or are at increased risk for chronic physical, developmental, behavioral, or emotional condition and who also require health and related services of a type or amount beyond that required by children generally."[1] It is well established that raising a special needs child causes great stress on marriages and other romantic relationships.[2]

This impact on relationships has been described as "one moment, you and your lover are singing along in bad Italian with Venetians in a crowded bar . . . red wine pouring out of nowhere. And the next minute, the two of you are filling out disability forms for your tiny son."[3] It is little wonder that most marriages do not survive this type of jolt.[4]

Divorce rates in families with special needs children have been estimated to be between 85 and 90 percent.[5] The stress level within families raising special needs children is extremely high.[6] It has been estimated that up to 31 percent of children under 18 years old, or nearly 20 million children in the United States, have special health

1. McPherson, M., Arango, P., Fox, H., Lauver, C., Newacheck, P. W., Perrin, J. M., Shonkoff, J. P., & Strickland, B. (1998). A new definition of children with special health care needs. *Pediatrics, 102*, 137–140; cited in P. Newacheck, J. Rising, & S. Kim (2006), Children at risk for special health care needs, *Pediatrics, 118*(1), 334–342.

2. Brown, C., Goodman, S., & Kupper, L. (2003). The unplanned journey: When you learn that your child has a disability. *News Digest 20* (3rd ed.). http://www.nichcy.org/pubs/newsdig/nd20txt.htm.

3. *Id.*

4. Hodapp, R., & Krasner, D. (1994). Families of children with disabilities: Findings from a national sample of eighth-grade students, *Exceptionality, 5*(2), 71–81.

5. Kraus, M. (2005). Planning is important even when life doesn't go the way we plan. *Family Court Review, 43*(4), 607–611.

6. Kazak, A. (1986). Families with physically handicapped children: Social ecology and family systems. *Family Process, 25*(2), 265–281.

needs—and 30 percent of these children have two or more special health needs.[7] It is important to understand the types of special needs[8] and how they can affect a family law case when a relationship does break down.

I. LEGISLATION REGARDING DISABILITIES

Before beginning an in-depth discussion of how these special needs situations can affect a divorce or other family law case, it is helpful to have an overview of the legislation that currently exists in the subject area of disabilities. Please note that none of this legislation directly addresses the issue of special needs and the family courts. The two primary areas of law that have applied to the subject area of disabilities are title V of the Social Security Act[9] and the Individuals with Disabilities Education and Improvement Act (IDEA) of 2004.[10]

Title V of the Social Security Act authorizes grants-in-aid to states for health programs for mothers and children (title V, part 1) that include crippled children (title V, part 2) and welfare services for children (title V, part 3). Title V of the Social Security Act was passed in the 1930s.[11] Additional federal legislation since that time has provided additional health care benefits for mothers and children.[12] Health care programs, not the family courts, are the focus of these statutes.

The Individuals with Disabilities Education Improvement Act (IDEA) of 1997, amended in 2004,[13] is intended to ensure that all children with disabilities receive a free appropriate public education, with specially designed instruction provided at no cost to the parents, tailored to meet the individual needs of a child with a disability.[14] Education, not the family court system, is the focus of this legislation.

While these federal legislative programs provide much-needed health care and educational supports for children with disabilities, no federal legislation protects these

---

7. Sneed, R., May, W., & Stencel, C. (2000). Training of pediatricians in care of physical disabilities in children with special health needs: Results of a two-state survey of practicing pediatricians and national resident training programs. *Pediatrics, 105*(3), 554–561.

8. McPherson, M., Arango, P., Fox, H., Lauver, C., McManus, M., Newacheck, P., Perrin, J. M., Shonkoff, J. P., & Strickland, B. (1998). Commentary: A new definition of children with special health care needs. *Pediatrics, 102*(1), 137–139.

9. 42 U.S.C. 7, subch. V §§ 701–710 (1989).

10. Pub. L. No. 108–446. Council on Children with Disabilities, Section on Developmental Behavioral Pediatrics, Bright Futures Steering Committee and Medical Home Initiatives for Children with Special Needs Project Advisory Committee. (2006). Identifying infants and young children with developmental disorders in the medical home: An algorithm for developmental surveillance and screening. *Pediatrics, 118*(1), 405–420.

11. van Dyck, P. (2003). A history of child health equity legislation in the United States. *Pediatrics, 112*(3), 727–730.

12. *Id.*

13. Pub. L. No. 108–446.

14. Karger, J., for National Center on Accessing the General Curriculum (NCAC). (n.d.). Access to the general curriculum for students with disabilities: A discussion of the interrelationship between IDEA '97 and NCLB; A Policy Paper for Educators and Families. U.S. Office of Special Education Programs.

National Center for Homeless Education (NCHE) at SERVE. (n.d.). Individuals with Disabilities Education Improvement Act (IDEA) of 2004 Provisions for Children and Youth with Disabilities Who Experience Homelessness. NCHE, P. O. Box 5367, Greensboro, NC 27435.

children when their families are going through divorce, paternity cases, and other family law cases. Further, the federal laws regarding health care and educational supports for children with disabilities each use different definitions for what constitutes a child with a disability. While this issue is complicated, it is vitally important to address the issue of special needs in family court cases.

A child's special needs may require tailoring the visitation schedule, parenting plan, child support amount, property distribution, and other factors that are often handled through a standard form, worksheet, or calculation. A child who cannot handle transitions well may need a parenting plan that involves fewer custody exchanges. A child who is receiving cancer treatment out of town may require more child support to help pay for uncovered out-of-network medical expenses, travel expenses, and the primary caregiver's time away from work to take the child to the treatments. A parent who has sacrificed her career to take care of a chronically ill child is no longer contributing to her 401(k) plan and will have greater financial need at the time of retirement. This may necessitate a greater portion of maintenance (alimony) or property distribution to this spouse. A child who will never be self-supporting or able to live independently will need support beyond the age at which child support usually terminates. Clearly, merely following the typical forms, worksheets, and calculations will not serve the needs of these families.

II. EVALUATING SPECIAL NEEDS IN FAMILY COURT CASES

There is a relatively simple approach to evaluating special needs in family court cases. First, we need to explore the situations in which a child's disability may be relevant in a family law case.

A child's disability may be relevant in family court cases when the child has (1) acute life-threatening medical conditions, (2) chronic developmental disorders, or (3) psychological or behavioral issues.[15] These situations may present as a child who is chronically or terminally ill; who is unlikely to be able to care for himself as an adult; who needs special therapy, medication, equipment, treatments, or other substantial modifications on a regular and ongoing basis; and/or who is at significant risk of harm to himself or others.

Sometimes a child has a condition or situation that is not an acute life-threatening medical condition, chronic developmental disorder, or psychological or behavioral issue yet may still warrant special attention in the family court case. Examples of these conditions or situations include when the individual child's condition is severe enough that special modifications are required for the child's best interests to be met during the processes of custody and visitation; when the child's condition or situation is such that the standard amount of child support will not be adequate; or when the child's situation affects the employment of one of the parents such that the parent (1) must reduce the hours he works, (2) must take a different job, (3) has his career negatively affected, and/or (4) has his pension or retirement negatively affected.

---

15. Saposnek, D., Perryman, H., Berkow, J., & Ellsworth, S. (2005). Special needs children in family court cases. *Family Court Review, 43*(4), 566–581.

A parent often must reduce her work hours to take care of a sick or disabled child, to take the child to therapy or treatments, and to handle crisis situations. With a child with significant special needs, it can be very difficult, if not impossible, for the primary caregiver parent to maintain full-time employment and provide the care the child needs. The caregiver parent often must take part-time status at work to avoid being fired completely. When the parent becomes a part-time employee, she also usually loses her health insurance, retirement, and other benefits. Often part-time employees are ineligible to participate in these benefits. These restrictions present a financial loss to this parent.

When caring for a child with significant special needs, a parent may have to take a different job. For example, a flight attendant, sales representative, or other person whose job involves travel may have to take a lower-paying job in order to stay local and take care of the child. To synchronize his or her work hours to the child's school and treatment or therapy schedule, a parent who worked shifts that do not synchronize with this schedule may have to take a different job. Work schedules that were workable with two parents raising the child out of the same home will often not work at all when there is only one parent living in the home with the child.

Changing jobs, changing shifts, decreasing hours, and not being available for overtime or extra projects can all negatively influence a parent's career. The parent may have the immediate impact of lower income than before—as well as fewer promotions, fewer raises, and less job security, all of which also negatively affect pension or retirement benefits. The parent may lose eligibility to participate in the employer's pension or retirement plans. Even if she is still allowed to participate, her rate of contribution will likely decrease, thus decreasing the amount of money she will have to live on when she retires. It may take more years for the parent to vest in her employer's pension or retirement plan when vesting is based on the number of hours worked.

A tricky area arises when there is no diagnosis yet, but perhaps there should be. Often a child has not yet been diagnosed with a special need at the time his parents start the divorce process. One reason for this is the difficulty of diagnosing some conditions until a child reaches a certain age or developmental stage. Another reason may be that the parents have a gut feeling that something is wrong, but they have not yet fully explored the problem and received a diagnosis. Another factor causing this situation is that the parents are too involved in their marital difficulties to fully appreciate the severity of the child's problem. Regardless of the reason for the lack of diagnosis, the lawyer can do a great service to the family and the child in sending the child for an evaluation, because early diagnosis and intervention are critical to a child's long-term prognosis.[16]

The lawyer should consider talking with her client and exploring the possibility of having the child evaluated for a special need when the following factors are present, or other factors that cause the lawyer to have concerns that more may be going on than is readily apparent:

---

16. Glass, N. (1999). Sure Start: The development of an early intervention programme for young children in the United Kingdom. *Children & Society, 13*(4), 257–264; McCabe, L., Therrell, B., & McCabe, E. (2002). Newborn screening: rationale for a comprehensive, fully integrated public health system. *Molecular Genetics and Metabolism, 77*(4), 267–273; Health Resources Services Administration, the American Academy of Pediatrics, et al. (2000). Serving the family from birth to the medical home: a report from the Newborn Screening Task Force convened in Washington, D.C., May 10–11, 1999. *Pediatrics*, 106 (2, Supp.), 383–427.

- *The child is having ongoing problems in school.* The child may have repeated discipline issues that are incorrectly treated as behavior issues when the true cause may be an undiagnosed special need. The child may be getting bad grades when he actually has a learning disability, a hearing impairment, or an undiagnosed chronic medical or psychiatric issue.
- *The child is having ongoing problems with law enforcement or other authority.* When a child has run-ins with the police, teachers, or school administrators, there may be an undiagnosed special need. The child might not be able to learn in the way in which the material is being taught at school, and she may feel frustrated or embarrassed, so she "acts out" to mask that frustration or embarrassment. If a child is being abused, she may behave in a manner that seems inappropriate to an adult who is unaware of the abuse.
- *The parents have difficulty "handling" the child.* A child who is hyperactive and has difficulty focusing or paying attention may have ADHD (attention deficit hyperactivity disorder). If this condition has not been diagnosed yet, the child might get punished for things he cannot help doing. A child who has sensory integration issues may refuse to eat all but four or five foods—not because he is trying to be demanding or difficult, but because he truly cannot tolerate the taste, texture, or feel of most foods due to a neurological condition. This child might frequently take off his clothes because he cannot tolerate the scratchy feeling of the seams or labels. He may have to turn away from the rest of the class because the visual stimuli are overwhelming. He may cover his ears and shriek uncontrollably because in a restaurant he can hear all the conversations at the same volume and cannot filter out the people at other tables.
- *The child is frequently sick or misses school.* Children with special needs are rarely diagnosed on the first day that their special need arrives. Often it takes a long time—months or even years—for the parents to figure out there is a problem, try to understand what the problem is, and find the proper medical specialists to diagnose and treat the child. Sometimes a child just says she does not feel well, but she cannot explain in more detail. She may have low energy for months, and then the parents will notice that she is drinking a lot of liquids, and she may become very ill before she is eventually diagnosed with diabetes. Sometimes people even think the child is faking illness when there has not yet been a diagnosis.
- *The parents or others express the concern that the child is not performing up to what others perceive as the child's abilities—that is, the child is underachieving.* When the parents or educators feel the child could be doing better in school, a closer look is warranted. If a child is underachieving due to a learning disability or processing issue, he may feel he is stupid and may then give up on getting good grades. Often the child's obstacles to meeting his potential can be overcome when a correct and accurate diagnosis is made, treatment commenced, and modifications put in place.
- *The child is not developing with her peers—this includes physical, emotional, academic, and skills development.* Parents tend to compare their children to other children. While all children develop at their own pace, a child whose development is significantly behind that of her peers—whether it be physical development, emotional development, or academic or skills development—deserves a closer look. If a child is significantly smaller than her peers and not growing at the same rate, she may have a metabolic, endocrine, or pituitary issue that can be treated. If she seems to still be in her "terrible twos" when she is eight years old, there may be a medical or psychological cause. If she cannot seem to grasp the basic academic concepts that her peers have mastered, whether the concepts are recognizing colors and animals or being able to read and do simple math, there may be an issue with learning or processing. If she cannot tie her shoes, eat with a spoon, write, do jumping jacks, or skip across the room, there may be fine or gross motor delay, neurological issues, or

other developmental issues that need to be explored. If a child is not developing socially, does not engage in typical play, and does not interact with other children, there may be a neurological issue such as autism—or there may be a psychological issue.

- *The client, lawyer, teacher, or a significant caregiver expresses the concern that "something is not quite right."* Sometimes it is merely a "gut feeling" that sends a child for an evaluation. A good professional will not make you feel stupid when you request an evaluation although you cannot list clear reasons or use the correct medical terminology. If you had all that information, you would be the medical professional. After you express your concerns as best you can, then the professionals should take it from there and do their jobs. Visual impairments, diabetes, and even brain tumors have been discovered in children when their parents simply knew something was wrong but did not know what it was.

These concerns must be balanced with the reality that it is difficult on children when their parents divorce.[17] Children often experience anger, fear, frustration, isolation, stomachaches, headaches, insomnia, loss of appetite, and emotional outbursts when their parents are going through divorce.[18]

Think of how difficult divorce can be on the adults going through the divorce. Now imagine being a child, and the two people you love the most are breaking up, perhaps yelling and fighting. You are scared and worried. Will you ever see your mom again? Will you ever see your dad again? Will one parent keep you from seeing your grandparents or cousins on the other parent's side? Why do they have to divorce? Was it your fault? If only you had been better behaved or gotten better grades or helped out more around the house or not broken that window or not gotten sick so much, maybe they would not be divorcing. Since they stopped loving each other, will they one day stop loving you too? If one of them gets married to someone else, will the new person be mean, or will they like you? Will your parents get so busy with their new boyfriend or girlfriend they have no time for you? Obviously, these deep and legitimate emotions can wreak havoc upon a child's psyche and even cause physical problems for the child.[19] If, after considering these factors, the lawyer feels there might be something else or something more involved, they should defer to the professionals and get the child evaluated.

III. CASE MANAGEMENT FOR THE COURTS

Upon identifying the case as one involving a special needs child, the courts should immediately put the case on a different track with a different timeline from typical family law cases.[20] The court needs time to properly gather sufficient information about the individual child's particular special needs and how these special needs should be addressed in the family law case. Failure to get sufficient information before entering even a temporary or short-term court order can have tragic and devastating effects.[21] Do not expect the litigants to present to the court all the information it needs to properly adjudicate these cases.

---

17. Committee on Psychosocial Aspects of Child and Family Health. (1999). American Academy of Pediatrics: The child in court: A subject review. *Pediatrics, 104*(5), 1145–1148.

18. *Id.*

19. *Id.*

20. Brown, Goodman, & Kupper, *supra* note 2.

21. *Id.*

Approximately 75 percent of family court litigants do not have a lawyer and are not adequately prepared for the initial hearing.[22] Divorce is extremely expensive, and many people simply cannot afford to hire a lawyer to represent them in court.[23]

A. What Types of Special Needs Can a Child Have?

Many of the same types of disabilities or special needs that should be evaluated and considered by the court as a factor in a divorce are the ones that the public education system considers as rendering a child eligible for special education services. The *Parents Guide to Special Education in Missouri* explains that the Individuals with Disabilities Education Act (IDEA) Part B and the Missouri State Plan list the following diagnoses as special needs that are eligible for special education services:

- **Autism** is a "developmental disability significantly affecting verbal or nonverbal communication and social interaction, generally evident before age 3, that adversely affects a child's educational performance. Other characteristics often associated with autism are engagement in repetitive activities and stereotyped movements, resistance to environmental change or change in daily routines, and unusual response to sensory experiences."[24]
- **Deafness/blindness** is a category for children with both visual and auditory impairments who cannot have their needs adequately met in special education programs for only one of the impairments.[25]
- **Emotional disturbance** is "a condition exhibiting one or more of the following characteristics over a long period of time and to a marked degree that adversely affects a child's educational performance:
    1. An inability to learn that cannot be explained by intellectual, sensory or health factors.
    2. An inability to build or maintain satisfactory interpersonal relationships with peers and teachers.
    3. Inappropriate types of behavior or feelings under normal circumstances.
    4. A general pervasive mood of unhappiness or depression.
    5. A tendency to develop physical symptoms or fears associated with personal or social problems."[26]
- **Hearing impairment or deafness.** Hearing impairment is an impairment in hearing that adversely affects the child's educational performance but is not as severe as deafness. Deafness is "a hearing impairment that is so severe that the child is impaired in processing linguistic information through hearing, with or without amplification, adversely affecting a child's educational performance."[27]
- **Mental retardation** is "significantly sub-average general intellectual functioning existing concurrently with deficits in adaptive behavior manifested through the developmental period that adversely affects a child's educational performance."[28]

---

22. *Id.*

23. S. Katz. (1994). Historical perspective and current trends in the legal process of divorce: The future of children. *Children and Divorce, 4*(1), 44–62.

24. Parent's Guide to Special Education in Missouri (2002). Missouri Department of Elementary and Secondary Education (Jefferson City, Missouri), p. 32.

25. *Id.*

26. *Id.* at 33.

27. *Id.*

28. *Id.*

- **Multiple disabilities** are defined as "concomitant impairments (such as mental retardation-blindness, mental retardation-orthopedic impairment, etc.) the combination of which causes such severe educational needs that the child cannot be accommodated in special education programs solely for one of the impairments. The term does not include deaf/blindness."[29]
- **Orthopedic impairment** must be severe enough to adversely affect the child's educational performance. This category includes "impairments caused by congenital anomaly (e.g., club foot, absence of some member, etc.) impairments caused by disease (poliomyelitis, bone tuberculosis, etc.) and impairments from other causes (e.g., cerebral palsy, amputations and fractures, or burns that cause contractures)."[30]
- **Other health impairment** is defined as "having limited strength, vitality or alertness, including a heightened alertness to environmental stimuli that results in limited alertness to the educational environment that is due to chronic or acute health problems, such as asthma, attention deficit disorder, or attention deficit hyperactivity disorder, diabetes, epilepsy, a heart condition, hemophilia, lead poisoning, leukemia, nephritis, rheumatic fever, and sickle cell anemia; and adversely affects a child's educational performance."[31]
- **Specific learning disability** involves "a disorder in one or more of the basic psychological processes involved in understanding or in using language, spoken or written, which may manifest itself in an imperfect ability to listen, think, speak, read, write, spell or do mathematical calculations. The term includes such conditions as perceptual disabilities, brain injury, minimal brain dysfunction, dyslexia, and developmental aphasia. The term does not include learning problems that are primarily the result of visual, hearing, or motor disabilities, of mental retardation, of emotional disturbance, or environmental, cultural or economic disadvantage."[32]
- **Speech or language impairment** is a communication disorder that adversely affects a child's educational performance. This can include such conditions as stuttering, impaired articulation, language impairment, or voice impairment.[33]
- **Traumatic brain injury (TBI)** is an "injury to the brain caused by an external physical force, resulting in total or partial functional disability or psychosocial impairment, or both, that adversely affects a child's education."[34] A traumatic brain injury may include open head injury or closed head injury and may result in impairment in one or more of the following areas: "cognition, language, memory, attention, reasoning, abstract thinking, judgment, problem solving, sensory, perceptual and motor abilities, psychological behavior, physical functions, information processing and speech."[35] It does not include brain injuries from birth trauma or brain injuries that are congenital or degenerative.[36]
- **Visual impairment/blindness** is an impairment of vision, including both partial sight and blindness, that—even with correction—adversely affects a child's education.[37]
- **Young child with developmental delay** is a category for a child age three to five years who has developmental delays in one or more of the following areas: "physical development, cognitive development, communication development, social or emotional

29. *Id.* at 34.
30. *Id.*
31. *Id.*
32. *Id.*
33. *Id.*
34. *Id.* at 35.
35. *Id.*
36. *Id.*
37. *Id.*

development or adaptive development; and who needs special education and related services."[38]

Of course, there may be diagnoses that do not appear in the preceding list that require special attention in a divorce case. Besides the categories discussed earlier, a child's special needs could fit into one or more of these categories:

- Infectious disease of chronic or ongoing nature (such as tuberculosis, septic shock, parasitic infection, herpes, systemic fungal disease, Lyme disease, or sexually transmitted disease);[39]
- Immunological disorders (that can occur in children with sickle-cell disease, diabetes, congenital cardiac defects, bronchial asthma, allergic rhinitis, cystic fibrosis, celiac abnormalities, malnutrition, immunosuppressive therapy, or chronic viral diseases);[40]
- Cardiovascular disorders (cardiac arrhythmia, congenital heart defects);[41]
- Pulmonary disorders (asthma, chronic bronchitis, chronic pneumonia, or pneumonitis);[42]
- Gastrointestinal disorders (digestive disorders, tumors, celiac disease, Crohn's disease, ulcerative colitis, irritable bowel syndrome, diverticulosis, diverticulitis);[43]
- Hepatic and biliary disorders (liver disease, hepatitis, tumors, cholecystitis, cancer, gallbladder disease);[44]
- Nutritional and metabolic disorders (malnutrition, vitamin deficiency, obesity, pigment disorders);[45]
- Endocrine disorders (pituitary disorders, diabetes, thyroid disorders, adrenal disorders);[46]
- Hematology disorders (anemia, hemophilia, platelet disorders, sickle-cell anemia, leukemia, lymphomas, Hodgkin's disease, spleen disorders, tumors) and oncology disorders (cancer);[47]
- Musculoskeletal and connective tissue disorders (lupus, tumors of bones or joints, bone and cartilage disorders, juvenile chronic arthritis);[48]
- Neurological disorders (chronic migraine headaches, insomnia, head injury, spinal cord injury, meningitis, encephalitis, brain hemorrhagic syndromes, multiple sclerosis, tics, spinal cord disorders, neuropathies, muscular dystrophies);[49]
- Psychiatric disorders (neurosis, mood disorders, depression, mania, suicidal behavior, anxiety, phobias, obsessive-compulsive disorder, posttraumatic stress disorder, psychosis, hallucinations, drug and alcohol dependence);[50]
- Genitourinary disorders (kidney disease, urinary tract disorders, fungal disease, obstructions, incontinence, trauma, tumors);[51]

38. *Id.*

39. Berkow, R. (1992). *The Merck manual of diagnosis and therapy* (16th ed., pp. 4–275). Merck Publishing Group.

40. *Id.* at 279–363.

41. *Id.* at 367–594.

42. *Id.* at 596–731.

43. *Id.* at 739–860.

44. *Id.* at 864–930.

45. *Id.* at 932–1052.

46. *Id.* at 1055–1132.

47. *Id.* at 1136–1291.

48. *Id.* at 1294–1377.

49. *Id.* at 1380–1526.

50. *Id.* at 1532–1635.

51. *Id.* at 1646–1751.

- Gynecologic and obstetric conditions (pregnancy, rape, miscarriage, abortion);[52]
- Conditions usually associated with pediatrics or genetics (respiratory distress, birth trauma, fetal alcohol syndrome, drug addiction from fetal exposure, seizure disorders, hearing loss, congenital heart defect, heart failure, gastrointestinal defects, congenital eye defects, failure to thrive, behavioral problems, learning disorders (including attention deficit disorder and dyslexia, mental retardation, child abuse, and neglect), HIV in children, tumors, cystic fibrosis, childhood peptic ulcer, autism, cerebral palsy, eating disorders, Down syndrome, fragile X syndrome, chromosomal or genetic disorders);[53]
- Otolaryngology disorders (hearing impairment, chronic ear infections, rhinitis, sinusitis);[54]
- Ophthalmologic disorders (visual impairment, ocular injury, chronic conjunctivitis, retinal disorders, optic nerve disorders).[55]

B. How Can the Lawyer or Judge Know When a Particular Case Should Be Considered a Special Needs Case?

Lawyers and judges are not medical, psychological, or behavioral experts. How do we know when it is not just a situation in which a child is having a hard time because of the divorce, but because of other things in the child's life? Since so many children are diagnosed with something today, will all cases end up being considered special needs cases? No, they will not, because it is in the best interest of a typical child to be treated as a typical child, and it is in the best interest of a special needs child to be treated as a special needs child. Courts are required to act in the best interests of the child, so it logically follows that if they are acting in the best interests of the child, they are treating the case the way it should be handled.

Lawyers and judges must make every reasonable effort to evaluate the issue of special needs when it is appropriate in a family court case. When evaluating a case in which there is a potential special needs issue, it is better to err on the side of having an evaluation performed than to press forward, ignoring the issue and hoping everything will turn out right.

The ultimate standard:

When it is in the best interest of the child to be considered a special needs case, the child should be considered as such.

---

52. *Id.* at 1755–1911.
53. *Id.* at 1918–2316.
54. *Id.* at 2318–2357.
55. *Id.* at 2360–2397.

CHAPTER 2

How to Recognize and Handle Issues of Special Needs in Family Law Cases

Family court judges and lawyers are frequently facing the issue of special needs in their cases. Critical to the task of handling special needs cases competently is the skill of being able to identify or recognize special needs. You cannot properly handle an issue if you are unaware of the issue. Since "little to nothing [has been] published on this topic in the professional literature as guidance, divorce professionals have been at a loss as to how to accurately and effectively identify and manage these cases."[1] The number of special needs children is increasing,[2] therefore it is more important than ever for lawyers, judges, and other family court professionals to become well educated on this subject and become skilled at recognizing and handling special needs.[3] The number of children who receive special education services grew from 6.5 million to 7.3 million from 2009 to 2020.[4] More than 40 percent of school-aged children suffer from chronic health conditions.[5] The rate of illness in children in the United States has increased in the last 20 years.[6] The CDC reports that 61 million adults live with a disability, which is one in four American adults.[7] The U.S. Census Bureau says that the childhood disability rate went up between 2009 and 2019 to more than three million children with difficulty seeing,

1. Saposnek, D. (2005). Editorial preface to special issue of Family Court Review. *Family Court Review, 43*(4), 563–565.

2. Newacheck, P. W., Strickland, B., Shonkoff, J. P., Perrin, J. M., McPherson, M., & McManus, M., Lauver, C., Fox, H., & Arango, P. (1998). An epidemiologic profile of children with special health care needs. *Pediatrics, 102*(1), 117–123.

3. Saposnek, *supra* note 1.

4. National Center for Education Statistics. Retrieved May 24, 2022. https://nces.ed.gov/fastfacts/display.asp?id=64.

5. https://www.cdc.gov/healthyschools/chronicconditions.htm#:~:text=In%20the%20United%20States%2C%20more,%2C%20and%20behavior%2Flearning%20problems. Retrieved May 24, 2022. CDC's reference: National Survey of Children's Health. NSCH 2018 19: Number of Current or Lifelong Health Conditions, Nationwide, Age in 3 Groups website. childhealthdata.org. Accessed February 24, 2021.

6. Landrigan, P., Trasande, L., Thorpe, L., Gwynn, C., Loiy, P., & D'Alton, M., et al. (2006). The National Children's Study: A 21 year prospective study of 100,000 American children. *Pediatrics, 118*(5), 2173–2186.

7. https://www.cdc.gov/ncbddd/disabilityandhealth/infographic-disability-impacts-all.html#:~:text=61%20million%20adults%20in%20the,is%20highest%20in%20the%20South. Retrieved May 24, 2022.

hearing, concentrating, remembering, walking, climbing stairs, or performing self-care tasks like dressing or bathing (age five and above).[8]

Many people have things going on in their lives that do not amount to special needs. Lawyers and judges must learn how to recognize special needs and how to differentiate them from everyday situations. One of the best and most obvious means of recognizing special needs is simply to ask. This seems painfully basic, yet a successful skip tracer once said his best tool was the phone book. Sometimes things are hiding out in the open. Surprisingly, clients often do not tell their lawyers about a child's significant special need until they are specifically asked about special needs.

I. THE INITIAL CLIENT INTERVIEW

As part of their initial intake questionnaire with a client, lawyers should include a question about special needs. Simply ask, "Do any of the children or the parents have any special needs?" Sometimes clients are not entirely sure what this means, so explain your question by telling them that special needs can include any physical, mental, or emotional disability; learning disability; behavior or mood disorder; or any other issue that might require special consideration in the divorce for purposes of medication or medical treatment, visitation, child support, or maintenance.

PRACTICE TIP

What to ask the client about special needs in the initial interview:

1. Do any of the children receive special assistance at school?
2. Do any of the children have an **Individualized Education Plan (IEP)**[9] (specialized instruction plan) or **504 Plan** (reasonable accommodations plan) at school?
3. Are any of the children on medication?
4. Are any of the children in counseling—physical therapy, behavior therapy, or psychological counseling?
5. Do any of the children have a diagnosed medical condition, psychiatric condition, or learning disability?

---

8. https://www.census.gov/library/stories/2021/03/united-states-childhood-disability-rate-up-in-2019-from-2008.html#:~:text=Over%20three%20million%20children%20(4.3,Hearing. Retrieved May 24, 2022.

9. An IEP is a legal document mandated by IDEA, which controls the procedural requirements. It is more involved than a 504 Plan. An IEP is required for students with disabilities who require specialized instruction. A 504 Plan is a written plan that is required for students with disabilities needing only reasonable accommodation. It is less involved than an IEP. An excellent explanation may be found in L. Wilmhurst & A. W. Brue, *A Parent's Guide to Special Education* (2005, Amacom). See also "IEP's vs. 504 Plans," and the entire Sevier County Special Education website. Retrieved September 10, 2008, from https://www.sevier.org/site/default.aspx?PageType=2&PageModuleInstanceID=486&ViewID=838b13a1-2ccb-4c74-83cb-0b9f098d6937&RenderLoc=0&FlexDataID=7938. Additional helpful materials include the Learning Disabilities OnLine website, http://www.LDonline.org (especially the materials on accommodations and modifications) and the Cleveland Heights Teachers Union website materials on 504 Plan Frequently Asked Questions, http://www.chtu.org. (Both websites retrieved on September 10, 2008).

If any of the children or parents have a diagnosed medical condition, psychiatric condition, or learning disability, then the lawyer needs to ask further questions. There is much more information the lawyer needs to obtain and understand in order to appropriately assess the situation and draft the necessary pleadings.

PRACTICE TIP

Additional questions the lawyer needs to ask if any of the children have a diagnosed medical condition, psychiatric condition, or learning disability:

1. What is the official diagnosis?
2. Who made the diagnosis?
3. When was the diagnosis made?
4. When did the first symptoms appear?
5. What testing was done to evaluate the child's condition?
6. Why was the child seen by the person who made the diagnosis? (What made the parents think the child needed to be evaluated?)
7. Has any other professional confirmed the diagnosis?
8. What follow-up has been done since the initial diagnosis?
9. What treatment has been done since the additional diagnosis?

The necessary information merely begins at the point of diagnosis. Much more information needs to be gathered and assimilated when handling a case involving a child with special needs. The lawyer needs to obtain information regarding the child's actual condition and prognosis.

PRACTICE TIP

Questions to ask about the child's condition and prognosis:

1. What is the child's current condition, as of the time the lawyer has become involved in the case?
2. What is the child's prognosis (expected outcome)?
3. Is the condition curable (can they make it "go away")?
4. Is the condition treatable (it will not go away, but things can be made better or perhaps not made worse for the patient)?
5. Is the condition terminal (fatal)?

Merely having the foregoing information in a vacuum is of extremely limited value to the courts and lawyers involved. In addition to having the information concerning the diagnosis, current condition, and prognosis, the court needs to know how the condition will impact the child, siblings, and parents. The lawyer should thoroughly question the client regarding the impact on the family.

PRACTICE TIP

Questions to ask a client concerning the impact of special needs on the family:

1. What is the child's life expectancy?
2. How does this condition affect the child's life now?
3. How is it expected to impact the child's life in the future?
4. How does this condition affect siblings' lives now?
5. How is this condition expected to impact siblings' lives in the future?
6. How does this condition affect the parents' lives now?
7. How is this condition expected to impact the parents' lives in the future?
8. Who is the primary caregiver? (This could be a parent, a grandparent, or another person.)
9. Of the parents, which one contributes more time and care to the child?
10. How has the child's condition impacted the careers of the parents?
11. How is the child's condition expected to impact the parents' career advancement and retirement plan contributions in the future?

The lawyer must be prepared to answer detailed questions concerning the child's specific special needs. To do this, the lawyer must know which questions to ask the family in order to have this information in the client file. This information should first be gathered and then read and thoroughly understood. Understanding this material may require the lawyer to conduct additional research or to hire a medical professional to explain the terminology and concepts relevant to the individual child.

FILE MANAGEMENT TIP

Once the lawyer clearly understands the material, he should organize it as a separate subsection of the client's file. This subsection may be entitled "Medical Records" or "Special Needs."

PRACTICE TIP

Detailed questions to ask concerning the child's individual special needs:

1. What are the names, addresses, telephone numbers, and credentials of all persons the child currently sees for this condition?
2. List all medications the child currently takes, the frequency and dosage, the reason for the medication, the expected result of the medication, and the amount of time the child is anticipated to remain on the medication.
3. List all therapies the child currently receives, including therapies received at home and at school. For each therapy, identify
   - the person or organization who provides the therapy;
   - the entity who referred the child to that person or organization for the therapy;
   - where the therapy is received;
   - the type of therapy and methodology used (for example, behavior therapy using ABA—applied behavior analysis—methodology);

- the frequency and duration of therapy (for example, three times per week, one hour per session);
- the length of time this therapy is expected to continue (for example, for the entire school year, first six weeks after the cast is removed, indefinitely, for six months);
- the cost of the therapy;
- how this cost is paid (private pay, funding program);
- the amount of uncovered cost of this therapy;
- incidental costs of this therapy—and transportation, time, and cost of caregiver, supplies, meals, equipment;
- the identity of the person who takes the child to the therapy.

4. What are the expectations regarding future therapies and medications?
5. Is the child on any waiting list for any therapy, program, school, or funding?
6. Itemize all direct and indirect costs resulting from the child's special needs, including therapy, doctors, other practitioners, medications, supplements, equipment, supplies, caregiver training, special nutritional requirements, special clothing and personal care item requirements, home modifications, vehicle modifications, modifications at school, nonparental caregiver costs, transportation, and any other costs.

SAMPLE DETAILED CHECKLIST FOR INITIAL INTERVIEW IN CASES INVOLVING SPECIAL NEEDS CHILD

INITIAL INTERVIEW—What to ask the client

- Do any of the children have special needs? These can include any physical, mental, or emotional disability; learning disability; behavior or mood disorder; or any other issue that might require special consideration in the divorce for purposes of medication, medical treatment, therapy, custody, visitation, or child support.
- Do any of the children receive special **assistance at school**?
- Do any of the children have an **Individualized Education Plan (IEP)** or **504 Plan** at school? (See footnote 9 for an explanation of IEPs and 504 Plans.)
- Are any of the children on **medication**?
- Are any of the children in **counseling**, physical **therapy**, behavior therapy, or psychological counseling?
- What is the official **diagnosis**?
- **Who** made the diagnosis?
- **When** was the diagnosis made?
- When did the **first symptoms** appear?
- What **testing** was done to evaluate the child's condition?
- **Why** was the child seen by the person who made the diagnosis? (What made the parents think the child **needed to be evaluated**?)
- Has any other professional **confirmed** the diagnosis?
- What is the child's **current condition**?
- What is the child's **prognosis**? (expected outcome)
- Is the condition **curable**?
- Is the condition **treatable**?
- Is the condition **terminal**?
- Is the child expected ever to get a high school **diploma**, get a college degree, live on her own, hold a regular job, **live** completely **independently**, marry, have children?
- What is the child's **life expectancy**?
- How does this condition **affect** the child's life **now**?
- How is it expected to **impact** the child's life in the **future**?
- How does this condition **affect siblings**' lives **now**?
- How is it expected to **impact siblings**' lives in the **future**?
- How does this condition **affect** the **parents**' lives **now**?
- How is it expected to **impact** the **parents**' lives in the **future**?
- Who is the **primary caregiver**?
- How has the condition **impacted** the **careers** of the **parents**?
- How will the condition impact the **parents**' **career advancement** and **retirement plan contributions**?
- What are the names, addresses, telephone numbers, and credentials of all **persons the child currently sees** for this condition?
- List all **medications** the child currently takes, the frequency and dosage, the reason for the medication, and the expected result from the medication.

- List all **therapies** the child currently receives, including therapies received at home and at school. For each therapy, identify
    a. the **person** or **organization** who provides the therapy;
    b. who **referred** the child to that person or organization;
    c. **where** the therapy is received;
    d. the **type** of therapy and **methodology** used (for example, behavior therapy using ABA—applied behavior analysis method);
    e. the **frequency** and **duration** of therapy (for example, three times per week, one hour each time);
    f. the **length of time** therapy is **expected to continue** (for example, for the entire school year, for six weeks after the cast is removed, indefinitely, for six months);
    g. **cost** of the therapy;
    h. **how** is this **paid** (private pay, insurance, funding program);
    i. amount of **uncovered cost** of this therapy;
    j. **incidental costs** of this therapy—transportation, caregiver, supplies, meals, equipment;
    k. **who takes** the child to the therapy.
- What are the expectations regarding future therapies and medications?
- Is the child on a **waiting list** for any therapy, program, school, or funding?

Itemize all **direct and indirect costs** resulting from the child's special needs, including therapy, doctors, other practitioners, medications, supplements, equipment, supplies, caregiver training, special nutritional requirements, special clothing and personal care item requirements, home modifications, vehicle modifications, modifications at school, nonparental caregiver costs, transportation, and any other costs.

II. DRAFTING DIVORCE PETITIONS AND ANSWERS

State family law statutes require that certain allegations be made in the Petition for Dissolution. Here is a sample Petition for Dissolution for use in a case not involving special needs children.

SAMPLE PETITION FOR DISSOLUTION TYPICAL CASE, NOT INVOLVING SPECIAL NEEDS

IN THE FAMILY COURT OF THE COUNTY OF ____________
STATE OF ____________

In Re the Marriage of:	)	For File Stamp Only
	)	
______________________,	)	
______________Street	)	
City, State ZIP	)	
____________	)	
Petitioner,	)	
and	)	Case No. ____________
______________________,	)	
______________Street	)	
City, State ZIP	)	Division: __________
____________	)	
Respondent.	)	

SERVE AT:
Office/Home
Street Address
City, State ZIP

PETITION FOR DISSOLUTION OF MARRIAGE

Comes now the Petitioner, ________________, and for her cause of action, states to the Court as follows:

1. Petitioner has been a resident of the State of _________ for _____ days/months immediately preceding the filing of this Petition for Dissolution, and has been a resident of _______ County, State, for _____ days/months immediately preceding the filing of this Petition for Dissolution.
2. Respondent has been a resident of the State of __________ for _____ days/months immediately preceding the filing of this Petition for Dissolution, and has been a resident of ____________ County, State, for _____ days/months immediately preceding the filing of this Petition for Dissolution.
3. Petitioner resides at ___________Street, City, County, State. Petitioner is currently employed at _____________.
4. Respondent is currently residing at _____________Street, City, County, State. Respondent is currently employed at ________________.

5. Petitioner states that the parties were married on ____________Month, Day, Year, in the City of _______________, State, and that said marriage was registered in the County of _____________, State.
6. Petitioner and Respondent are residing in the same residence, but are no longer living together as husband and wife, and separated on or about______________ Month, Day, Year.
7. Petitioner states that neither Petitioner nor Respondent are members of the armed forces of the United States of America on active duty and are not entitled to any benefits or immunities of the Servicemembers Civil Relief Act.
8. Petitioner states that there is no reasonable likelihood that the marriage can be preserved and, therefore, the marriage is irretrievably broken.
9. Petitioner and Respondent have acquired certain property and certain debts during the marriage and have not yet entered into a property settlement agreement that disposes of all matters between them, financial or otherwise.
10. Petitioner states that there was one unemancipated child born of the marriage, namely:
    Child's Name, DOB _________________
11. That Petitioner is not now pregnant.
12. For sixty days immediately preceding the filing of the Petition for Dissolution of Marriage, the minor child of the parties resided with Petitioner and Respondent at __________________ Dr., City, County, State.
13. The Petitioner requests that the Court award the parties joint care and custody of the minor child with the child's principal residence being with Petitioner.
14. There have been no arrangements made as to the custody and support of the parties' child.
15. The Petitioner has not participated in any capacity in any other litigation concerning the custody of the child in this or any other state; Petitioner has no information of any custody proceeding concerning the child pending in a court of this or any other state; and Petitioner knows of no person not a party to these proceedings who has physical custody of the child or claims to have custody or visitation rights with respect to the child.
16. That Respondent is hereby notified pursuant to Section _______________ that he may not terminate coverage for Petitioner or any minor child born of the marriage under any existing policy of health, dental, or vision insurance.
17. That the Court make provision for the maintenance of a health benefit plan for the minor child and for payment of noncovered medical, orthodontic, health, dental, and optical expenses incurred with regard to the minor child all pursuant to the provisions of Section ________________.
18. That Petitioner requests that all child support payments be made through the Family Support Payment Center, P.O. Box ___________, City, State, ZIP.
19. That this Court order the Sheriff or other law enforcement office to enforce this Court's custody and/or visitation orders.
20. That this Court order terms of custody and visitation pursuant to the terms contained in Petitioner's Parenting Plan.
21. That this Court order Child Support pursuant to Petitioner's Child Support Chart.

WHEREFORE, Petitioner prays for a Judgment dissolving the marriage of the parties; that the Court set aside to Petitioner and Respondent their separate nonmarital property; that the marital property and marital debts be divided in a fair and equitable manner; that the Court award custody of the minor child pursuant to Petitioner's Parenting Plan; that the Court order Respondent to pay to Petitioner child support pursuant to Petitioner's Child Support Chart retroactive to the date of filing; and for further and different relief as this Court deems just and proper in the premises.

STATE OF ______________

ss.

COUNTY OF ____________

Comes now ________________, Petitioner, being first duly sworn according to law, and states that she has read the foregoing Petition for Dissolution of Marriage and states that the facts contained therein are true and correct according to her best knowledge, information, and belief.

____

Petitioner

Subscribed and sworn to before me this _____ day of ___________, 20___

____

Notary Public

My commission expires:

Respectfully submitted,
[Attorney Signature Block]
ATTORNEY FOR PETITIONER

NOTICE TO PETITIONER AND RESPONDENT

Please take notice that pursuant to Section _________ of the ______________ Statutes, from the date of filing the petition for dissolution of marriage or legal separation, no party shall terminate coverage during the pendency of the proceeding for any other party or any minor child of the marriage under any existing policy of health, dental, or vision insurance.

A typical petition includes allegations regarding

- facts establishing the court's jurisdiction over the parties and property;
- employer and Social Security information (some states);
- dates and place of the marriage and registration thereof;
- date of separation;
- active duty military service;
- irretrievably broken marriage;
- marital and separate property and debts;

- names, dates of birth, and Social Security numbers of children born of the marriage;
- emancipation status of the children;
- whether the wife is pregnant;
- where the children have resided before the filing of the divorce Petition or Motion to Modify;
- prior litigation concerning custody of the children;
- legal and physical custody of the children;
- child support;
- need for or waiver of maintenance;
- health, dental, or vision insurance for the children;
- payment agency for child support and/or maintenance;
- enforcement of custody and visitation orders;
- restoration of maiden name.

In a case involving special needs, additional items should be addressed in the pleadings. State family law statutes should be amended to require these suggested provisions addressing special needs. To address these issues, the lawyer must make sure she understands the information she gathered at the initial intake interview as well as the information contained in the additional documentation gathered for her file. If necessary, lawyers may consult an expert in the particular field their case involves so they will feel comfortable discussing the issues inherent in the child's condition and arguing the merits of the case to the judge.

In the best interests of the special needs child, the issue of special needs should be raised immediately in the case. Lawyers should not "save" this issue to spring it on the other side at trial. Properly addressing the issues raised by special needs requires much more time than does a case not involving special needs. If the issue of special needs is raised at trial for some perceived tactical advantage, the children will suffer.

SAMPLE PETITION FOR DISSOLUTION INVOLVING SPECIAL NEEDS

IN THE FAMILY COURT OF THE COUNTY OF ____________
STATE OF ____________

In Re the Marriage of:	)	For File Stamp Only
	)	
______________________,	)	
______________Street	)	
City, State ZIP	)	
_____________	)	
Petitioner,	)	
and	)	Case No. ______________
______________________,	)	
_____________Street	)	
City, State ZIP	)	Division: __________
____________	)	
Respondent.	)	

SERVE AT:
Office/Home
Street Address
City, State ZIP

PETITION FOR DISSOLUTION OF MARRIAGE

Comes now the Petitioner, _________________, and for her cause of action, states to the Court as follows:

1. Petitioner has been a resident of the State of _________ for _____ days/months immediately preceding the filing of this Petition for Dissolution, and has been a resident of _______ County, State, for _____ days/months immediately preceding the filing of this Petition for Dissolution.
2. Respondent has been a resident of the State of __________ for _____ days/months immediately preceding the filing of this Petition for Dissolution, and has been a resident of ____________ County, State, for ____ days/months immediately preceding the filing of this Petition for Dissolution.
3. Petitioner resides at ___________Street, City, County, State. Petitioner is currently employed at _____________.
4. Respondent is currently residing at _____________Street, City, County, State. Respondent is currently employed at ________________.
5. Petitioner states that the parties were married on ___________Month, Day, Year, in the City of _______________, State, and that said marriage was registered in the County of _____________, State.

6. Petitioner and Respondent are residing in the same residence, but are no longer living together as husband and wife, and separated on or about ___________ Month, Day, Year.
7. Petitioner states that neither Petitioner nor Respondent are members of the armed forces of the United States of America on active duty and are not entitled to any benefits or immunities of the Servicemembers Civil Relief Act.
8. Petitioner states that there is no reasonable likelihood that the marriage can be preserved and, therefore, the marriage is irretrievably broken.
9. Petitioner and Respondent have acquired certain property and certain debts during the marriage and have not yet entered into a property settlement agreement that disposes of all matters between them, financial or otherwise.
10. Petitioner states that there was one unemancipated child born of the marriage, namely:
    Child's Name, DOB ________________
    AND THAT SUCH CHILD HAS SPECIAL NEEDS, SPECIFICALLY __________.
11. That Petitioner is not now pregnant.
12. For sixty days immediately preceding the filing of the Petition for Dissolution of Marriage, the minor child of the parties resided with Petitioner and Respondent at _________________ Dr., City, County, State.
13. The Petitioner requests that the Court award the parties joint care and custody of the minor child with the child's principal residence being with Petitioner.
14. There have been no arrangements made as to the custody and support of the parties' child.
15. The Petitioner has not participated in any capacity in any other litigation concerning the custody of the child in this or any other state; Petitioner has no information of any custody proceeding concerning the child pending in a court of this or any other state; and Petitioner knows of no person not a party to these proceedings who has physical custody of the child or claims to have custody or visitation rights with respect to the child.
16. That Respondent is hereby notified pursuant to Section _______________ that he may not terminate coverage for Petitioner or any minor child born of the marriage under any existing policy of health, dental, or vision insurance.
17. That the Court make provision for the maintenance of a health benefit plan for the minor child and for payment of noncovered medical, orthodontic, health, dental, and optical expenses incurred with regard to the minor child all pursuant to the provisions of Section ________________.
18. That Petitioner requests that all child support payments be made through the Family Support Payment Center, P.O. Box ______________, City, State, ZIP.
19. That this Court order the Sheriff or other law enforcement office to enforce this Court's custody and/or visitation orders.
20. That this Court order terms of custody and visitation pursuant to the terms contained in Petitioner's Parenting Plan for Special Needs.
21. That this Court order Child Support pursuant to Petitioner's Child Support Chart for Special Needs.

WHEREFORE, Petitioner prays for a Judgment dissolving the marriage of the parties; that the Court set aside to Petitioner and Respondent their separate nonmarital property; that the marital property and marital debts be divided in a fair and equitable manner; that the Court award custody of the minor child pursuant to Petitioner's Parenting Plan for Special Needs; that the Court order Respondent to pay to Petitioner child support pursuant to Petitioner's Child Support Chart for Special Needs retroactive to the date of filing; and for further and different relief as this Court deems just and proper in the premises.

STATE OF ______________

ss.

COUNTY OF ____________

Comes now ________________, Petitioner, being first duly sworn according to law, and states that she has read the foregoing Petition for Dissolution of Marriage and states that the facts contained therein are true and correct according to her best knowledge, information, and belief.

____
Petitioner

Subscribed and sworn to before me this _____ day of ____________, 20___

____
Notary Public

My commission expires:

Respectfully submitted,
[Attorney Signature Block]
ATTORNEY FOR PETITIONER

NOTICE TO PETITIONER AND RESPONDENT

Please take notice that pursuant to Section _________ of the ______________ Statutes, from the date of filing the petition for dissolution of marriage or legal separation, <u>no party</u> shall terminate coverage during the pendency of the proceeding for any other party or any minor child of the marriage under any existing policy of health, dental, or vision insurance.

PRACTICE TIP

In addition to the usual items contained in a standard petition, assess the following topics and include them in the petition if relevant:

- a recital of the child's special needs
- a recital of the need to use a different child support amount
- a recital of the need to use a different parenting plan
- a statement of the type of physical custody appropriate
- a statement of the type of legal custody appropriate
- a statement of the type of visitation appropriate
- a statement of the need for maintenance

Since lawyers are already required to plead many subjects in a divorce petition, simply adding the requirement that the pleadings contain either an allegation that there are no known or suspected special needs, or an allegation that there are known special needs and a brief statement of the facts concerning them, would not be burdensome. It would, of course, be required in the responsive pleading as well.

SAMPLE ANSWER TO PETITION FOR DISSOLUTION AND CROSS PETITION FOR DISSOLUTION OF MARRIAGE FOR USE IN TYPICAL CASE NOT INVOLVING SPECIAL NEEDS

IN THE FAMILY COURT OF THE COUNTY OF ____________
STATE OF ____________

In Re the Marriage of:	)	
	)	
____________________,	)	
____________,	)	
Petitioner,	)	
vs.	)	Case No. ____________________
____________________,	)	Division: ________
____________,	)	
Respondent.	)	

ANSWER TO PETITION FOR DISSOLUTION

Comes now the Respondent, ________________________, by and through his attorney, ___________________________, and in Answer to the Petition for Dissolution of Marriage, states to the Court as follows:

1. Respondent admits each and every allegation contained in paragraphs 1, 2, 3, 4, 5, 6, 7, 8, and 9 of the Petition, including every subpart thereof.

WHEREFORE, Respondent having fully answered Petitioner's Petition for Dissolution of Marriage prays the Court find the marriage of the parties to be irretrievably broken and enter a Judgment dissolving the marriage; that the Court set aside to Petitioner and Respondent their separate nonmarital property; that the marital property and marital debts be divided in a fair and equitable manner; that the Court award the parties joint care and custody of the minor child with the child's principal residence being with Petitioner; that the Court order child support pursuant to Respondent's Model Child Support Chart and visitation pursuant to Respondent's Model Parenting Plan; and for further and different relief as this Court deems just and proper in the premises.

STATE OF ______________

ss.

COUNTY OF ____________

Comes now ______________________, Respondent, being first duly sworn according to law, and states that the facts in the foregoing are true and correct to his best knowledge and belief.

____
Respondent

Subscribed and sworn to before me this _____ day of ___________, 20___.

____
Notary Public

My commission expires:

Respectfully submitted,
[Attorney Signature Block]
ATTORNEY FOR RESPONDENT

CERTIFICATE OF SERVICE

I hereby certify that a true and correct copy of the foregoing was deposited in the U.S. Mail, postage prepaid to:
Opposing Counsel's Name, Street Address, City, State ZIP
this ______ day of _________________, 20___.

____
Attorney for Respondent

IN THE FAMILY COURT OF THE COUNTY OF _____________
STATE OF ______________

In Re the Marriage of:	)	
	)	
___________________,	)	
____________,	)	
Petitioner,	)	
vs.	)	Case No. ___________________
___________________,	)	Division: ________
____________,	)	
Respondent.	)	

COUNTER-PETITION FOR DISSOLUTION OF MARRIAGE

Comes now the Respondent, ______________________, and for his cause of action, states to the Court as follows:

1. Respondent has been a resident of the State of ______________ for _____ days/months immediately preceding the filing of this Petition for Dissolution, and has been a resident of _____________ County, __________, for _____ days/months immediately preceding the filing of this Petition for Dissolution.
2. Petitioner has been a resident of the State of __________ for _____ days/months immediately preceding the filing of this Petition for Dissolution, and has been a resident of ___________ County, ___________, for _____ days/months immediately preceding the filing of this Petition for Dissolution.

3. Respondent is currently residing at ________________Road, City, State. Respondent is currently employed by ___________________.
4. Petitioner is currently residing at ______________ Dr., City, County, State. Petitioner is currently employed by _______________________.
5. Respondent states that the parties were married on ___________Month, Day, Year, in _________________________City, County, State, and that said marriage was registered in __________________County, State.
6. Petitioner and Respondent are residing in the same residence, but are no longer living together as husband and wife, and separated on _______________ Month, Day, Year.
7. Respondent states that neither Petitioner nor Respondent are members of the armed forces of the United States of America on active duty and are not entitled to any benefits or immunities of the Servicemembers Civil Relief Act.
8. Respondent states that there is no reasonable likelihood that the marriage can be preserved and, therefore, the marriage is irretrievably broken.
9. Petitioner and Respondent have acquired certain property and certain debts during the marriage but have not yet entered into a property settlement agreement.
10. Respondent states that there is one unemancipated child born of this marriage, to wit:
    Child's Name, DOB ______________
11. That Petitioner is not now pregnant.
12. For sixty days immediately preceding the filing of the Petition for Dissolution of Marriage, the minor child of the parties resided with Respondent and Petitioner at __________________ Dr., City, County, State.
13. The Respondent requests that the Court award the parties joint care and custody of the minor child with the child's principal residence being with Respondent.
14. There have been no arrangements made as to the custody and support of the parties' child.
15. The Respondent has not participated in any capacity in any other litigation concerning the custody of the child in this or any other state; Respondent has no information of any custody proceeding concerning the child pending in a court of this or any other state; and Respondent knows of no person not a party to these proceedings who has physical custody of the child or claims to have custody or visitation rights with respect to the child.
16. That Petitioner is hereby notified pursuant to Section _______________ that she may not terminate coverage for Respondent or any minor child born of the marriage under any existing policy of health, dental, or vision insurance.
17. That the Court make provision for the maintenance of a health benefit plan for the minor child and for payment of noncovered medical, orthodontic, health, dental, and optical expenses incurred with regard to the minor child all pursuant to the provisions of Section _________________.
18. That Respondent requests that all child support payments be made through the Family Support Payment Center, P.O. Box _____________, City, State, ZIP.
19. That this Court order the Sheriff or other law enforcement office to enforce this Court's custody and/or visitation orders.
20. That this Court order terms of custody and visitation pursuant to the terms contained in Respondent's Parenting Plan.

21. That this Court order Child Support pursuant to Respondent's Child Support Chart.

WHEREFORE, Respondent prays for a Judgment dissolving the marriage of the parties; that the Court set aside to Petitioner and Respondent their separate nonmarital property; that the marital property and marital debts be divided in a fair and equitable manner; that the Court award custody of the minor child pursuant to Respondent's Parenting Plan; that the Court order Petitioner to pay to Respondent child support pursuant to Respondent's Child Support Chart retroactive to the date of filing; and for further and different relief as this Court deems just and proper in the premises.

STATE OF ______________
ss.
COUNTY OF ____________

Comes now ______________________, Respondent, being first duly sworn according to law, and states that the facts in the foregoing are true and correct to his best knowledge and belief.

____
Respondent

Subscribed and sworn to before me this _____ day of ___________, 20___.

____
Notary Public

My commission expires:

Respectfully submitted,
[Attorney Signature Block]
ATTORNEY FOR RESPONDENT

<u>CERTIFICATE OF SERVICE</u>

I hereby certify that a true and correct copy of the foregoing was deposited in the U.S. Mail, postage prepaid to:
Opposing Counsel's Name, Street Address, City, State ZIP
this ______ day of ________________, 20___.

____
Attorney for Respondent

NOTICE TO PETITIONER AND RESPONDENT

Please take notice that pursuant to Section _________ of the _____________ Statutes, from the date of filing the petition for dissolution of marriage or legal separation, <u>no party</u> shall terminate coverage during the pendency of the proceeding for any other party or any minor child of the marriage under any existing policy of health, dental, or vision insurance.

SAMPLE ANSWER TO PETITION FOR DISSOLUTION AND CROSS PETITION FOR DISSOLUTION OF MARRIAGE FOR USE IN CASE INVOLVING SPECIAL NEEDS

IN THE FAMILY COURT OF ________________ COUNTY
STATE OF ________________

In Re the Marriage of:	)	
	)	
________________,	)	
___________,	)	
Petitioner,	)	
vs.	)	Case No. ________________
________________,	)	Division: _______
___________,	)	
Respondent.	)	

<u>ANSWER TO PETITION FOR DISSOLUTION</u>

Comes now the Respondent, ____________________, by and through his attorney, ______________________, and in Answer to the Petition for Dissolution of Marriage, states to the Court as follows:

1. Respondent admits each and every allegation contained in paragraphs 1, 2, 3, 4, 5, 6, 7, 8, and 9 of the Petition, including every subpart thereof.
2. In further response to paragraph 4 of said Petition, Respondent states that the minor child, ________________________, has **<u>special needs</u>, namely**, ___________, therefore the use of the standard child support guidelines and standard parenting plan would be unjust and inappropriate.

WHEREFORE, Respondent having fully answered Petitioner's Petition for Dissolution of Marriage prays the Court find the marriage of the parties to be irretrievably broken and enter a Judgment dissolving the marriage; that the Court set aside to Petitioner and Respondent their separate nonmarital property; that the marital property and marital debts be divided in a fair and equitable manner; that the Court award the parties joint care and custody of the minor child with the child's principal residence being with Petitioner; that the Court order child support pursuant to Respondent's Model Child Support Chart for Special Needs and visitation pursuant to Respondent's Model Parenting Plan for Special Needs; and for further and different relief as this Court deems just and proper in the premises.

STATE OF ____________

ss.

COUNTY OF ___________

Comes now ____________________, Respondent, being first duly sworn according to law, and states that the facts in the foregoing are true and correct to his best knowledge and belief.

____
Respondent

Subscribed and sworn to before me this _____ day of ___________, 20___.

____
Notary Public

My commission expires:

Respectfully submitted,
[Attorney Signature Block]
ATTORNEY FOR RESPONDENT

CERTIFICATE OF SERVICE

I hereby certify that a true and correct copy of the foregoing was deposited in the U.S. Mail, postage prepaid to:
Opposing Counsel's Name, Street Address, City, State ZIP
this ______ day of ________________, 20___.

____
Attorney for Respondent

IN THE FAMILY COURT OF ___________________ COUNTY
STATE OF ___________________

In Re the Marriage of:)
)
__________________,)
____________,)
Petitioner,)
vs.) Case No. ___________________
__________________,) Division: _______
____________,)
Respondent.)

COUNTER-PETITION FOR DISSOLUTION OF MARRIAGE

Comes now the Respondent, ____________________, and for his cause of action, states to the Court as follows:

1. Respondent has been a resident of the State of _____________ for _____ days/months immediately preceding the filing of this Petition for Dissolution, and has been a resident of ____________ County, _________, for _____ days/months immediately preceding the filing of this Petition for Dissolution.

2. Petitioner has been a resident of the State of __________ for _____ days/months immediately preceding the filing of this Petition for Dissolution, and has been a resident of ___________ County, ___________, for _____ days/months immediately preceding the filing of this Petition for Dissolution.
3. Respondent is currently residing at __________________Road, City, State. Respondent is currently employed by ___________________.
4. Petitioner is currently residing at ________________ Dr., City, County, State. Petitioner is currently employed by _______________________.
5. Respondent states that the parties were married on Month, Day, Year, in City, County, State, and that said marriage was registered in County, State.
6. Petitioner and Respondent are residing in the same residence, but are no longer living together as husband and wife, and separated on Month, Day, Year.
7. Respondent states that neither Petitioner nor Respondent are members of the armed forces of the United States of America on active duty and are not entitled to any benefits or immunities of the Servicemembers Civil Relief Act.
8. Respondent states that there is no reasonable likelihood that the marriage can be preserved and, therefore, the marriage is irretrievably broken.
9. Petitioner and Respondent have acquired certain property and certain debts during the marriage but have not yet entered into a property settlement agreement.
10. Respondent states that there is one unemancipated child born of this marriage, to wit:
    Child's Name, DOB ________________
    AND THAT SUCH CHILD HAS SPECIAL NEEDS, NAMELY, ________.
11. That Petitioner is not now pregnant.
12. For sixty days immediately preceding the filing of the Petition for Dissolution of Marriage, the minor child of the parties resided with Respondent and Petitioner at ___________________ Dr., City, County, State.
13. The Respondent requests that the Court award the parties joint care and custody of the minor child with the child's principal residence being with Respondent.
14. There have been no arrangements made as to the custody and support of the parties' child.
15. The Respondent has not participated in any capacity in any other litigation concerning the custody of the child in this or any other state; Respondent has no information of any custody proceeding concerning the child pending in a court of this or any other state; and Respondent knows of no person not a party to these proceedings who has physical custody of the child or claims to have custody or visitation rights with respect to the child.
16. That Petitioner is hereby notified pursuant to Section ________________ that she may not terminate coverage for Respondent or any minor child born of the marriage under any existing policy of health, dental, or vision insurance.
17. That the Court make provision for the maintenance of a health benefit plan for the minor child and for payment of noncovered medical, orthodontic, health, dental, and optical expenses incurred with regard to the minor child all pursuant to the provisions of Section __________________.

18. That Respondent requests that all child support payments be made through the Family Support Payment Center, P.O. Box ____________, City, State, ZIP.
19. That this Court order the Sheriff or other law enforcement office to enforce this Court's custody and/or visitation orders.
20. That this Court order terms of custody and visitation pursuant to the terms contained in Respondent's Parenting Plan for Special Needs.
21. That this Court order Child Support pursuant to Respondent's Child Support Chart for Special Needs.

WHEREFORE, Respondent prays for a Judgment dissolving the marriage of the parties; that the Court set aside to Petitioner and Respondent their separate nonmarital property; that the marital property and marital debts be divided in a fair and equitable manner; that the Court award custody of the minor child pursuant to Respondent's Parenting Plan for Special Needs; that the Court order Petitioner to pay to Respondent child support pursuant to Respondent's Child Support Chart for Special Needs retroactive to the date of filing; and for further and different relief as this Court deems just and proper in the premises.

STATE OF ____________

ss.

COUNTY OF ___________

Comes now ____________________, Respondent, being first duly sworn according to law, and states that the facts in the foregoing are true and correct to his best knowledge and belief.

____
Respondent

Subscribed and sworn to before me this _____ day of ___________, 20___.

____
Notary Public

My commission expires:

Respectfully submitted,
[Attorney Signature Block]
ATTORNEY FOR RESPONDENT

CERTIFICATE OF SERVICE

I hereby certify that a true and correct copy of the foregoing was deposited in the U.S. Mail, postage prepaid to:

Opposing Counsel's Name, Street Address, City, State ZIP
this ______ day of ________________, 20___.

____
Attorney for Respondent

NOTICE TO PETITIONER AND RESPONDENT

Please take notice that pursuant to Section _________ of the _____________ Statutes, from the date of filing the petition for dissolution of marriage or legal separation, no party shall terminate coverage during the pendency of the proceeding for any other party or any minor child of the marriage under any existing policy of health, dental, or vision insurance.

Requiring the parties to raise or eliminate the subject of special needs in the initial pleading and responsive pleading will cause the parties to think about the issue early on and will bring the issue to the court's attention. By wording the allegation to address *known or suspected* special needs, the parties would be able to amend their pleadings in the event a child became diagnosed during the pendency of the litigation. There should also be legislative provision for amending pleadings during the pendency of litigation in the event that a special need worsens during that time.

CHECKLIST FOR DRAFTING THE ANSWER AND CROSS-PETITION IN CASES INVOLVING SPECIAL NEEDS CHILD

HOW TO PREPARE THE ANSWER AND CROSS-PETITION

1. If the child's **special needs** have not been recited in the Petition, they should be alleged in the Answer and Cross-Petition.
2. If the child's special needs have been recited in the Petition **accurately**, this should be acknowledged in the Answer and Cross-Petition.
3. If the child's special needs have been **inaccurately alleged** in the Petition, this should be alleged in the Answer and Cross-Petition, with the **Respondent's view** of the child's condition.
4. If the need to use a **different child support amount** is appropriate but not alleged in the Petition, this should be alleged in the Answer and Cross-Petition.
5. If the need to use a different child support amount is **not appropriate** but is alleged in the Petition, this should be alleged in the Answer and Cross-Petition.
6. If the need to use a **different parenting plan** is appropriate but not alleged in the Petition, this should be alleged in the Answer and Cross-Petition.
7. If the need to use a different parenting plan is **not appropriate** but is alleged in the Petition, this should be alleged in the Answer and Cross-Petition.
8. Appropriate **physical custody** should be addressed in the Answer and Cross-Petition.
9. Appropriate **legal custody** should be addressed in the Answer and Cross-Petition.
10. Appropriate **visitation** should be addressed in the Answer and Cross-Petition.
11. The need for **maintenance** should be addressed in the Answer and Cross-Petition.

III. ADDITIONAL LITIGATION STAGES

The issue of special needs must be raised in other stages of litigation. State family law statutes should require the issue of special needs to be raised automatically in litigation pleadings, documents, and worksheets.

A. Interrogatories—Standard Question for Form Interrogatories

Interrogatories should address the issue of special needs. This could be accomplished by requiring a *standard question* in form **interrogatories.**

STANDARD FORM INTERROGATORY QUESTION:

Q: Do you allege that any of the parties or children of the parties have any special needs? If so, please state the nature of each such special need, as well as

a. the identity of the person with such special need;
b. the date of onset;
c. the date of diagnosis;
d. the identity of the diagnosing person with full address and telephone number;

e. any modifications currently employed;
f. all modifications you allege are necessary in addition to the current modifications;
g. all medications taken for such special need;
h. all therapy and treatment this person is receiving for this special need, including location, organization, frequency, duration, and cost;
i. prognosis and source of such prognosis;
j. financial impact of this special need;
k. public services and assistance currently received for this special need;
l. private services and assistance currently received for this special need;
m. breakdown of parental involvement in the care of this child, in percentage;
n. factual statement of the impact of this special need on daily life of the family;
o. impact of this special need on the current and future career of Mother;
p. impact of this special need on the current and future career of Father; and
q. any other information on this special need relevant to this divorce.

B. Discovery in General

Often, the documentation the clients provide to the lawyers is incomplete. In addition to the usual items that may be explored during a standard divorce, special needs cases demand exploring special subjects through the discovery process. Many of these are subject areas a lawyer may never deal with in the ordinary practice of law. The discovery requirements can be massive and overwhelming, especially if the lawyer is not familiar with special needs.

The lawyer must determine all the special needs of all children in the family. Often there will be more than one special need within a family. Special assistance received at the school must be explored. Individualized Education Plans (IEPs) and 504 Plans must be obtained from the schools. (See footnote 9 for an explanation of IEPs and 504 Plans.) Information on all medications, physical therapy, behavior therapy, psychological counseling, and other therapy and counseling must be obtained. The lawyer must obtain thorough information and documentation as to diagnosis, symptoms, testing, and evaluations.

The child's current condition and prognosis must be determined and documented. Information must be obtained on whether the child's condition is curable, treatable, or terminal. The likelihood of the child to attain a high school diploma, live independently, or be employed must be explored. The child's life expectancy needs to be determined.

The current and future impact of the special needs on the child must be explored, as well as current and future impact on the lives of the parents and siblings. These issues can be important factors in determining the amount of child support and/or maintenance as well as property distribution, including retirement plans.

The lawyer needs to obtain scholarly and authoritative materials concerning these subject areas, in order to educate the lawyer as well as the judge. The lawyer also needs to obtain documentation, medical records, and proof of costs. All of these materials, documentation, records, and proofs of costs need to be obtained in such a manner as to be admissible in court.

PRACTICE TIP

Subjects to explore through the discovery process:

(This list is for guidance only and is not intended to be considered exhaustive. This list may need to be expanded on a case-by-case basis.)

1. *Do any of the children have special needs?* Determine with regard to all of the children whether they have any physical, mental, or emotional disability; learning disability; behavior or mood disorder. Often there will be more than one special need within a family. Ask about this subject through interrogatories and/or depositions. Follow up with Request for Production of Documents. Obtain signed and notarized releases so you can obtain medical records of all medical and therapeutic professionals and record keepers.
2. *Do any of the children receive special assistance at school?* Ask about this subject through interrogatories and/or depositions. Follow up with Request for Production of Documents. Obtain signed and notarized releases of school records.
3. *Do any of the children have an Individualized Education Plan (IEP) or 504 Plan at school?* (See footnote 9 for an explanation of IEPs and 504 Plans.) Ask about this subject through interrogatories and/or depositions. Follow up with Request for Production of Documents. Obtain signed and notarized release of school records. In some educational settings, you may need to obtain two releases, one for the general education program and one for the entity that provides the special education/therapy in the school setting.
4. *Are any of the children on medication?* Ask about this subject through interrogatories and/or depositions. Follow up with Request for Production of Documents. Obtain signed and notarized releases of medical records.
5. *Are any of the children in counseling, physical therapy, behavior therapy, or psychological counseling?* Ask about this subject through interrogatories and/or depositions. Follow up with Request for Production of Documents. Obtain signed and notarized releases so you may obtain the records of all counselors and therapists.
6. *What is the official diagnosis?* Ask about this subject through interrogatories and/or depositions. Follow up with Request for Production of Documents. Obtain signed and notarized release so you may obtain the records of the diagnostician. Sometimes this may be a doctor or therapist. Other times, it may be a diagnostic clinic or other entity.
7. *Who made the diagnosis?* Ask about this subject through interrogatories and/or depositions. Follow up with Request for Production of Documents. Obtain signed and notarized release so you may obtain the records of the diagnostician. Sometimes this may be a doctor or therapist. Other times, it may be a diagnostic clinic or other entity.
8. *When was the diagnosis made?* Ask about this subject through interrogatories and/or depositions. Follow up with Request for Production of Documents. Obtain signed and notarized release so you may obtain the records of the diagnostician. Sometimes this may be a doctor or therapist. At other times, it may be a diagnostic clinic or other entity.
9. *When did the first symptoms appear?* Ask about this subject through interrogatories and/or depositions. Follow up with Request for Production of Documents. Be prepared to follow up with discovery on all persons or entities involved in the first

appearance of symptoms. These may be preschools and their personnel, babysitters, pediatricians, emergency room personnel, law enforcement personnel, relatives of the child, Parents As Teachers, or other early childhood programs. Obtain all appropriate releases.

10. *What testing was done to evaluate the child's condition?* Ask about this subject through interrogatories and/or depositions. Follow up with Request for Production of Documents. Obtain all appropriate releases.
11. *Why was the child seen by the person who made the diagnosis?* (What made the parents think the child needed to be evaluated?) Ask about this subject through interrogatories and/or depositions. Follow up with Request for Production of Documents. Obtain all appropriate releases.
12. *Has any other professional confirmed the diagnosis?* Ask about this subject through interrogatories and/or depositions. Follow up with Request for Production of Documents. Obtain all appropriate releases.
13. *What is the child's current condition?* Ask about this subject through interrogatories and/or depositions. Follow up with Request for Production of Documents. Obtain all appropriate releases. Do research on the child's actual condition. Obtain authoritative and scholarly materials to educate yourself and the court on the child's particular condition. Research your state and local court evidentiary rules regarding admissibility of this evidence.
14. *What is the child's prognosis (expected outcome)?* Ask about this subject through interrogatories and/or depositions. Follow up with Request for Production of Documents. Obtain all appropriate releases. Obtain authoritative and scholarly materials to educate yourself and the court on the child's particular prognosis. Research your state and local court evidentiary rules regarding admissibility of this evidence.
15. *Is the condition curable (can they make it "go away")?* Ask about this subject through interrogatories and/or depositions. Follow up with Request for Production of Documents. Obtain all appropriate releases. Obtain authoritative and scholarly materials to educate yourself and the court on the curability of the child's particular condition. Research your state and local court evidentiary rules regarding admissibility of this evidence.
16. *Is the condition treatable (they can't make it go away but they can make things better or perhaps make things not get worse for the patient)?* Ask about this subject through interrogatories and/or depositions. Follow up with Request for Production of Documents. Obtain authoritative and scholarly materials to educate yourself and the court on the treatment of the child's particular condition. Research your state and local court evidentiary rules regarding admissibility of this evidence.
17. *Is the condition terminal (fatal)?* Ask about this subject through interrogatories and/or depositions. Follow up with Request for Production of Documents. Obtain authoritative and scholarly materials to educate yourself and the court on whether the child's particular condition is terminal. Research your state and local court evidentiary rules regarding admissibility of this evidence.
18. *Is the child expected ever to get a high school diploma, get a college degree, live on her own, hold a regular job, live completely independently, marry, have children?* Ask about this subject through interrogatories and/or depositions. Follow up with Request for Production of Documents. Obtain authoritative and scholarly materials to educate yourself and the court on the lifetime implications of the child's particu-

lar condition. Research your state and local court evidentiary rules regarding admissibility of this evidence.

19. *What is the child's life expectancy?* Ask about this subject through interrogatories and/or depositions. Follow up with Request for Production of Documents. Obtain authoritative and scholarly materials to educate yourself and the court on the life expectancy of the child's particular condition. Research your state and local court evidentiary rules regarding admissibility of this evidence.
20. *How does this condition impact the child's life now?* Ask about this subject through interrogatories and/or depositions. Follow up with Request for Production of Documents. Obtain authoritative and scholarly materials to educate yourself and the court on the current impact of the child's particular condition. Research your state and local court evidentiary rules regarding admissibility of this evidence.
21. *How is this condition expected to impact the child's life in the future?* Ask about this subject through interrogatories and/or depositions. Follow up with Request for Production of Documents. Obtain authoritative and scholarly materials to educate yourself and the court on the future impact of the child's particular condition. Research your state and local court evidentiary rules regarding admissibility of this evidence.
22. *How does this condition impact siblings' lives now?* Ask about this subject through interrogatories and/or depositions. Follow up with Request for Production of Documents. Obtain authoritative and scholarly materials to educate yourself and the court on the impact of the child's particular condition on siblings. Research your state and local court evidentiary rules regarding admissibility of this evidence.
23. *How is it expected to impact siblings' lives in the future?* Ask about this subject through interrogatories and/or depositions. Follow up with Request for Production of Documents. Obtain authoritative and scholarly materials to educate yourself and the court on the future impact of the child's particular condition on siblings. Research your state and local court evidentiary rules regarding admissibility of this evidence.
24. *How does this condition impact the parents' lives now?* Ask about this subject through interrogatories and/or depositions. Follow up with Request for Production of Documents. Obtain authoritative and scholarly materials to educate yourself and the court on the current impact of the child's particular condition on parents. Research your state and local court evidentiary rules regarding admissibility of this evidence.
25. *How is it expected to impact the parents' lives in the future?* Ask about this subject through interrogatories and/or depositions. Follow up with Request for Production of Documents. Obtain authoritative and scholarly materials to educate yourself and the court on the future impact of the child's particular condition on parents. Research your state and local court evidentiary rules regarding admissibility of this evidence.
26. *Who is the primary caregiver?* Ask about this subject through interrogatories and/or depositions. Follow up with Request for Production of Documents. Obtain all appropriate releases.
27. *How has the condition impacted the careers of the parents?* Ask about this subject through interrogatories and/or depositions. Follow up with Request for Production of Documents. Obtain authoritative and scholarly materials to educate yourself and

the court on the impact of the child's particular condition on careers of the parents. Research your state and local court evidentiary rules regarding admissibility of this evidence. Obtain employer and retirement account records from three time periods: (a) prior to the child's special need; (b) at the time the child's special need occurred; and (c) at the current time.

28. *How will the condition impact the parents' career advancement and retirement plan contributions?* Ask about this subject through interrogatories and/or depositions. Follow up with Request for Production of Documents. Obtain authoritative and scholarly materials to educate yourself and the court on the impact of the child's particular condition on career advancement and retirement plan contributions of the parents. Research your state and local court evidentiary rules regarding admissibility of this evidence. Obtain employer and retirement account records from three time periods: (a) prior to the child's special need; (b) the time the child's special need occurred; and (c) at the current time.
29. *What are the names, addresses, telephone numbers, and credentials of all persons the child currently sees for this condition?* Ask about this subject through interrogatories and/or depositions. Follow up with Request for Production of Documents. Obtain all appropriate releases.
30. *List all medications the child currently takes, the frequency and dosage, the reason for the medication, and the expected result from the medication.* Ask about this subject through interrogatories and/or depositions. Follow up with Request for Production of Documents. Obtain all appropriate releases.
31. *List all therapies the child currently receives, including therapies received at home and at school.* Ask about this subject through interrogatories and/or depositions. Follow up with Request for Production of Documents. Obtain authoritative and scholarly materials to educate yourself and the court on each of the child's particular therapies. Research your state and local court evidentiary rules regarding admissibility of this evidence. Obtain all appropriate releases and records from all therapists, service providers, referral entities, and funding sources. Obtain admissible evidence for all billing, invoices, and receipts. For each therapy, identify
    a. the person or organization who provides the therapy;
    b. who referred the child to that person or organization;
    c. where the therapy is received;
    d. the type of therapy and methodology used (for example, behavior therapy using ABA—applied behavior analysis method);
    e. the frequency and duration of therapy (for example, three times per week, one hour each time);
    f. the length of time therapy is expected to continue (for example, for the entire school year, for six weeks after the cast is removed, indefinitely, for six months);
    g. cost of the therapy;
    h. how is this paid (private pay, insurance, funding program);
    i. amount of uncovered cost of this therapy;
    j. incidental costs of this therapy—transportation, caregiver, supplies, meals, equipment;
    k. who takes the child to the therapy.
32. *What are the expectations regarding future therapies and medications?* Ask about this subject through interrogatories and/or depositions. Follow up with Request for Production of Documents. Obtain authoritative and scholarly materials to edu-

cate yourself and the court on the future therapies and medications relative to the child's particular condition. Research your state and local court evidentiary rules regarding admissibility of this evidence. Obtain all appropriate releases.

33. *Is the child on a waiting list for any therapy, program, school, or funding?* Ask about this subject through interrogatories and/or depositions. Follow up with Request for Production of Documents. Obtain all appropriate releases.
34. *Itemize all direct and indirect costs resulting from the child's special needs, including therapy, doctors, other practitioners, medications, supplements, equipment, supplies, caregiver training, special nutritional requirements, special clothing and personal care item requirements, home modifications, vehicle modifications, modifications at school, nonparental caregiver costs, transportation, and any other costs.* Ask about this subject through interrogatories and/or depositions. Follow up with Request for Production of Documents. Obtain all appropriate releases. Obtain admissible evidence for all billing, invoices, and receipts.
35. Laundry list of items the discovery file should contain:
    - medical reports, test results, diagnoses
    - evaluations
    - treatment plans
    - therapy plans
    - medication plans
    - child's safety plans for home, school, and away
    - medical bills
    - documentation of all costs (see preceding checklist)
    - IEPs (Individual Education Plans), 504 Plans current and previous (see footnote 9)
    - information on every treating professional (see preceding checklist)
    - copies of articles or book excerpts providing basic information on child's particular condition
    - detailed therapy and treatment schedule
    - detailed daily schedule

Ask about these "laundry list" subjects through interrogatories and/or depositions. Follow up with Request for Production of Documents. Obtain all appropriate releases. Obtain admissible evidence for all reports, documents, billing, invoices, and receipts.

Motions for the Appointment of a Guardian ad Litem (GAL) certainly should address the issue of special needs, to put the guardian ad litem on notice of the issue and to prevent unnecessary delay caused by the issue being raised later in the case. State family law statutes should require courts to raise and consider the issue of the appointment of a guardian ad litem in special needs cases, as many state statutes do in cases involving abuse. The Motion form should contain a box to check if the party requesting the appointment of the guardian ad litem is aware of any special needs of any of the children, with a few lines for brief explanation and another box to check if the requesting party is not aware of any special needs of any of the children. If a party submits a request for appointment of a guardian ad litem without using the court's form, the party would be required to state the same information regarding special needs that would be required on the court's form.

SAMPLE GUARDIAN AD LITEM MOTION SPECIAL NEEDS CASE

IN THE FAMILY COURT OF ________________ COUNTY
STATE OF ________________

In Re the Marriage of:	)	
	)	
________________,	)	
___________,	)	
Petitioner,	)	
vs.	)	Case No. ________________
________________,	)	Division: _______
___________,	)	
Respondent.	)	

MOTION FOR APPOINTMENT OF GUARDIAN AD LITEM

Comes now the Petitioner, ____________________, by and through his attorney, ______________________, and respectfully requests the Court appoint a Guardian Ad Litem for the minor children:

CHILD ONE
CHILD TWO
for the following reasons:

_____ credible allegations of child neglect
_____ credible allegations of child abuse
_____ special needs of the child(ren), specifically: ____________________
____

I AM/AM NOT AWARE OF ANY SPECIAL NEEDS OF THE CHILD(REN), SPECIFICALLY: ____
____

_____ other

This Motion for Appointment of Guardian Ad Litem is supported by a sworn affidavit, a true and correct copy of which is attached hereto and marked as Exhibit 1.

Respectfully submitted,
[Attorney Signature Block]
ATTORNEY FOR RESPONDENT

<u>CERTIFICATE OF SERVICE</u>

I hereby certify that a true and correct copy of the foregoing was deposited in the U.S. Mail, postage prepaid to:

Opposing Counsel's Name, Street Address, City, State ZIP

this ______ day of ________________, 20___.

____

Attorney for Respondent

The *Order Appointing a Guardian ad Litem* should also contain a similar set of boxes for the judge to check, to put the judge on notice of the possibility of special needs issues being raised in the case. This is especially relevant when the judge is determining the amount of the initial fees deposit the parties must make for the guardian ad litem.

SAMPLE GUARDIAN AD LITEM ORDER SPECIAL NEEDS CASE

IN THE FAMILY COURT OF __________________ COUNTY
STATE OF __________________

In Re the Marriage of:	)	
	)	
__________________,	)	
____________,	)	
Petitioner,	)	
vs.	)	Case No. __________________
__________________,	)	Division: _______
____________,	)	
Respondent.	)	

ORDER APPOINTING GUARDIAN AD LITEM

IT IS HEREBY ORDERED that __________________________ shall be appointed as Guardian Ad Litem for the minor children:

CHILD ONE
CHILD TWO
for the following reasons:

_____ credible allegations of child neglect
_____ credible allegations of child abuse
_____ special needs of the child(ren), specifically: ________________________
THE PARTIES STATE THAT THEY ARE/ARE NOT AWARE OF ANY SPECIAL NEEDS OF THE CHILD(REN), SPECIFICALLY:
____
____
____
_____ other

SO ORDERED:

____
The Honorable ____________________

Statements of Income and Expenses and similar required financial filings of the parties should address the issues of special needs. This can be accomplished by having an expense category for Special Needs with separate line items for such expenses.

Example:

(This list is for guidance only, and is not intended to be considered exhaustive. This list may need to be expanded on a case-by-case basis.)

- cost of actual physical modifications at home (both homes);
- cost of actual physical modifications as well as other (such as testing) modifications at school;
- cost of medications (both homes);
- cost of supplements;
- cost of special diet;
- cost of therapy;
- cost of treatment;
- cost of special equipment and supplies—includes special shoes, clothes, sensory items, medical supplies other than medication, therapy items, wigs, orthopedic devices, helper dogs, and any other items required. These can vary at different stages of therapy or treatment (both homes);
- cost of training of caregivers;
- amount that special needs care has decreased caregiver's income and retirement;
- public services and assistance received;
- private services and assistance received.

SAMPLE STATEMENT OF INCOME AND EXPENSES

IN THE FAMILY COURT OF ____________________ COUNTY
STATE OF ____________________

In Re the Marriage of:	)	
	)	
____________________,	)	
	)	
Petitioner,	)	
and	)	Case No. ____________________
	)	
____________________,	)	Division: _______
	)	
Respondent.	)	

STATEMENT OF INCOME AND EXPENSES OF PETITIONER SPECIAL NEEDS CASE

1. **INCOME**

   A. Name and Address of Employer: ______________________________

Gross Wages or Salary and Commission Each Pay Period $__________

PAID: ___ Weekly ___ Biweekly ___ Semimonthly ___ Monthly

Number of Dependents Claimed: _____

   B. Payroll Deductions:
   FICA (Social Security Tax) $_____
   Federal Withholding Tax $_____
   State Withholding Tax $_____
   City Earnings Tax (If Applicable) $_____
   Union Dues $_____
   Others: $_____
   ______________ $_____
   ______________ $_____
   Total Deductions Each Pay Period $_____
   Net Take Home Pay Each Pay Period $_____

Additional Income from Rentals, Dividends and Business Enterprises, Social Security, A.F.D.C. V.A. Benefits, Pensions, Annuities, Bonuses, "Commissions and all Other Sources" (give monthly average and list sources of income). $__________
   Average Monthly Total
   C. Total Average Net Monthly Income $
   D. Your Share of the Gross Income Shown on Last Year's Federal Income Tax Return $ ___________

2. **EXPENSES REQUIRED TO MAINTAIN PREVIOUS STANDARD OF LIVING STATED ON A MONTHLY AVERAGE**
   A. Rent or Mortgage Payments
   B. Utilities
      1. Gas
      2. Water
      3. Electricity
      4. Telephone
      5. Trash Service
   C. Automobiles
      1. Gas and Oil
      2. Maintenance (Routine)
      3. Taxes and License
      4. Payment on the Auto Loan

D. Insurance
1. Life
2. Health & Accident
3. Disability
4. Homeowners (If Not Included in Mortgage Payment)
5. Automobile

E. Total Payment Installments Contracts

F. Child Support Paid to Others for Children Not in Your Custody (Excluding Children of This Marriage)

G. Maintenance or Alimony (Excluding Petitioner or Respondent Herein)

H. Church and Charitable Contributions

I. Other Living Expenses (Total of Items 1–7 Listed Below)

YOURS	CHILDREN IN YOUR CUSTODY

1. Food
2. Clothing
3. Medical Care, Dental Care, and Drugs
4. Recreation
5. Laundry and Cleaning
6. Barber Shop or Beauty Shop
7. School and Books

J. Day Care Center or Babysitter

K. All Other Expenses Not Presently Identified (Give as Monthly Average)

L. Special Needs Expenses (Give as Monthly Average)
1. Medical treatment
2. Doctors
3. Therapy
4. Other medical expenses
5. Equipment
6. Supplies
7. Training
8. Transportation
9. Caregiver
10. Companion
11. Professionals
12. Medication
13. Supplements
14. Dietary modifications
15. Household modifications
16. Daily/personal care items
17. Respite care
18. Activities
19. Meals
20. Sensory items
21. Other special needs items
22. Total special needs items

M. Total Average Monthly Expenses

STATE OF ______________

SS

COUNTY OF ____________

COMES NOW _________, being of lawful age and after being duly sworn, states that Affiant has read the foregoing **STATEMENT OF INCOME AND EXPENSES**, and that the facts therein are true and correct according to the Affiant's best knowledge and belief.

____

Affiant

Subscribed and sworn to before me, the undersigned Notary Public, on this ___day of_________, 20___.

____

Notary Public

My commission expires:

PRACTICE TIP

What should be included in the Statement of Income and Expenses?

In addition to the standard items disclosed in the Statement of Expenses, the Statement of Income and Expenses should also disclose *all direct and indirect costs resulting from the child's special needs, including*

- therapy
- doctors
- other practitioners
- medications
- supplements
- equipment
- supplies
- caregiver training
- special nutritional requirements
- special clothing and personal care item requirements
- home modifications
- vehicle modifications
- modifications at school
- nonparental caregiver costs
- transportation
- any other costs

Child Support Guidelines should have a separate section for Special Needs and should include all of the costs just listed in the Statement of Income and Expenses. Another option is that a different form should be used for calculating child support in cases involving children with special needs.

MODEL CHILD SUPPORT CHART FOR USE IN SPECIAL NEEDS CASES

In re the Marriage of: ______________________________

Form 14SN—CHILD SUPPORT AMOUNT CALCULATION WORKSHEET

CHILDREN	DATE OF BIRTH	CHILDREN	DATE OF BIRTH
Name		Name	

	Parent Receiving Support	Parent Paying Support	Combined
1. MONTHLY GROSS INCOME	$	$	
a. Court-ordered maintenance being received	$	$	
2. ADJUSTMENTS (per month)	($)	($)	
a. Other court or administratively ordered child support being paid			
b. Court-ordered maintenance being paid	($)	($)	
c. Support obligation for other children in parent's primary physical custody	($)	($)	
3. ADJUSTED MONTHLY GROSS INCOME (sum of lines 1 and 1a, minus lines 2a, 2b, and 2c)	$	$	$
4. PROPORTIONATE SHARE OF COMBINED ADJUSTED MONTHLY GROSS INCOME (each parent's line 3 income divided by combined line 3 income)	%	%	
5. BASIC CHILD SUPPORT AMOUNT (from support chart using combined line 3 income)			$
6. ADDITIONAL CHILD-REARING COSTS (per month)			
a. Reasonable work-related childcare costs of the parent receiving support less any child care tax credit	$		

b. Reasonable work-related childcare costs of the parent paying support		$	
c. Health insurance costs for the children who are subjects of this proceeding	$	$	
d. Uninsured extraordinary medical costs (agreed by parents or ordered by court)	$	$	
e. Other extraordinary child-rearing costs (agreed by parents or ordered by court)	$	$	
f. Special needs expenses and costs: therapy equipment medications supplements dietary costs sensory items respite care other reasonable items	$	$	
7. TOTAL ADDITIONAL CHILD SUPPORT COSTS (sum of lines 6a, 6b, 6c, 6d, and 6e)	$	$	$
8. TOTAL COMBINED CHILD SUPPORT COSTS (sum of line 5 and combined line 7)			$
9. EACH PARENT'S SUPPORT OBLIGATION (multiply line 8 by each parent's line 4)	$	$	
10. CREDIT FOR ADDITIONAL CHILD-REARING COSTS (line 7 of parent paying support)		$	
11. ADJUSTMENTS FOR A PORTION OF THE AMOUNTS EXPENDED DURING PERIODS OF OVERNIGHT VISITATION OR CUSTODY (multiply line 5 by ____%)		$	
12. ADJUSTMENT FOR RESPITE CARE AND OTHER EXPENSES IF VISITATION IS NOT REGULARLY EXERCISED		$	
13. PRESUMED CHILD SUPPORT AMOUNT (line 9 minus line 10 and 11 plus line 12)		$	
PREPARED BY: Attorney for			
EXHIBIT # __________			

PRACTICE TIP

Special considerations regarding child support

In addition to the standard child support considerations, the following items should be considered when determining the amount of child support needed in a *divorce involving a special needs child:*

- costs of therapy
- doctor bills, uncovered amounts, and co-pays
- bills of other practitioners, uncovered amounts and co-pays
- medications, uncovered medications and co-pays
- cost of supplements
- cost of equipment
- expenditures for supplies
- expenses of caregiver training
- extra cost of special nutritional requirements
- extra cost of special clothing and personal care item requirements
- cost of home modifications
- cost of vehicle modifications
- cost of modifications at school
- nonparental caregiver costs
- transportation expenses
- any other costs

C. Maintenance/Alimony Calculations

Giving up one's career and retirement contributions to care for a special needs child can have a dramatic impact on the primary caregiver parent's immediate and lifelong financial picture. Accordingly, calculations regarding the amount of maintenance to be awarded should include thorough consideration of the impact that caring for the person with special needs has on the career, both short- and long-term, of the caregiver.

Managing the care of a special needs child can be a full-time job. When a parent is frequently spending time taking the child to doctor appointments, taking the child to therapy, scheduling appointments for the child, dealing with concerns of therapists and teachers, and responding to crisis after crisis, it is difficult if not impossible to keep a full-time job. The primary caregiver spouse is frequently exhausted, sleep deprived, and stressed out. A primary caregiver spouse may be unemployed, underemployed, or have unstable employment due to caring for the special needs of the child. It can be difficult or cost prohibitive to obtain appropriate child care for a special needs child. A case that might otherwise not look like a maintenance case may be one in which maintenance is appropriate for the primary caregiver parent. In short, the primary caregiver parent often gives up her current career, her future career potential, her current and future economic opportunity, and current and future contributions to retirement accounts. If these special needs cases are not treated differently, primary caregiver parents will be penalized financially and may be destitute in their old age.

D. Parenting Plan

Lawyers should also discuss the issue of special needs with their clients at the stage of preparing the Parenting Plan. Standard parenting plans must be modified when dealing with children with special needs. It is pointless merely to submit a standard or form parenting plan that does not meet the needs of a special needs child.

PRACTICE TIP

To draft an appropriate Parenting Plan in a family law case involving special needs, the lawyers should have the following items in their client file (in addition to the usual client file items):

- Medical reports, test results, diagnoses
- Evaluations
- Treatment plans
- Therapy plans
- Medication plans
- Child's safety plans for home, school, and away
- Medical bills
- Documentation of all direct and indirect costs resulting from the child's special needs, including therapy, doctors, other practitioners, medications, supplements, equipment, supplies, caregiver training, special nutritional requirements, special clothing and personal care items or requirements, home modifications, vehicle modifications, modifications at school, nonparental caregiver costs, transportation, and any other costs
- IEPs and 504 Plans, current and previous (See footnote 9 for an explanation of IEPs and 504 Plans.)
- Information on every treating professional—the names, addresses, telephone numbers, and credentials of all persons the child currently sees for this condition
- Copies of articles or book excerpts providing basic information on child's particular condition
- Detailed therapy and treatment schedule
- Detailed daily schedule
- Documentation for all other special needs items discussed at the initial intake interview

SAMPLE SPECIAL NEEDS PARENTING PLAN

IN THE FAMILY COURT OF ____________________ COUNTY
STATE OF ____________________

In Re the Marriage of:	)	
	)	
____________________,	)	
_____________,	)	
Petitioner,	)	
vs.	)	Case No. ____________________
____________________,	)	Division: ________
_____________,	)	
Respondent.	)	

<u>CONSENT PARENTING PLAN FOR SPECIAL NEEDS</u>

For purposes of this Parenting Plan, "Minor Children" refers to CHILD ONE, born Month, Day, Year, and CHILD TWO, born Month, Day, Year, either collectively, or either child separately, as is appropriate.

Mother and Father shall have joint legal custody and Father shall have sole physical custody of said minor children.

Father's residence shall be designated as the primary residence of the minor children for mailing and educational purposes.

CUSTODY

PARENTING TIME SCHEDULE

Due to the special needs of the children, the standard visitation schedule is not in the best interests of the children. The girls are 12-year-old twins. One of the children, CHILD ONE, has cerebral palsy. She receives intensive therapy for many hours every week, and, by necessity, her life is extremely structured.

The two most important aspects of this Parenting Plan are:

- The best interests of the children, and
- Cooperation of the parents.

CUSTODY, VISITATION AND RESIDENTIAL TIME FOR EACH CHILD WITH EACH PARENT SHALL BE AT SUCH TIMES AS THE PARTIES SHALL AGREE. The parties are strongly encouraged to work together cooperatively and flexibly to reach by amicable agreement such custody, visitation and residential times as shall be in the best interests of the children and keeping in mind their special needs. In the event the parties cannot agree, Mother shall have custody, visitation, or residential time as set forth below and Father shall have all other time as his custody, visitation, or residential time.

EACH PARENT IS STRONGLY ENCOURAGED TO PUT THE CHILDREN FIRST AND TO MAKE EVERY REASONABLE EFFORT TO MEET THE UNIQUE NEEDS OF THE SPECIAL NEEDS CHILD(REN). Each parent is strongly encouraged to take time every week to spend one-on-one time with the special needs child and to spend one-on-one time with the non–special needs child.

WEEKDAY VISITATION

Mother may come to Father's house to visit the children during the evenings whenever her schedule permits, as long as the parties shall so agree. In the event the parties cannot agree upon the night or nights of this visitation, Mother shall visit the children at Father's house or pick them up at Father's house on Wednesday evenings. Mother shall visit/pick up children at 6:00 PM and return them to Father's house by 7:15 PM, when she is welcome to participate in their bedtime routine, which usually lasts until 8:00 PM. Mother may extend this weekday visitation to overnight visitation. In the event the parties agree upon overnight visitation during the week, Mother shall either return the children to Father's house the next morning or take them to their morning activity, as agreed to by the parties.

WEEKENDS

The children are involved in many activities due to their special needs. These activities require great flexibility and cooperation by the parents regarding the weekend visitation. The general goal is that Mother shall have the children for approximately half of the weekends, although this will often not be every other weekend. The parties shall frequently consult each other regarding the scheduled activities and arrange the weekend visitation around the schedules and best interests of the children. If the parties cannot agree, Mother shall have visitation of the children every other weekend beginning at 6:00 PM on Friday through and ending at 6:00 PM. on Sunday, beginning the weekend following the date of the judgment. If either parent's holiday weekend, as set forth below, conflicts with this, then the parent losing their regular weekend shall receive the other parent's next regular weekend to thereafter be followed by the original schedule so that each would have two consecutive weekends.

SUMMER

The children attend summer school for six weeks every year. This usually runs from June through August. There is a week or two between the regular school year letting out and the start of summer school, and there is a week or two between the end of summer school and the beginning of the next school year. During these weeks, the girls usually attend a special needs summer day camp. It is important for the girls to attend summer school. If they are registered for summer school but do not attend consistently, they will not be eligible to attend in subsequent years.

Mother may exercise periods of summer visitation during the summer regardless of whether it is during the weeks of summer school, as long as she shall take the children to summer school if her time periods fall during those weeks.

Since these arrangements must be made well in advance, Mother shall notify Father of her choice of option in writing by March 1st every year.

Mother may have liberal summer visitation as the parties shall agree. In the event the parties cannot agree, subject to the above provisions, Mother shall have three weeks each summer (to be divided into three 7 consecutive day periods) to coincide with the children's school summer vacation. Mother may select the first week of this summer vacation by notifying Father of same (each notification herein to be in writing) by February 1st of each year, one week may then be excluded by Father by February 15th and then the next week may be selected by Mother by March lst, one more week may then be excluded by Father by March 15th, the final week may be selected by Mother by April lst. Father's excluded weeks shall prevail over Mother's weekend and weekday periods set forth above.

HOLIDAYS AND SPECIAL DAYS

1. Holiday and special day custody shall prevail over weekend, weekday, and summer vacation set forth above. Birthday periods shall not prevail when in conflict with other Holidays and Special Days.
2. Mother shall have the minor children on her birthday and on Mother's Day of each year from 9:00 AM to 9:00 PM; plus "Holiday Group A" in even-numbered years and "Holiday Group B" in odd-numbered years.
3. Father shall have the minor children on his birthday and on Father's Day of each year from 9:00 AM to 9:00 PM; plus "Holiday Group A" in odd-numbered years and "Holiday Group B" in even-numbered years.
4. Mother and Father are encouraged to communicate to attempt to arrange a combined event/activity for the children's birthday. In the event they cannot agree, the following provisions regarding the children's birthday shall apply.
5. Due to the serious special needs of the children, the conditions stated in the above paragraphs concerning WEEKDAY, WEEKEND, and SUMMER visitation shall apply to HOLIDAY GROUPS A & B.

HOLIDAY GROUP A

1. PRESIDENT'S DAY/WASHINGTON'S BIRTHDAY (OBSERVED) weekend from 5:00 PM the Friday prior to 8:00 AM the following Tuesday.
2. A period of 7 (seven) days during the children's school spring break, the exact days to be selected and notice given in writing to the other parent by February lst.
3. INDEPENDENCE DAY if July 4th falls on a (a) Tuesday, Wednesday, or Thursday from 5:00 PM on July 3rd until 9:00 AM on July 5th; (b) Friday or Saturday from 5:00 PM on the Thursday before until 9:00 AM on the following Monday; (c) Sunday or Monday from 5:00 PM on the Friday before until 9:00 AM on the following Tuesday.
4. HALLOWEEN (October 31st) night from 4:00 PM until 9:00 AM the following day.
5. CHRISTMAS VACATION from December 25th beginning at 10:00 AM through 9:00 AM on December 31st.
6. Each child's birthday from 9:00 AM until 9:00 AM the following day.

HOLIDAY GROUP B

1. MARTIN LUTHER KING weekend from 5:00 PM the Friday prior through 8:00 AM the following Tuesday.
2. MEMORIAL DAY weekend from 5:00 PM the Friday prior through 8:00 AM the following Tuesday.

3. LABOR DAY weekend from 5:00 PM the Friday prior through 8:00 AM the following Tuesday.
4. THANKSGIVING weekend from 5:00 PM the Wednesday prior through 8:00 AM the following Monday.
5. CHRISTMAS VACATION from 5:00 PM the day the children's school Christmas vacation begins through 10:00 AM on December 25th and December 31st beginning at 9:00 AM through 8:00 AM the day the children's school Christmas vacation ends.
6. The day prior to each child's birthday beginning at 9:00 AM through 9:00 AM the day of the birthday.

The serious special needs of the children require that Mother and Father be far more cooperative and flexible than the parents of children without special needs.

<u>EXCHANGES</u>
[X] When school is in session:

Exchanges of all children from Mother to Father shall occur at:
[ ] Residence of Mother [X] Residence of Father [ ] School
[ ] Other Location—Parents currently reside at same location, exchanges not applicable.

Exchanges of all children from Father to Mother shall occur at:
[ ] Residence of Mother [X] Residence of Father [ ] School
[ ] Other Location

[ ] When school is not in session or if all children are not school age:

Exchange of all children from Mother to Father shall occur at:
[ ] Residence of Mother [X] Residence of Father
[ ] Other Location

Exchange of all children from Father to Mother shall occur at:
[ ] Residence of Mother [X] Residence of Father
[ ] Other Location

[ ] If an exchange occurs at a location other than a parent's residence, the parent scheduled to have time with the children shall pick up and return the children to the specified location and the other parent shall be responsible for assuring the children are at the specified location for pick up, unless other arrangements are described.

<u>TRANSPORTATION</u>
Transportation arrangements for all children for all scheduled parenting times, including weekdays, weekends, holidays and vacation times, shall be as follows:

[X] Mother shall be responsible for transportation of the children at the beginning of the visit. Mother shall be responsible for transportation of the children at the end of the visit.

Mother and Father shall share responsibility for all transportation of the children, including cost, as follows:

[ ] Extraordinary Transportation Costs (bus, taxi, train, airfare) shall be the responsibility of Mother [ ] Father [ ] Shared % Mother % Father

CHANGES

The parents' schedules and commitments may require occasional changes in the parenting time schedule. Parents shall attempt to agree on any changes, but the parent receiving a request for a change shall have the final decision on whether the change shall occur.

The parent making the request may make such request
[X] in person [X] by phone [X] in writing to the other parent [X] other—email

The request for change shall be made no later than:
[ ] 24 hours [X] one week [ ] two weeks [ ] other
prior to the date of the requested change.

The parent receiving the request shall respond no later than:
24 hours [ ] one week [ ] two weeks [X] other—72 hours
after receiving the requested change.

The response to the request may be made
[X] in person [X] by phone [X] in writing to the other parent [X] other—email

Any parent requesting a change of schedule shall be responsible for any additional child care or transportation costs resulting from the change.

Mother and Father shall cooperate to allow the children to meet their therapeutic, school, and social commitments.

TELEPHONE CONTACTS

Each parent shall have reasonable access to all children by telephone during any period in which the children are with the other parent, unless otherwise specified.

RELOCATION

Absent exigent circumstances as determined by a Court with jurisdiction, you, as a party to this action, are ordered to notify, in writing by certified mail, return receipt requested, and at least sixty days prior to the proposed relocation, each party to this action of any proposed relocation of the principal residence of the children, including the following information: (1) The intended new residence, including the specific address and mailing address, if known, and if not known, the city; (2) The home telephone number of the new residence, if known; (3) The date of the intended move or proposed relocation; (4) A brief statement of the specific reasons for the proposed relocation of the children; and (5) A proposal for a revised schedule of custody or visitation with the children. Your obligation to provide this information to each party continues as long as you or any other party by virtue of this order is entitled to custody of a child covered by this order. Your failure to obey the order of this Court regarding the proposed relocation may result in further litigation to enforce such order, including contempt of court. In addition, your failure to notify a party of a relocation of the child may be considered in a proceeding to modify custody or visitation with the children. Reasonable costs and attorney fees shall be assessed against you if you fail to give the required notice.

LEGAL CUSTODY

Legal Custody: The parties shall agree before making any final decisions on issues affecting the growth and development of the children; including, but not limited to, choice of religious upbringing, choice of child care provider, choice of school, course of study, special tutoring, extracurricular activities, including but not limited to, music, art, dance, and other cultural lessons or activities and gymnastics or other athletic activities, choice of camp or other comparable summer activity, nonemergency medical and dental treatment, psychological, psychiatric, or like treatment or counseling, the choice of particular health care providers, the extent of any travel away from home, part- or full-time employment, purchase or operation of a motor vehicle, contraception and sex education, and decisions relating to actual or potential litigation on behalf of the children. However, each parent may make decisions regarding the day-to-day care and control of the children and in emergencies affecting the health and safety of the children while the children are residing with him or her. The parents shall endeavor, whenever reasonable, to be consistent in such day-to-day decisions.

Communication: Each parent shall ensure that the other parent is provided with copies of all communications or information received from a child's school, and if a second copy of the communication is not provided by the school, shall make a copy for the other parent. Each parent shall notify the other of any activity such as school conferences, programs, sporting and other special events, etc., where parents are invited to attend and each shall encourage and welcome the presence of the other.

Children Not Involved in Court or Financial Communications: The parties shall not talk about adult issues, parenting matters, financial issues, and other Court-related topics when the children are present. Such discussions shall not be had during custody exchanges of the children or during telephone visits. The children shall not be used to carry such messages, written communication, or child support payments between the parents.

Medical Care Information: Each parent shall have the authority to seek any emergency medical treatment for the children when in his or her custody. Each shall advise the other of any medical emergency or serious illness or injury suffered by the minor children as soon as possible after learning of the same, and shall give the other parent details of the emergency, injury, or illness and the name and telephone numbers of all treating doctors. Each parent shall inform the other before any routine medical care, treatment, or examination by a health care provider, including said provider's name and telephone number. Each party shall direct all doctors involved in the care and treatment of the minor children to give the other parent all information regarding any injury or illness and the medical treatment or examination, if requested. For purposes of this paragraph, a serious injury or illness is one that requires a child (1) to be confined to home for more than 48 hours, or (2) to be admitted to, or treated at, a hospital or surgical facility, or (3) to receive any type of general anesthesia or invasive surgical procedure or test.

Child Care Provider: If both parents will need to use a child care provider during periods of custody or visitation, they shall use the same child care provider, unless the distances between their residences or places of employment make the use of the same child care provider unreasonable.

Access to Records: Each parent shall be entitled to immediate access from the other or from a third party to records and information pertaining to the children, including but not limited to medical, dental, health, child care, school or educational records; and each shall take whatever steps are necessary to ensure that the other parent has such access.

Activities to Not Conflict with Custody or Visitation: The parties shall enroll the children in activities, particularly outside of school, which, to the extent possible, are scheduled at times and places that avoid interruption and disruption of the custody or visitation time of the other party unless consented to by that parent. The special needs of the children require far greater cooperation and flexibility by the parents than is required of the parents of children without special needs.

Resolution of Disputes: If the parties fail to agree on the interpretation of the Parenting Plan, or are unable to agree upon a final decision on issues affecting the growth and development or health and safety of the children, they shall submit the dispute to a mutually agreed-upon Special Needs Coordinator who shall hear and arbitrate the issue. In the event they are not able to agree on a Special Needs Coordinator, they shall each select a Special Needs Coordinator from the list of approved Special Needs Coordinators maintained by the ___________ County Family Court and the two Special Needs Coordinators shall determine who shall arbitrate the case. The Special Needs Coordinator shall be a quick and informal tribunal to arbitrate issues that may arise in the future, including but not limited to increasing or decreasing child support; changes in therapy, treatment, education, custody and/or visitation; and issues relating to expenses.

<u>CHILD SUPPORT AND OTHER EXPENSES</u>

Due to the special needs of the children, the application of Standard Child Support Guidelines would be inappropriate and/or unjust. The initial amount of child support shall be $_________ per month, payable by Mother to Father. This amount shall be modifiable. This is the base amount, which DOES include the current amount for nutritional supplements/regimens, and DOES NOT include additional support for therapy, activities, camps, or other expenses necessitated by their special needs. Parents shall pay for these additional items based upon their proportional share of income. Parents acknowledge that future nutritional supplements/regimens may involve an increased cost, and parents agree to pay such increased cost based upon their proportional income.

Child support shall terminate for CHILD TWO in accordance with § _______ [Statutes of state of _______________].

The Parties recognize that due to the special needs of CHILD ONE, child support may not terminate at age 18 or at any particular age and may continue if the child is physically or mentally incapacitated from supporting herself and insolvent and unmarried as per § _______ [Statutes of state of _______________].

In addition, each party will continue to contribute to child support as long as they are able to provide child support.

The child support shall be paid 50% on the 1st and 50% on the 15th day of each month.

<u>HEALTH CARE COSTS</u>

The children are currently covered by _______________ medical insurance through Father's employer. Both parents shall cooperate to keep the children covered under this insurance or under another plan. In the event it becomes appropriate to obtain other health insurance for the children, the parents shall pay the expense of such coverage based upon their proportionate share of income. Both parents shall cooperate to provide insurance ID cards to the other parent as applicable, and to complete all forms required by the coverage.

Unless both parties have agreed to use a health care provider that is not covered by the health benefit plan, if a parent incurs an expense to a health care provider that is not covered by the health benefit plan that would have been covered, or covered at a more favorable rate, if a provider included in the plan had been used, then that parent shall pay seventy-five percent (75%) and the other parent twenty-five percent (25%) of the uncovered expenses.

"Health expenses" shall be defined in accordance with Internal Revenue Code (1987) § 213 "Medical, Dental, etc., Expenses" or any other section enacted in replacement, in addition or in substitution thereof, and/or any Internal Revenue Regulation, including but not limited to § 1.213-1 or any relevant Regulation enacted in replacement, in addition or in substitution thereof, or any relevant Treasury Decision, Regulation, or any Revenue Ruling defining those types or kinds of medical costs that are deductible under the Internal Revenue Code, and shall also include orthodontia and optical care (including but not limited to prescription eyeglasses or contact lenses and eye examinations conducted by an optician, optometrist, or ophthalmologist), treatment, and appliances. Psychological and counseling expenses shall be paid as the parties agree, or absent agreement to the extent they are included as "Health Expenses" defined above or are determined by the child's case manager to be in the best interests of the child.

All health expenses incurred on behalf of the children and not paid by the health benefit plan shall be paid based upon each parent's proportionate share of income. The health expenses covered by this paragraph are not limited to just the usual medical, dental, orthodontic, optical, and psychological expenses of children without special needs. Due to the special needs of the children, they have and are expected to continue to have extraordinary medical, therapeutic, and other expenses that shall be paid by the parents based upon proportionate share of income, in addition to the base amount of child support.

The Parties recognize that due to the special needs of CHILD ONE, payment of health care costs may not terminate at age 18 or at any particular age and may continue if the child is physically or mentally incapacitated from supporting herself and insolvent and unmarried as per § _______ [Statutes of state of _______________].

In addition, each party will continue to contribute to health care as long as they are able to provide health care.

FOR EACH CHILD WITH SPECIAL NEEDS, ATTACH AN EXHIBIT CONTAINING A SUMMARY OF:

[ ] Diagnosis

[ ] Doctors, therapists, and other professionals

[ ] Child's current daily schedule and routine
[ ] Child's current therapy plan
[ ] Summary of how special needs affect the child's daily life
[ ] Itemization and explanation of the costs involved in or caused by the special needs
[ ] Who is the primary caregiver of the child
[ ] Primary caregiver's daily schedule
[ ] Statement as to the impact of transitions and schedule changes on the child
[ ] List of equipment and special items needed by the child and the location of such items
[ ] Suggested physical custody arrangement
[ ] Suggested legal custody arrangement
[ ] Suggested visitation—daily, weekly, weekends, holidays, summers, and special days

<u>EDUCATION AND EXTRAORDINARY EXPENSES</u>

Due to the special needs of the children, they currently incur and are expected to continue to incur extraordinary educational and other expenses. These shall be paid by the parties based upon their proportionate share of income. If the parties cannot agree on the extraordinary expenses for education, therapy, activities, equipment, supplements, and/or other items, the parties agree to pay (based upon their proportionate share of income) for the items determined by the child's/children's Special Needs Coordinator to be in the best interest of the child/children.

____________________ ____________________

Petitioner Respondent

____________________ ____________________

Attorney for Petitioner Attorney for Respondent

[Adapted from Special Needs Parenting Plan, coauthored with Kieran Coyne, attorney in St. Louis, Missouri.]

Property Distribution Worksheets should address the issue of special needs. This can be accomplished by including line items for the current and future impact on the career and ability to contribute to retirement accounts of the caregiver. Again, thorough consideration should be given to this subject when awarding property to either party.

Settlement Agreements should contain a recital of whether there are any known special needs, just as they contain a statement that there either will be maintenance or that it is waived. This recital will add clarity to Settlement Agreements and will be another opportunity for the judge to be made aware of the issue of special needs when deciding the case, whether by trial or by approval of settlement.

SAMPLE SETTLEMENT AGREEMENT

IN THE FAMILY COURT OF ________________ COUNTY
STATE OF ________________

In Re the Marriage of:	)	
	)	
________________,	)	
____________,	)	
Petitioner,	)	
vs.	)	Case No. ________________
________________,	)	Division: _______
____________,	)	
Respondent.	)	

MARITAL SETTLEMENT AGREEMENT

This MARITAL SETTLEMENT AGREEMENT (hereinafter the "AGREEMENT") is made on the _______ day of ____________, 2005, between __________, (hereinafter the "WIFE"), and _____________, (hereinafter the "HUSBAND"), and collectively referred to as the "PARTIES."

WITNESSETH that:

WHEREAS, the PARTIES to this AGREEMENT were married on the ____ day of ___________, ______, and because of irreconcilable differences that have arisen between them, which render it impossible for them to live together as husband and wife, and

WHEREAS, the PARTIES believe there is no reasonable likelihood that the marriage of the PARTIES can be preserved, and that the marriage is irretrievably broken, and

WHEREAS, there are two Children born of the marriage to wit: Child One, born Month, Day, Year, and Child Two, born Month, Day, Year, (hereinafter the "Minor Children"), and

WHEREAS, there is now pending an action in the Family Court of the County of _____________, State of ____________ praying that the marriage of the PARTIES be dissolved, and

WHEREAS, the PARTIES hereby desire to fully and finally settle all property rights, and claims between them and make provisions regarding the disposition of their property, maintenance, child support, child custody, attorneys' fees, and the costs of these proceedings;

NOW, THEREFORE, for valuable consideration, each received by the other and for mutual promises herein contained, it is agreed as follows;

I. **AGREEMENT CONTINGENT UPON COURT REVIEW:**

All of the stipulations, conditions, and agreements hereinafter contained are contingent upon the Family Court of the County of __________, State of _______, entering an order and judgment dissolving the marriage of the PARTIES and are contingent upon the Court's determination that this AGREEMENT is not unconscionable.

II. **CHILD CUSTODY AND SUPPORT MATTERS:**

The PARTIES agree that the provisions of the PARENTING PLAN (hereinafter the 'PLAN') attached as Exhibit 'A' shall govern the terms of the Minor Children's custody, visitation, and support arrangements. The PARTIES agree that they will abide by the terms of the PLAN. (Mother shall Pay Father the sum of $_________ per month in child support.)

III. **DIVISION OF PROPERTY:**

A. **NONMARITAL PROPERTY:**

The PARTIES agree that there is nonmarital property to be set apart by the Court, which property is divided as indicated on Exhibit B attached.

B. **MARITAL PROPERTY:**

1. **PERSONAL PROPERTY**

a. **Division of Personal Property**

The PARTIES make specific reference to the division of personal property identified on Exhibit B attached, with the property being awarded to the PARTY indicated. Any household goods and personal effects not identified on said exhibit or awarded by this Agreement are awarded to the party who has possession or control of such unidentified goods or personal effects. Each PARTY is to be responsible for the payment of personal property taxes, if any, that are due for the personal property they are awarded by this agreement.

1998 Dodge Caravan

The PARTIES agree that HUSBAND is awarded the 1998 Dodge Caravan as his sole and separate property. Further, HUSBAND shall pay and be responsible for any loan or obligation secured by said vehicle, any personal property tax obligations for said vehicle, any leases for said vehicle, and the cost of insuring and operating said vehicle and shall indemnify and hold harmless WIFE for such debts.

2002 Toyota Camry

The PARTIES agree that WIFE is awarded the 2002 Toyota Camry as her sole and separate property. Further, WIFE shall pay and be responsible for any loan or obligation secured by said vehicle, any personal property tax obligations for said vehicle, any leases for said vehicle, and the cost of insuring and operating said vehicle and shall indemnify and hold harmless HUSBAND for such debts.

Bank A (Savings)

The PARTIES agree that the parties will close this account and share the proceeds from this account equally.

Bank B (Sav) and (Chk)

The PARTIES agree that HUSBAND is awarded the checking and savings accounts at Bank B as his sole and separate property.

Bank C (Sav)(W) (in Wife's name)

The PARTIES agree that WIFE is awarded the account at Bank C (Sav)(W) as her sole and separate property.

Bank D (Chk) (in Wife's name)

The PARTIES agree that WIFE is awarded the account at Bank D (Chk) as her sole and separate property.

Bank E (Sav)(H) (in Husband's name)

The PARTIES agree that HUSBAND is awarded the account at Bank E (Sav)(H) as his sole and separate property.

Bank F (Chk)(H) (in Husband's name)

The PARTIES agree that HUSBAND is awarded the account at Bank F (Chk)(H) as his sole and separate property.

Pensions and IRAs

The PARTIES acknowledge that each Party is currently receiving retirement and/or disability benefits as a result of their respective military services and the PARTIES agree that each Party shall be awarded their own retirement/pension/disability benefits as their respective property. Neither Party will make any claims for any portion of the retirement/pension/disability benefits in the name of the other Party, and both Parties do hereby waive and release any interest they have in the retirement/pension/disability benefits in the name of the other Party. HUSBAND is awarded the IRA in his name as his property. Even though Father is the primary caregiver for Child One, the child with Special Needs, and thus is unable to work to his otherwise full ability, thereby decreasing the amount he is able to contribute to a retirement plan for his future benefit, the parties agree that this is a fair and equitable distribution of the Pensions and IRAs, for the reason that both parties have full military pensions.

Life Insurance

The PARTIES are each awarded the life insurance policies in their respective names (on their respective lives) as their property. The PARTIES agree that they will continue to maintain their children as the sole beneficiaries on the existing life insurance policies until their children are emancipated by law. Further, Each Party shall provide the other Party documentation regarding the terms of the POLICY and its current status, upon the other Party's request. Further, The PARTIES consent to the insurance company issuing, and/or managing, such POLICY providing to the OTHER PARTY such information about the POLICY that is reasonably necessary to determine the existence, terms, beneficiaries, and status of the POLICY.

Additionally, the PARTIES agree that there are GERBER life insurance policies insuring each of their children, and the PARTIES agree to maintain such insurance POLICIES and to each pay one-half of the insurance premiums for said POLICIES until the insured minor child is emancipated. The PARTIES further agree that they will each be designated as equal co-beneficiaries on such POLICIES, and in the event of the death of an insured minor child, the insurance proceeds will be used to satisfy the burial costs of the child, the child's outstanding uninsured medical bills, if any, the child's outstanding educational expenses, and thereafter such remaining proceeds shall be shared equally between the PARTIES.

b. Titles and Papers

Each PARTY shall promptly deliver to the other all property or documents evidencing ownership of property, which by the terms of this AGREEMENT is to remain or become the property of the other. Each PARTY shall execute and deliver to the other PARTY such Affidavits of Gift and Limited Powers of Attorney that are reasonably required to transfer each PARTY'S interest in the cars, automobiles, and vehicles awarded the other PARTY and to permit the other PARTY to act as attorney in fact for the sole purpose of transferring title of the car, automobile, or vehicle awarded by this AGREEMENT.

Further, each party agrees to keep all property, and documents evidencing ownership of property, which by the terms of this AGREEMENT is to remain or become the property of the other in good condition, normal wear and tear excepted, until such time as delivery of such property and documentation to the other PARTY has occurred. The PARTIES agree that neither PARTY shall be obligated to store or keep the property or documentation of ownership of such property, which by the terms of this AGREEMENT is to remain or become the property of the other, for more than 30 days after written notice of a request to pick up such property and documentation has been mailed by certified mail, return receipt requested, to the PARTY to whom such property and documentation is awarded by this AGREEMENT. (Such notice to pick up property shall be addressed to the last known mailing address of the recipient PARTY and shall specify a date, time, and place where the property and documentation in question is to be picked up, which date and time shall be reasonable, and not sooner than five days from the date of mailing of such notice.)

2. REAL PROPERTY

a. Identification of Real Property

The PARTIES acknowledge that they now own or have a marital interest in the following real property:

i. 1234 AnyStreet, City, State, located in the County of ________, State of __________, with the legal description contained on Exhibit ___ attached (hereinafter the "MARITAL RESIDENCE") Which real property is security for an obligation, evidenced by a Deed of Trust, in favor of XYZ Bank (hereinafter the "MORTGAGEE FOR MARITAL RESIDENCE").

b. Division of Real Property

The PARTIES agree that the real property in which they have a marital interest shall be disposed of as follows:

i. **MARITAL RESIDENCE**

The PARTIES agree that the *MARITAL RESIDENCE* is awarded to HUSBAND as his sole and exclusive property.

HUSBAND shall assume and pay the unpaid balance of approximately $_______, owing on the *MARITAL RESIDENCE,* to XYZ Credit Union (hereinafter the "MORTGAGEE FOR MARITAL RESIDENCE"). HUSBAND shall also assume and pay the unpaid balance of any other obligation or line of credit that is secured by the *MARITAL RESIDENCE* and shall indemnify and hold WIFE harmless for such other obligations, if any.

HUSBAND shall indemnify and hold WIFE harmless should the MORTGAGEE FOR MARITAL RESIDENCE, or its assigns or successors, proceed against WIFE upon HUSBAND'S failure to assume or pay the obligation owed to the MORTGAGEE FOR MARITAL RESIDENCE, or upon HUSBAND'S default under any provision of the loan instruments, promissory notes, or Deed of Trust evidencing or securing the obligation to the MORTGAGEE FOR MARITAL RESIDENCE.

HUSBAND shall also be responsible for any obligation for taxes, subdivision dues, insurance costs, repair costs and utility costs, and any other costs associated with the ownership, possession, or use of the *MARITAL RESIDENCE.* HUSBAND shall indemnify and hold WIFE harmless on such costs.

HUSBAND agrees to take such reasonable action as is necessary to remove WIFE'S name from the obligation to the MORTGAGEE FOR MARITAL RESIDENCE, including, but not limited to, refinancing the obligation. WIFE'S name shall be removed from the obligation within four weeks of the date of a Judgment of Dissolution of Marriage between the parties.

WIFE shall deliver a Quitclaim Deed, transferring her interest in the MARITAL RESIDENCE to HUSBAND concurrently with the removal of her name from the mortgage obligation.

WIFE shall pay all unpaid mortgage payments due on the MARITAL RESIDENCE for any period prior to the delivery of a Quitclaim Deed to HUSBAND.

WIFE does herewith assign, transfer, and set over to the HUSBAND all of her interest in the Escrow fund, if any, held on MARITAL RESIDENCE and further the WIFE assigns, transfers, and sets over to the HUSBAND all of WIFE'S interest in all existing insurance on the MARITAL RESIDENCE.

WIFE waives any interest in any deposit previously paid to any utility service providers, whether for phone, water, trash, electric, gas, and sewer service, for service to the MARITAL RESIDENCE. WIFE agrees to cooperate with HUSBAND and to do all things reasonably necessary to have the water, phone, electric, gas, sewer, and trash utilities for the MARITAL RESIDENCE put in the name of the HUSBAND.

c. Other Real Property

The PARTIES each acknowledge and represent to the other that neither party has any interest in any real property in the State of __________ or elsewhere, whether in their names alone or with others, except as identified above.

3. NATURE OF PROPERTY DIVIDED

The PARTIES agree that all of the property divided by Section B above is marital property (except for property listed on Petitioner's Statement of Property filed with the Court as being separate/nonmarital property). The transfers represent fair and equitable divisions of property after consideration of the other financial provisions of this AGREEMENT.

4. TRANSFERS OF PROPERTY INTEREST

The PARTIES stipulate and agree that the transfers of property interests, which take place in order to satisfy the terms of this Agreement, shall be transfers pursuant to Section 1041 of the Internal Revenue Code, and the PARTIES agree to execute any forms or other documents as might be necessary to establish this intent.

IV. **MAINTENANCE:**

The PARTIES agree, after examining all relevant factors, including the factors specified under Section __________ (statutes of state of _________), that WIFE shall pay to HUSBAND the sum of $________ per month as and for maintenance; such payments are due on the first day of each month, beginning on first of ______, 20___. The PARTIES agree that this provision as to maintenance shall be modifiable. Maintenance shall automatically terminate upon the first of the following to occur: HUSBAND'S death, WIFE'S death, HUSBAND'S remarriage. The PARTIES agree that no wage withholding orders are required at this time, although the PARTIES understand that in the event maintenance or child support is not paid in a timely fashion, then a wage withholding order may be applied for by HUSBAND.

V. **DEBTS:**

A. **Assumption of Debts and Liabilities:** From and after the date the petition in this case was filed, each PARTY will be solely liable for the debts acquired by him or her.

B. **Terms of Payments:** The PARTIES' debts and liabilities will be assumed and paid as provided on the exhibits attached hereto (i.e., Exhibit "B") and incorporated herein by reference. Each PARTY is responsible for any debt or obligation that is incurred in connection with the ownership, possession, or use of an asset of property, whether real or personal, unless specifically indicated otherwise in this Agreement.

C. **Indemnification:** The PARTIES agree to indemnify and hold harmless each other and defend the other from and against all claims and liabilities and will reimburse the other for any and all expenses made or incurred by the other, either directly or indirectly, including a reasonable attorney's fee, as a result of his or her failure to pay or otherwise satisfy the debts and liabilities assumed by each in this AGREEMENT.

D. **No Undisclosed Debts:** The PARTIES warrant to each other that he or she has not incurred any debt or obligation that is either (1) an obligation on or for which the other PARTY is or may become personally liable, or (2) an obligation that could be enforced at any time against an asset held or to be received under this AGREEMENT by the other PARTY, except as disclosed on attached Exhibit B. Each PARTY covenants not to incur any such obligations or debts on or after the execution of this AGREEMENT.

VI. **INCORPORATION IN DECREE:**

It is the intent of the PARTIES that the terms of this AGREEMENT be incorporated and fully set forth in any Decree of Dissolution of Marriage entered by the Court, and the Parties shall be ordered to perform the terms thereof.

VII. **SEVERABILITY OF PROVISIONS:**

In the event that any provision of the AGREEMENT is unenforceable when incorporated as part of the Court's judgment, it shall be considered severable and enforceable by an action based on contractual obligation, and it shall not invalidate the remainder of this AGREEMENT as incorporated in any Decree.

VIII. **PROVISIONS FOR FAILURE TO PERFORM WITH NOTICE REQUIRED:**

In the event that either PARTY brings an action for failure to perform any of the obligations imposed by the AGREEMENT due him or her, or for enforcement or clarification of the AGREEMENT, the prevailing PARTY in such action shall have the right to recover his or her reasonable attorney's fees and litigation costs reasonably expended in prosecuting or defending the action. However, no attorney fees shall be so recovered by a PARTY filing an action unless the PARTY seeking to recover said attorney fees and costs shall have mailed to the other PARTY written notice of the alleged failure to perform and said alleged failure was not cured within ten (10) days after the date of mailing of said notice by certified mail to the alleged breaching PARTY'S residential address. Provided further, that no such notice shall be necessary as to any periodic child support obligation that Petitioner has failed to perform in a timely fashion in accordance with this Agreement on more than two occasions. Provided further, that no such notice shall be necessary as to any periodic maintenance obligation that Wife has failed to perform in a timely fashion in accordance with this AGREEMENT on more than two occasions.

No fees or costs authorized by this paragraph shall be recovered except as determined and awarded by the Court in an action brought for enforcement, breach, or clarification of the AGREEMENT.

IX. **MODIFICATION AND APPROVAL:**

The terms of this AGREEMENT shall be subject to modification or change only by a mutual agreement of the PARTIES in writing. It is understood that this provision is not applicable to the terms of the AGREEMENT dealing with child custody, visitation, and child support. The PARTIES recognize that the provisions relating to custody, visitation, and child support are subject to the approval of the Court, and may be modified by the Court regardless of this paragraph.

X. **MUTUAL RELEASE:**

Subject to the provisions of the AGREEMENT, each PARTY has remised, released, and forever discharged and, by these presents, does himself or herself and his or her heirs, legal representatives, executors, administrators, and assigns remise, release, and forever discharge the other PARTY, and the other PARTY'S family, employees, agents, and attorneys, of and from all cause or causes of action, claims, rights, or demands whatsoever in law or equity, which either PARTY hereto ever had or now has against the other, except any and all cause or causes of action for dissolution of marriage or rights arising from this AGREEMENT or subsequent Court Order.

XI. **MUTUAL WAIVER OF RIGHTS IN ESTATES**:

Except as otherwise provided in this AGREEMENT, each PARTY shall have the right to dispose of his or her property of whatsoever nature, real or personal, and each PARTY, for himself or herself, respectively, and for their respective heirs, legal representatives, executors, administrators, personal representatives, and assigns, hereby waives any right of election that he or she may have or hereafter acquire regarding the estate of the other or to take against any Last Will and Testament of the other or any codicil thereto, whether heretofore or hereafter executed, as provided for in any law now or hereinafter effective of this state or any other state or territory of the United States or any foreign country and renounces and releases all interest, right, or claim of distributive share or interstate succession or dower or courtesy, or community property or statutory exemption or allowance or otherwise, that he or she now has or might otherwise have against the other or the estate of the other, or the property of whatsoever nature, real or personal, of the other PARTY under or by virtue of the laws of any state or country. Nothing contained in this particular paragraph, however, shall affect any obligation undertaken in the other paragraphs of the AGREEMENT by either PARTY.

XII. **DISPOSAL OF PROPERTY**:

Except as set forth in this agreement, each of the PARTIES shall, from the date of the execution of this AGREEMENT, have the right to dispose of his or her property by *inter vivos* conveyance, gift, Last Will or otherwise, as though a single person.

XIII. **EXECUTION OF PAPERS**:

The PARTIES agree that they shall take any and all steps to execute, acknowledge, and deliver to the other any and all instruments, assurances, and affidavits that the other PARTY may reasonably require or find convenient, expedient, or businesslike for the purpose of giving full force and effect to the provisions of this AGREEMENT.

XIV. **PERFORMANCE OF ACTS REQUIRED IN AGREEMENT**:

Where acts and things are required to be performed under the terms of this Agreement and no time is specified for their performance, they shall be done as soon as practical after a judgment of dissolution of marriage is entered between the PARTIES, or within 15 days of the date of judgment of dissolution of marriage is entered between the PARTIES, whichever is sooner.

XV. **VOLUNTARY AGREEMENT AND INVESTIGATION AND DISCLOSURE**:

Each of the PARTIES hereby affirms that they each are entering into this AGREEMENT freely and voluntarily; that they have ascertained and weighed all the facts and circumstances likely to influence his or her judgment herein; that they have given due consideration to such provisions in question; that they have sought independent advice of counsel in regard to all details and particulars of the AGREEMENT (or, they had an opportunity to seek independent advice of counsel) and the underlying facts; and that they clearly understand and assent to all the provisions hereof.

Each PARTY further warrants that they have each disclosed to the other the full extent of their respective properties and income, either on the Statements of Property and/or Statements of Income and Expenses filed with the Court, or on the attachments to this AGREEMENT. Each PARTY further warrants that they have not secreted, hidden, transferred, or disposed of any assets that either PARTY may have an interest in. Each PARTY warrants that neither PARTY has since the ___ day of ________, 20___ withdrawn, consumed, or borrowed, except for ordinary, regular, and normal living expenses, funds from the bank accounts, stock holdings, retirement plans, 401k plans, pension plans, and Thrift Savings Plans, in their respective names or control. Each PARTY warrants that the equity values or balances of the bank accounts, stock holdings, retirement plans, 401k plans, pension plans, and Thrift Savings Plans, except as values fluctuate with the market or accounts are subject to third-party charges, are as disclosed on each PARTY'S Statements of Property filed with the Court, or as disclosed on the account statements or documentation provided the other PARTY in response to Requests for the Production of Documents, whichever documentation contains the most current information.

Each PARTY agrees that in the event property, assets, or interests are discovered that have not been disclosed on their Statements of Property or on attachments to this AGREEMENT, and which property, assets, or interests were acquired in whole or in part during the marriage and not by way of inheritance or gift or in exchange for non-marital property, that such property, assets, or interests shall be divided equally between the PARTIES promptly after the discovery of the same.

XVI. **WAIVER OF DISCOVERY:**

Each party acknowledges that he or she has had the opportunity to complete the discovery each as Interrogatories, Request for Production of Documents, appraisals, real estate and other property, and depositions, and has chosen not to do same. Each party acknowledges the risks of proceeding without completion of such discovery. Each party has, nevertheless, directed his or her attorneys to proceed without completion of such discovery. Each party acknowledges that without such completed discovery, his or her counsel has not conducted any investigation or analysis that would permit his or her counsel to determine the full extent and value of the parties' marital property, debts, income, and expenses, and whether there is any marital component in any nonmarital property. The settlement has been based on the personal knowledge of each party, and the review of limited documents exchanged between the parties and Statement of Income and Expenses and Statement of Property filed by each party herein.

XVII. **RIGHTS TO TRIAL:**

Both Parties understand they have a right to trial. The Parties agree and stipulate, having been fully advised by their respective attorneys of the consequences and considerations that could result if fully litigated and that trying the case could be more favorable or could be less favorable than the terms of this Property Settlement and Separation Agreement. Nevertheless, the Parties have agreed it is in their respective best interests to waive any trial of this matter and settle the case.

XVIII. LIVING APART:

The PARTIES shall continue to live separate and apart and from the date of the execution of this AGREEMENT, free from any interference by the other, as if fully unmarried, and further, neither will molest, malign, annoy, or trouble the other in any manner.

XIX. **JOINT INCOME TAX RETURNS:**

The PARTIES agree to file joint income tax returns for the tax year ending December 31, 20 ___, and each shall be entitled to one-half (1/2) of any refund on any joint returns filed for said tax year and will likewise be responsible for one-half (1/2) of any taxes, interest, and penalties on returns that are jointly filed.

The PARTIES agree that in the event any jointly filed income tax return is audited by the appropriate taxing authorities, they will cooperate with each other and their respective attorneys, and accountants, to investigate, respond to, or comply with such audit. Any noncooperating PARTY shall indemnify and hold harmless the other PARTY for failure to perform any reasonable request to assist the attorney/accountants in investigating, responding to, or complying with said audit.

The PARTIES agree that in the event either PARTY receives any notice or documentation from the Internal Revenue Service, or any state taxing authority, that references or involves an income tax return that was filed by either PARTY, or the PARTIES jointly, during the course of the marriage, they shall promptly forward a copy of such notice or documentation to the other PARTY at their last known mailing address. In the event a PARTY fails to promptly forward a copy of such notice or documentation to the other PARTY and additional taxes, interest, or penalties are assessed against the other PARTY after the date of receipt of such notice or documentation by the non-forwarding PARTY, then the non-forwarding PARTY shall indemnify and hold harmless the other PARTY for such additional taxes, interest, and penalties.

XX. **PAYMENT OF ATTORNEY'S FEES:**

The PARTIES agree that they shall each pay their own respective attorney fees incurred in this case.

XXI. **PAYMENT OF COURT COSTS:**

The PARTIES agree that the court costs, excluding deposition costs, of this proceeding shall be equally shared between the PARTIES. Any deposition costs shall be borne solely by the PARTY taking the deposition. In the event the Court orders court costs paid from any deposits already on hand with the Court, then the Respondent shall indemnify, hold harmless, and reimburse Petitioner for Respondent's share of court costs as agreed to in this paragraph.

XXII. **BINDING EFFECT:**

This AGREEMENT shall be binding on the heirs, representatives, and assigns of the PARTIES hereto except as to the specific paragraphs that contain provisions for termination of obligations on the death of one or both of the PARTIES.

XXIII. **EXECUTION:**

Each PARTY hereto acknowledges that each of them is making this AGREEMENT of his or her own free will and volition and acknowledges that no coercion, force, pressure, or undue influence has been used against either PARTY in the making of this AGREEMENT or by any other person or persons.

XXIV. **STATUTORY COMPLIANCE:**

The validity and construction of this AGREEMENT shall be determined in accordance with the laws of the State of ____________.

XXV. **SIGNATURES:**

IN WITNESS WHEREOF, the PARTIES set their signatures to this document hereafter.

STATE OF ______________)
)ss.
COUNTY OF ____________)

_____________, of lawful age, being first duly sworn on her oath, states that she is the Petitioner (and Wife) named herein and that she has read the above and foregoing Agreement; she further states that the facts and matters contained therein are true and correct to the best of her knowledge, information, and belief, and she has executed this document voluntarily and of her free will.

____

Petitioner

On this ____ day of _______________, 20___, before me a Notary Public in and for said State personally appeared _____________ to me known to be the person described in and who executed the foregoing instrument, and acknowledged and stated under oath and/or affirmed that she executed the same as her free act and deed, and that the facts and matters contained therein are true and correct to the best of her knowledge, information, and belief.

IN TESTIMONY WHEREOF, I have hereunto set my hand and affixed my official seal in the County and State aforesaid, the day and year first above written.

____

Notary Public

My commission expires:

____

STATE OF _____________)
)ss.
COUNTY OF ____________)

____________, of lawful age, being first duly sworn on his oath, states that he is the Respondent (and Husband) named herein and that he has read the above and foregoing Agreement; he further states that the facts and matters contained therein are true and correct to the best of his knowledge, information, and belief, and he has executed this document voluntarily and of his free will.

____
Respondent

On this ____ day of ________________, 20___, before me a Notary Public in and for said State personally appeared ____________ to me known to be the person described in and who executed the foregoing instrument, and acknowledged and stated under oath and/or affirmed that he executed the same as his free act and deed, and that the facts and matters contained therein are true and correct to the best of his knowledge, information, and belief.

IN TESTIMONY WHEREOF, I have hereunto set my hand and affixed my official seal in the County and State aforesaid, the day and year first above written.

____
Notary Public

My commission expires:

____

EXHIBIT "A"
PARENTING PLAN

EXHIBIT "B"
DIVISION OF PROPERTY

EXHIBIT "C"
Legal Description for MARITAL RESIDENCE

[Adapted from Settlement Agreement coauthored with Kieran Coyne, an attorney in St. Louis, Missouri.]

The issue of special needs should be raised in *Affidavits for Judgment* and in *Judgment forms*. Affidavits for Judgment should contain a similar recital of whether there are any known special needs.

SAMPLE SPECIAL NEEDS AFFIDAVIT FOR JUDGMENT

IN THE FAMILY COURT OF __________________ COUNTY
STATE OF __________________

In Re the Marriage of:	)	For File Stamp Only
	)	
______________________	)	
	)	
Petitioner,	)	
	)	
vs.	)	Case No. ______________
______________________	)	Division: __________
	)	
Respondent.	)	

AFFIDAVIT OF PETITIONER REQUESTING DISSOLUTION
OF MARRIAGE – SPECIAL NEEDS CASE

Petitioner, upon her oath, submits the following affidavit pursuant to local rules, to form a basis for the court's entering a judgment in this case upon affidavit and without the necessity of a formal hearing.

1. The Petition in this case was filed on ______________, 20___.
2. Respondent was served with summons in this case on ________ (date) and filed a responsive pleading on _________ (date).
3. Respondent is and has been a resident of the State of __________ for more than _______ days/months immediately preceding the filing of the petition in this case.
4. Both parties are over eighteen years of age.
5. At the time of filing, Petitioner resided at ___________ (street address, city, county, state, zip code).
6. At the time of filing, Respondent resided at ___________ (street address, city, county, state, zip code).
7. Petitioner's social security number is XXX-XX-XXXX (if applicable).
8. Respondent's social security number is XXX-XX-XXXX (if applicable).
9. Petitioner is represented by ____________ (attorney name and address).
10. Respondent is represented by _____________ (attorney name and address).
11. Petitioner is employed as a _________ (occupation) at _______ (employer name) located at ____________________ (employer address).
12. Respondent is employed as a _________ (occupation) at _______ (employer name) located at ____________________ (employer address).

13. Petitioner and Respondent were married on __________ (date) at __________ (city, county, state). The marriage was recorded in the County of ________, State of ______.
14. Petitioner and Respondent separated on or about ________, 20___.
15. Petitioner believes that there is no reasonable likelihood that the marriage of Petitioner and Respondent can be preserved and, therefore, believes that the marriage is irretrievably broken.
16. Petitioner is not on active duty with the Armed Forces of the United States of America or its allies.
17. Respondent is not on active duty with the Armed Forces of the United States of America or its allies.
18. Petitioner is not pregnant.
19. The parties have entered into a written agreement for the division of their property that includes all assets and debts and identifies and divides the marital property and debts and sets apart to each party his or her nonmarital property. This agreement is attached to this affidavit and incorporated herein by reference.
20. Petitioner and Respondent have agreed to spousal maintenance payable by Respondent to Petitioner in the amount of $ _____ per month as and for Petitioner's maintenance until further order of the Court. Said maintenance obligation shall be modifiable. The parties ask that the court incorporate this agreed-upon spousal maintenance in the Judgment of Dissolution.
21. Petitioner is unaware of any genuine issue as to any material fact in this proceeding.
22. There are 2 minor, unemancipated children of the marriage, to wit:
    CHILD ONE DOB: ______
    CHILD TWO DOB: ______
23. CHILD ONE (Child's name) HAS SPECIAL NEEDS, NAMELY CEREBRAL PALSY, WHICH SPECIAL NEEDS HAVE BEEN COMPLETELY ADDRESSED IN THE SETTLEMENT AGREEMENT, PARENTING PLAN, AND PROPOSED JUDGMENT. THESE DOCUMENTS HAVE BEEN APPROVED BY THE SPECIAL NEEDS COORDINATOR ASSIGNED TO THIS CASE.
24. The children lived with Petitioner and Respondent at ____ (street address, city, county, state) for six months immediately preceding the filing of this petition.
25. Petitioner has not participated in any capacity in any other litigation concerning the custody of the children in this or any other state. Petitioner has no information of any custody proceeding concerning the children pending in a court of this or any other state; and knows of no person not a party to these proceedings who has physical custody of the children or claims to have custody or visitation rights with respect to the children.
26. Petitioner and Respondent have entered into a custody agreement, which is attached and incorporated herein by reference. Petitioner and Respondent request that the Court incorporate the terms of the custody agreement in the Judgment of Dissolution.

27. Attached hereto is a special needs child support worksheet (Form 14SN) that has been agreed to by both parties. Petitioner attests to the truth of the contents of the child support worksheet.
28. The parties agree that the amount of support calculated by the Child Support Guidelines as modified for Special Needs is not rebutted as being unjust or inappropriate and agree that Respondent shall pay $____ per month child support.
29. The child support rights have not been assigned to the State of ________.
30. Costs paid by Petitioner and Respondent equally.

____

Petitioner

STATE OF _____________)
)ss.
COUNTY OF ____________)

_______________ personally appeared before me on ___________________, who upon being duly sworn stated that the foregoing statements were true and accurate to their best knowledge and belief.

____

Notary Public

CERTIFICATE OF MAILING

I hereby certify that a copy of the foregoing was mailed on the ___ day of _____, 20__ by U.S. Mail, postage prepaid to: _________ (opposing counsel's name, street address, city, state, and zip code)

____

[Adapted from portions of Affidavit form, Missouri Attorney Assistant, Legal Easy, Inc.]

Finally, *Judgment forms* should address the issue of special needs. Judgment forms should contain a recital of whether there are any known special needs, and confirm that those needs have been fully met in the final documents.

SAMPLE SPECIAL NEEDS JUDGMENT

IN THE FAMILY COURT OF ____________________ COUNTY
STATE OF ____________________

In Re the Marriage of:	)	
	)	
____________________,	)	
______________,	)	
Petitioner,	)	
vs.	)	Case No. ____________________
____________________,	)	Division: ________
______________,	)	
Respondent.	)	

JUDGMENT OF DISSOLUTION

Now on this ____ day of (month), (year), this cause comes on for hearing; Petitioner, (name), appearing in person and with her attorney, (name). Respondent, (name), appearing in person and with his attorney, (name).

Whereupon, all matters contained in the petition are submitted to the Court for trial. All parties announce ready for hearing. After hearing all the evidence, reviewing the Property Settlement Agreement, and being fully advised in the premises, the Court finds that Petitioner has been a resident of the State of ____________ for more than ____ days/months next preceding the commencement of this proceeding and that more than ___ days have elapsed since the filing of the Petition. The Court finds that the Petitioner, ____________, is not now pregnant. The Court finds that there remains no reasonable likelihood that the marriage can be preserved and that the marriage is irretrievably broken.

IT IS THEREFORE ORDERED, ADJUDGED, AND DECREED by the Court that the parties hereto be and they are hereby granted the dissolution of their marriage and restored to all rights and privileges of single and unmarried persons.

The Court finds that the Property Settlement Agreement is presented to the Court and after being duly examined is found not to be unconscionable, and is to be made a part of the Judgment. The Court finds that said agreement disposes of all marital and nonmarital property and debt.

The Court finds that there were 2 children born of the marriage, namely;

CHILD ONE (name)born __________

CHILD TWO (name)born __________

THE COURT FINDS THAT CHILD ONE (Child's name) HAS SPECIAL NEEDS, NAMELY CEREBRAL PALSY, WHICH SPECIAL NEEDS HAVE BEEN COMPLETELY ADDRESSED IN THE SETTLEMENT AGREEMENT, PARENTING PLAN,

AND PROPOSED JUDGMENT. THESE DOCUMENTS HAVE BEEN APPROVED BY THE SPECIAL NEEDS COORDINATOR ASSIGNED TO THIS CASE.

The Court finds that it is in the best interests of the children for the parents to be awarded joint physical and joint legal custody of both children.

In determining the custody of the children, the Court has considered the wishes of the children's parents as to custody and the proposed parenting plan submitted by both parties; the needs of the children for a frequent, continuing, and meaningful relationship with both parents; and the ability and willingness of parents to actively perform their function as mother and father for the needs of the children; the interaction and interrelationship of the children with parents, siblings, and any other person who may significantly affect the children's best interests; which parent is more likely to allow the children frequent, continuing, and meaningful contact with the other parent; the children's adjustment to the children's home, school, community; the mental and physical health of all individuals involved, including any history of abuse of any individuals involved; the intention of either parent to relocate the principal residence of the children; and the wishes of the children as to the children's custodian.

In the event either party relocates their principal residence, then you are advised pursuant to Section ____ of the statutes of the State of ___________ as follows: Absent exigent circumstances as determined by a Court with jurisdiction, each party to this action is ordered to notify the other, in writing by certified mail, return receipt requested, and at least 60 days prior to the proposed relocation, of any proposed relocation of the principal residence of the children, including the following information:

a. The intended new residence, including the specific address and mailing address, if known, and if not known, the city;
b. The home telephone number of the new residence, if known;
c. The date of the intended move or proposed relocation;
d. A brief statement of the specific reasons for the proposed relocation of the children; and
e. A proposal for a revised schedule of custody or visitation with the children.

Your obligation to provide this information to each party continues as long as you or any other party by virtue of this order is entitled to custody of a child covered by this order. Your failure to obey this order of this court regarding the proposed relocation may result in further litigation to enforce such order, including contempt of court. In addition, your failure to notify a party of a relocation of the children may be considered in a proceeding to modify custody or visitation with the children. Reasonable costs and attorney fees may be accessed against you if you fail to give the required notice.

The Court orders that each party pay their respective pro rata share of the 20__ personal property taxes based upon the assessed value of the vehicles awarded to each party. Each party shall pay their share prior to December 31, 20__.

The Court orders the Sheriff or other Law Enforcement Officer to enforce visitation or custody rights.

The Court orders Petitioner to pay to Respondent the sum of $______ per month as and for Respondent's maintenance until further order of the Court. Said maintenance obligation shall be modifiable.

It is contemplated by and the intention and agreement of the parties that the amounts of maintenance payable by Petitioner to Respondent under this Section shall be deductible on Petitioner's Federal and (state) income tax returns and shall constitute income to Respondent for Federal and (state) income tax purposes.

The Court orders each party to pay their own attorney fees.

The Court orders Petitioner and Respondent to equally pay all court costs incurred herein.

The Court finds that this Judgment has disposed of all marital and nonmarital property and debts.

IT IS FURTHER ORDERED, ADJUDGED, AND DECREED by the Court that the parties shall sign any and all documents necessary to effectuate the terms of this Judgment Entry.

IT IS SO ORDERED.
Dated this _______ day of ___________________, 20____.

____
The Honorable _________________
Case No. ____________

APPROVED AS TO FORM:

ATTORNEY SIGNATURE BLOCK
ATTORNEY FOR PETITIONER

ATTORNEY SIGNATURE BLOCK
ATTORNEY FOR RESPONDENT

____

[Adapted from portions of Affidavit form, Missouri Attorney Assistant, Legal Easy, Inc.]

Having special needs incorporated into all layers of the litigation process will help prevent special needs cases from slipping through the cracks. Frequently, an issue is discussed early in a case but not considered later, when decisions are made and cases are resolved.

IV. POSTTRIAL MOTIONS

The issue of special needs may be addressed for the first time in a *Motion to Modify*. In the alternative, it may be raised in a Motion to Modify after being raised earlier in the underlying divorce or paternity action. State family law statutes require that certain allegations be contained in Motions to Modify. Frequently, the required allegations include

- Date of the divorce decree
- Dates of any subsequent modifications
- Divorce decree provisions for child support, custody, and visitation
- Divorce decree provisions concerning any other matters relevant to the modification
- Factual basis of the changed circumstances or need for modification
- Prior litigation concerning custody of the children
- Any other facts relevant to the modification

SAMPLE SPECIAL NEEDS MOTION TO MODIFY

IN THE FAMILY COURT OF ___________________ COUNTY
STATE OF ___________________

In Re the Marriage of:	)	For File Stamp Only
	)	
______________________,	)	
	)	
Petitioner,	)	
vs.	)	Case No. ______________
______________________,	)	Division: __________
	)	
Respondent.	)	

MOTION TO MODIFY – SPECIAL NEEDS

Comes now the Petitioner, _____________, by and through her counsel, ________, and for his cause of action, alleges and states:

1. On ______________ this Court entered a Decree of Dissolution in this matter. There were 2 children born of the marriage, namely;
   CHILD ONE (name) born _________
   CHILD TWO (name) born _________
   THE COURT FOUND THAT CHILD ONE (Child's name) HAS SPECIAL NEEDS, NAMELY CEREBRAL PALSY, AND FOUND THAT THE SPECIAL NEEDS HAD BEEN COMPLETELY ADDRESSED IN THE SETTLEMENT AGREEMENT, PARENTING PLAN, AND PROPOSED JUDGMENT. THESE DOCUMENTS WERE APPROVED BY THE SPECIAL NEEDS COORDINATOR ASSIGNED TO THIS CASE.
2. The Decree of Dissolution further awarded Petitioner and Respondent the joint physical and legal custody of the minor children.
3. The Decree of Dissolution awarded Respondent as support for said children the sum of $_____ per month.
4. The Decree of Dissolution further ordered Petitioner to pay maintenance to Respondent.
5. The Decree of Dissolution has not been modified.
6. Since the date of the original Decree of Dissolution was entered, there have been changed circumstances so substantial and continuing as to make the terms of said Decree of Dissolution unreasonable in regard to the children. As a result of such changed circumstances, a modification of the Decree of Dissolution is necessary to serve the best interests of the parties.

7. The changed circumstances include but are not limited to the following:
____

8. Petitioner requests the court award sole physical and legal custody of the minor child to her due to the change of circumstances listed above.
9. Petitioner requests the visitation schedule originally ordered be modified as follows:
____

10. Petitioner is unable to provide the ordered child support originally ordered due to the change of circumstances listed above.
11. Petitioner is unable to provide maintenance to Respondent.
12. Petitioner is presently employed by ____________.
13. Respondent is presently employed by ____________.
14. As a result of the above, all of which involve a substantial and continuing change of conditions and circumstances, the Petitioner prays that a new Order be entered by this Court.

WHEREFORE, Petitioner prays that the Court enter an Order modifying the decree of dissolution to award visitation as stated above to serve the best interests of the minor children; to decrease the child support paid by Petitioner, retroactive to the date of the service of this Motion, to a sum that is reasonable in light of the above-described changes in conditions and circumstances; to award custody of the minor children to Petitioner; to decrease the award of maintenance paid by Petitioner; and further Ordering that in all other respects, the Court's Order entered __________, 20___, shall remain in full force and effect; and for such further Orders as this Court shall deem just and proper.

____
ATTORNEY SIGNATURE BLOCK
ATTORNEY FOR PETITIONER

STATE OF ______________)
) ss.
COUNTY OF ____________)

Comes now _________, Petitioner, being first duly sworn according to law, and states that she has read the foregoing Motion to Modify and states that the facts contained therein are true and correct according to her best knowledge, information, and belief.

____

Subscribed and sworn to before me this _____ day of ________, 20___.

____
Notary Public

My commission expires:

V. UNDIAGNOSED SPECIAL NEEDS

Some special needs are obvious from birth; others become obvious in time, such as terminal illnesses and other extreme situations. Still other special needs are not as obvious and have not yet been diagnosed. Sometimes the family is in denial or hope that the child will grow out of it. Sometimes the current doctor has simply not made the diagnosis. The family may know there is a problem and be in the midst of evaluating the problem when they go through the divorce. For whatever reason, sometimes the lawyer or judge must be aware of certain special needs issues even when they have not yet been diagnosed. When they are made aware of the situation, a good family lawyer or family court judge will recognize when there is a situation that warrants evaluation by professionals. Of course, lawyers and judges do not learn medicine in law school and do not pretend to know as much as doctors. We should, however, know enough to determine when a child needs to be evaluated by a professional.

Acknowledging that we are not doctors, how do we know when to send a child for professional evaluation? Here are some general warning signs:

- The child is having ongoing problems in school.
- The child is having ongoing problems with law enforcement or other authority.
- The parents have difficulty "handling" the child.
- The child is frequently sick or misses school.
- The parents or others express the concern that the child is not performing up to what others perceive as the child's abilities (i.e., the child is underachieving).
- The child is not developing with her peers—this includes physical, emotional, academic, and skills development.
- The client, lawyer, teacher, or a significant caregiver expresses the concern that "something is not quite right."

These items are most likely communicated to the lawyer by the client, often when they are talking about things that lawyers try to avoid, in the interest of time. Rather than letting your client vent and ramble for hours on end out of fear that you might miss something important, it is better practice to make the subject of special needs part of the initial client interview questionnaire. It is also prudent to include the above list of issues on your initial interview checklist. It should enable you to get the information you need while keeping the client focused.

When you identify situations that need further evaluation by a professional, you must then evaluate and determine what type of professional would be most appropriate. You would not send someone with a brain tumor to an orthodontist. The discussion that follows is by no means exhaustive or complete, but it should get you started on the path to "special needs triage."

Autism, deaf/blindness, emotional disturbance, hearing impairment and deafness, mental retardation, multiple disabilities, orthopedic impairments, other health impairments, specific learning disabilities, speech or language impairment, traumatic brain injury, visual impairment including blindness, and developmental delay—a discussion of the diagnostic criteria for these conditions follows, with the important caveat that the author is not a physician and does not pretend to be.

Upon observing these symptoms in children whose parents are getting divorced, the lawyers should be aware that special needs may exist and that a medical professional should be involved to make such determination. The parents are often too overwhelmed by going through divorce to see clearly what is going on with their children.

In addition, this discussion of diagnostic criteria can be helpful when dealing with opposing counsel, who may throw around medical terminology incorrectly or inaccurately. Given this brief overview of diagnostic criteria, a practicing lawyer can be alerted to the possibility that the situation may not be as opposing counsel is characterizing it, and that further investigation is warranted.

This material does not include every possible condition or ailment that can give rise to a special needs situation for a child. There was no intent to slight or ignore or minimize any particular condition or category. For this material to be complete and fully inclusive, it would have to be several thousand pages long, like the *Merck Manual* is. This material is merely intended to give general guidelines, with the strong caution that we lawyers and judges are not doctors. If you have any reasonable concern that the child should see a medical professional, by all means send him.

A. Indicators That an Evaluation May Be Necessary

1. Autism

The incidence of **autism** is increasing at an alarming rate.[10] Some of the increase in diagnosis is due to increased awareness of the medical community, educators, and the general public regarding the characteristics of autism. The remainder of the increase is from currently unknown causes. Almost every person reading this will know someone whose family or circle of friends has been touched by autism. We do not yet know what causes autism, although this subject causes heated debate. There are many attempts to treat autism, yet the current rate of success is so low that most children with autism will be institutionalized by age 12. It is a severe neurological condition that can impact every aspect of a child's life and turn the family upside down. Anything in the environment—light, movement, sound, clothing, water, anything touching the skin, particular noises, types and textures of food and drink—can be excruciating, painful, and confusing to the child with autism. These are often referred to as sensory issues. Children with autism can be extremely oversensitive to these things, or they can be extremely under-sensitive to them—having a very high pain threshold, for example.

Communicating with a child with autism can be extremely difficult. Guardians ad litem need to be aware of this fact. When representing a child with autism, lawyers may need to utilize a professional or paraprofessional to help communicate with the child. Some children with autism are nonverbal. When a child with autism is verbal, the speech can be unusual—high-pitched, singsong, and echolalic (repeating what is said to them, instead of engaging in typical responsive speech). In a high-functioning child with autism who speaks well, there are often remaining vestiges of language impairment, in that the child speaks the native language as though it were a second language, not the native language. These children often speak without use of slang, idioms, or contractions, and they sometimes adopt a "professorial" tone.

---

10. National Institutes of Health, National Institute of Neurological Disorders and Stroke, Autism Fact Sheet. Retrieved October 1, 2005, from https://www.ninds.nih.gov/health-information/patient-caregiver-education/fact-sheets/autism-spectrum-disorder-fact-sheet.

Socialization is often extremely difficult for children with autism. In some severe cases the child is so withdrawn he isolates himself from everyone around him and does not interact. Attempts to bring the child into group play or activities can result in further withdrawal, shrieking, or tantrums. Without typical speech and language skills, social development is often delayed or impaired. Some of these children are perceived as "robotic" by their peers and are shunned, avoided, even taunted and bullied. These children often get along better with adults and with children much younger than they are.

Autism occurs across a broad spectrum of severity, from mild to severe. A child with autism may have only a few of the symptoms or many of them. Autism is difficult for the professionals to diagnose, so if there is a reasonable concern about any of these symptoms, send the child for an evaluation. Pediatric neurologists are well educated in autism. Speech therapists, occupational therapists, physical therapists, and special education specialists sometimes make the diagnosis and then send the child on to a neurologist. Sometimes children at the mild end of the spectrum are not diagnosed, or are misdiagnosed with something else, until they get in trouble at school or in trouble with law enforcement.

2. Hearing Deficits

Every newborn should have a thorough hearing evaluation. All children should have a hearing assessment done annually. Surprisingly, diagnosis is often significantly delayed for years.[11] Severe bilateral congenital hearing deficit is often noticed by the parents within the first few weeks of life because the child does not respond to voices or other sounds. Mild to moderate or unilateral hearing deficit can go for years, even until the child is in school, before it is diagnosed. Since most of a child's speech and language development takes place in the early years of life, failure to have a hearing deficit properly diagnosed and treated can result in lasting developmental problems for the child.[12] Often these children are sent only for speech and language therapy, with the underlying hearing deficit left unaddressed and untreated. Many children with vestibular disturbances that cause abnormal motor development are misdiagnosed as having developmental disorders, including mental retardation. A family practice doctor or pediatrician can perform a hearing evaluation on the child, and send the child to a specialist if necessary.

3. Visual Deficits

Every child should have regular eye exams. In addition, if the child is having difficulty with reading, art, or copying assignments from the classroom board, they may have visual problems.[13] A child with tracking, depth perception, or other visual problems may have trouble in gym class or recess.[14] Realize that often children are embarrassed

---

11. National Institutes of Health (NIH) Consensus Statements: 92. Early Identification of Hearing Impairment in Infants and Young Children; and Berkow, R. (1992). *The Merck manual of diagnosis and therapy* (16th ed., Section 19, Chapter 260, Disturbances in Newborns and Infants, Hearing Deficits in Children). Rahway, NJ: Merck Publishing Group.

12. *Id.*

13. "When to See an Eye M.D.," American Academy of Ophthalmology. Retrieved October 1, 2005, from http://www.medem.com.

14. *Id.*

by having difficulty, so they will mask it and say they dislike art, reading, gym class, or whatever is difficult.[15] It sometimes takes a little detective work to discover the source of the problem. Proper diagnosis and treatment are essential because these problems will not go away on their own, and the child may begin getting in trouble at school for refusing to participate in certain activities because of their undiagnosed impairments.[16] A family practice doctor or pediatrician can perform a vision evaluation on the child and send the child to a specialist if necessary.

4. Mental Retardation

The classification of mental retardation (MR) used to be based upon IQ alone—mild MR = an IQ of 52 to 68; moderate MR = 36 to 51, severe MR = 20 to 35; profound = less than 20.[17] In 1992 the American Association on Mental Retardation changed this definition.[18] The current definition of mental retardation now reflects adaptation to the environment and interaction with others as well as limited intellectual function.[19]

A child with mental retardation commonly presents with limitations in social, language, and self-help adaptive skills.[20] The child may also have seizures, psychiatric disorders, and behavioral disorders.[21] A mentally retarded adolescent may develop behavior disorders as a result of social rejection by other students or as a result of realizing that others see him as different and deficient.[22] The behavioral disorders may include explosive outbursts, temper tantrums, and physically aggressive behavior in response to normal stress.[23] A family practice doctor or pediatrician can perform an evaluation on the child and send the child to whatever specialists are necessary.

5. Learning Disabilities

The Merck Manual defines a **learning disorder** as the "[i]nability to acquire, retain, or generalize specific skills or sets of information because of deficiencies in attention, memory, perception, or reasoning."[24] This definition of learning disorder assumes normal cognitive abilities and refers to problems in reading (e.g., dyslexia), arithmetic (e.g., dyscalculia), spelling, written expression or handwriting (dysgraphia), and the use or comprehension of verbal abilities (e.g., dysphasia, dysnomia, expressive language) and

---

15. *Id.*

16. *Id.*

17. National Institutes of Health (NIH) National Institute of Child Health & Human Development, Mental Retardation and Developmental Disabilities Branch. Retrieved October 1, 2005, from www.nichd.nig.gov/health/topics/developmental_disabilities.cfm; and Berkow, *supra* note 11, at Ch. 262, Developmental Problems.

18. *Id.*

19. *Id.*

20. *Id.*

21. *Id.*

22. *Id.*

23. *Id.*

24. Berkow, R. (1992). *The Merck manual of diagnosis and therapy* (16th ed., Section 19, Chapter 262, Developmental Problems). Rahway, NJ: Merck Publishing Group.

nonverbal abilities.[25] *The Merck Manual* considers attention deficit disorder (ADD) as related to but separate from learning disabilities.[26]

Some learning disorders become apparent early in children who have several minor physical abnormalities and communication problems. Mild to moderate disorders, however, are often not diagnosed until the child enters school.[27]

Behavioral problems found frequently in children with learning disorders include difficulty with impulse control, discipline problems, withdrawal, avoidance, shyness, excessive fears, and aggressiveness.[28] Children with learning disabilities often have some **cognitive problems** (problems in thinking, reasoning, and problem solving).[29] There can be reasoning disabilities, which may include problems in conceptualizing, abstracting, generalizing, and organizing and planning information for problem solving.[30]

These children can also have problems with visual perception and auditory processing, including difficulty with spatial cognition and orientation, such as spatial memory, awareness of position and place, and object localization.[31] They can also struggle with visual attention and memory and with discriminating and analyzing sounds.[32]

Another area of difficulty for these children is memory function, including both short- and long-term memory.[33] In addition, the ability to use memory (rehearsal) and verbal recall or retrieval may be problematic.[34]

In the event that these or any other learning disabilities are suspected, a thorough evaluation and assessment should be performed. Usually the best place to have this assessment done is at the child's school. Thanks to federal and state legislation and forward-thinking parents and educators, many of today's schools have a broad range of professionals who can perform a thorough evaluation of possible learning disorders. The evaluation should include these components:

- *Medical evaluation.* This includes a detailed family history and a general physical examination as well as a traditional neurological or neurodevelopmental examination, and a complete medical, developmental, and school history of the child. Some portions or all of the medical evaluation may be performed by the child's pediatrician or a pediatric neurologist.
- *Intellectual evaluation.* This includes verbal intelligence testing and nonverbal intelligence testing. It is necessary to thoroughly evaluate and determine how the child processes information. Does she process information holistically or analytically? Is she a visual learner, or does she learn better auditorily (by hearing information)? A visual learner will have difficulty learning in a strictly lecture format, whereas an auditory learner will thrive in that setting. The auditory learner will tend to not perform as well on a written research and report project, whereas the visual learner will be quite

25. *Id.*
26. *Id.*
27. *Id.*
28. *Id.*
29. *Id.*
30. *Id.*
31. *Id.*
32. *Id.*
33. *Id.*
34. *Id.*

comfortable in that educational climate. The evaluator should also test the functioning of the right and left hemispheres of the brain.

- *Educational evaluation.* A professional should evaluate the child's abilities and needs in the areas of reading, writing, spelling, and arithmetic.
- *Linguistic evaluation.* A professional should evaluate the child's comprehension and use of language, phonological memory, and verbal memory.
- *Psychological evaluation.* A professional should explore conduct disorders, low self-esteem, anxiety disorders, and depression because these issues frequently occur in children with learning disabilities.

6. Attention-Deficit/Hyperactivity Disorder

The definition of *attention-deficit/hyperactivity disorder* changed in the new version of the DSM, the DSM-V. The current DSM-V definition of **attention-deficit/hyperactivity disorder** is:

A. A persistent pattern of inattention and/or hyperactivity-impulsivity that interferes with functioning or development, as characterized by (1) and/or (2):
   1. **Inattention:** Six (or more) of the following symptoms have persisted for at least 6 months to a degree that is inconsistent with developmental level and that negatively impacts directly on social and academic/occupational activities:
      - **Note:** The symptoms are not solely a manifestation of oppositional behavior, defiance, hostility, or failure to understand tasks or instructions. For older adolescents and adults (age 17 and older), at least five symptoms are required.

      a. Often fails to give close attention to details or makes careless mistakes in schoolwork, at work, or during other activities (e.g., overlooks or misses details, work is inaccurate).
      b. Often has difficulty sustaining attention in tasks or play activities (e.g., has difficulty remaining focused during lectures, conversations, or lengthy reading).
      c. Often does not seem to listen when spoken to directly (e.g., mind seems elsewhere, even in the absence of any obvious distraction).
      d. Often does not follow through on instructions and fails to finish schoolwork, chores, or duties in the workplace (e.g., starts tasks but quickly loses focus and is easily sidetracked).
      e. Often has difficulty organizing tasks and activities (e.g., difficulty managing sequential tasks; difficulty keeping materials and belongings in order; messy, disorganized work; has poor time management; fails to meet deadlines).
      f. Often avoids, dislikes, or is reluctant to engage in tasks that require sustained mental effort (e.g., schoolwork or homework; for older adolescents and adults, preparing reports, completing forms, reviewing lengthy papers).
      g. Often loses things necessary for tasks or activities (e.g., school materials, pencils, books, tools, wallets, keys, paperwork, eyeglasses, mobile telephones).
      h. Is often easily distracted by extraneous stimuli (for older adolescents and adults, may include unrelated thoughts).
      i. Is often forgetful in daily activities (e.g., doing chores, running errands; for older adolescents and adults, returning calls, paying bills, keeping appointments).

2. **Hyperactivity and impulsivity:** Six (or more) of the following symptoms have persisted for at least 6 months to a degree that is inconsistent with developmental level and that negatively impacts directly on social and academic/occupational activities:
   - **Note:** The symptoms are not solely a manifestation of oppositional behavior, defiance, hostility, or a failure to understand tasks or instructions. For older adolescents and adults (age 17 and older), at least five symptoms are required.

   a. Often fidgets with or taps hands or feet or squirms in seat.
   b. Often leaves seat in situations when remaining seated is expected (e.g., leaves his or her place in the classroom, in the office or other workplace, or in other situations that require remaining in place).
   c. Often runs about or climbs in situations where it is inappropriate. (**Note:** In adolescents or adults, may be limited to feeling restless.)
   d. Often unable to play or engage in leisure activities quietly.
   e. Is often "on the go," acting as if "driven by a motor" (e.g., is unable to be or uncomfortable being still for extended time, as in restaurants, meetings; may be experienced by others as being restless or difficult to keep up with).
   f. Often talks excessively.
   g. Often blurts out an answer before a question has been completed (e.g., completes people's sentences; cannot wait for turn in conversation).
   h. Often has difficulty waiting his or her turn (e.g., while waiting in line).
   i. Often interrupts or intrudes on others (e.g., butts into conversations, games, or activities; may start using other people's things without asking or receiving permission; for adolescents and adults, may intrude into or take over what others are doing).[35]

What used to be called ADD is how called attention-deficit/hyperactivity disorder—predominantly inattentive presentation if the hyperactivity criterion has not met for the past six months.[36]

7. Emotional Disturbances

Emotional disturbances are important special needs that must be addressed by lawyers and family courts. This section will discuss some of the more common emotional disturbances, but it is not exhaustive of the subject. The following psychiatric conditions or emotional disturbances are discussed:

- adjustment disorder
- posttraumatic stress disorder (PTSD)
- substance abuse disorders
- conduct disorders
- somatoform disorders
- depression
- bipolar disorder (manic-depressive psychosis)
- schizophrenia

---

35. American Psychiatric Association, (2013). *Diagnostic and statistical manual of mental disorders* (5th ed.). APA.

36. *Id.*

When any of these emotional disorders are suspected, prompt evaluation by the child's physician is *imperative*.[37] These disorders do not go away on their own—the child will not "grow out of it," and ignoring the situation usually results in it getting worse—so sticking your head in the sand about these issues is foolhardy at best. The child's physician may refer the child to a specialist for further evaluation and treatment.

Adjustment disorder is defined as "[a]n acute response to environmental stress by an adolescent with a basically good adaptive capacity; symptoms abate as stress diminishes."[38] *The Merck Manual* offers divorce and geographical relocation as examples of environmental stressors that may cause an adjustment disorder.[39]

Posttraumatic stress disorder (PTSD) can occur after major traumatic events even in otherwise stable children and adolescents.[40] The reaction can occur immediately or after several weeks,[41] months, or even years. PTSD generally has a more severe cause as well as a more severe reaction than adjustment disorder does.[42]

Substance abuse disorders are occurring in ever-younger children, even in preadolescents.[43] *Misuse* is the accepted term for illegal substance use by underage adolescents.[44] *Abuse* refers to repeated use with adverse consequences.[45]

Conduct disorder is defined as "[a] recurrent or persistent pattern of behavior that includes aggression toward people and animals, destruction of property, deceitfulness or theft, and serious violation of rules."[46] The particular behaviors differ by gender: boys tend to get into fighting, stealing, and vandalizing; girls tend to engage in lying, running away, and prostitution.[47]

Oppositional defiant disorder (ODD) has similar features to conduct disorder because it involves negative, angry, and defiant behavior toward authority figures, but it does not have a persistent pattern of behavior.[48] Be aware, though, that ODD may develop into conduct disorder.[49] Also be aware that suicidal ideation is common in children with conduct disorder, and their **suicide** attempts must be taken very seriously.[50]

The existence of **depression** in children is finally receiving acceptance by most medical professionals. Symptoms can include "a sad appearance, apathy and withdrawal, reduced capacity for pleasure, feeling rejected and unloved, somatic complaints (headaches, abdominal pain, insomnia), episodes of clowning or foolish behavior, and persistent self-blame."[51] Children with chronic depression can experience anorexia, weight

---

37. Berkow, *supra* note 11, at Ch. 274, Psychiatric Conditions in Childhood and Adolescence.
38. *Id.*
39. *Id.*
40. *Id.*
41. *Id.*
42. *Id.*
43. *Id.*
44. *Id.*
45. *Id.*
46. *Id.*
47. *Id.*
48. *Id.*
49. *Id.*
50. *Id.*
51. *Id.*

loss, despondency, and suicidal ideation.[52] Sometimes children with depression are actually overactive and engage in aggressive, antisocial behavior.[53]

Bipolar disorder is rare before puberty, but divorce often involves children who have reached puberty.[54] Episodes of depression, as well as stuporous or psychotic episodes, are a good indication that a child should be evaluated for bipolar disorder.[55] In adolescents the manic episode often presents as an excited psychotic attack.[56]

Childhood schizophrenia is characterized by withdrawal, flattened affect (lack of facial expression), apathy, thought disorder (blocking and perseveration), ideas of reference, hallucinations, delusions, and complaints of thought control.[57] Unlike some other psychiatric conditions, schizophrenia in a child looks like schizophrenia in an adult.[58]

8. Orthopedic Impairments

Orthopedic impairments vary widely and are best served by obtaining an assessment from the child's treating physician and therapists. This category can include congenital anomaly, such as clubfoot or absence of an extremity or a portion thereof; impairments caused by disease, such as poliomyelitis or bone tuberculosis; as well as impairments caused by other means, such as cerebral palsy, amputations, fractures, or burns with contractures.

9. Multiple Disabilities

This category pertains to when a child has more than one diagnosis (e.g., cerebral palsy and depression, or mental retardation and autism). These situations are much more complex because the combination of disabilities presents incredible challenges for the child, the family, medical professionals, and educators. These cases should be thoroughly and carefully assessed with consultations from all the professionals involved with the child. Only after such exhaustive evaluation should a specific plan be written for the child.

10. Traumatic Brain Injury

Traumatic brain injury (TBI) is a condition caused by external physical force. It can include either an open head injury or a closed head injury. It does not include brain injuries from birth trauma or brain injuries that are congenital or degenerative.

Head injury is the number one cause of death and disability in people younger than age 50.[59] It occurs in over 70 percent of accidents, which cause more deaths than anything else in men and boys younger than age 35.[60] Nearly half of the people who sustain severe head injury die from it, whether they receive treatment or not.[61] Treatment does not greatly improve the survival rates.[62]

---

52. *Id.*
53. *Id.*
54. *Id.*
55. *Id.*
56. *Id.*
57. *Id.*
58. *Id.*
59. Berkow, *supra* note 11, at Ch. 175, Trauma of the Head.
60. *Id.*
61. *Id.*
62. *Id.*

People dealing with children who have suffered severe head trauma should be aware of the potential residual disabilities it can cause.[63] The most common residual disabilities following severe head trauma are neuropsychological—problems with concentration, attention, and memory, as well as personality changes on a mild to moderate level.[64]

Most of the recovery for an adult will take place during the first six months following the injury.[65] After that, there is usually little improvement, although minor improvements can continue for up to two years.[66] Children tend to bounce back quicker from severe head injuries, and can continue to improve for more than two years following injury.[67]

11. Other Health Impairments

This is a huge catchall category that encompasses virtually everything that does not fit into the other categories. Some standards place attention deficit disorder in this category. ADD has been discussed in its own category because it is such a prevalent condition and there is a great deal of information we need to know about it.

The "Other Health Impairments" category can include either chronic or acute conditions, including **AIDS/HIV**, allergies, asthma, cancer, diabetes, epilepsy, heart disease, kidney disease, lead poisoning, rheumatic fever, sickle-cell anemia, and many other conditions that create a special needs situation. These conditions vary widely and are best served by obtaining an assessment from the child's treating physician and therapists.

Children who have been the victims of abuse will also need special consideration during divorce. Whether their abuse has been physical, sexual, or emotional, it will have caused them harm. Often children have been abused by their own relatives or by the friends or paramours of people in their family. Obviously, this situation must be taken into consideration when fashioning a parenting plan, custody, and visitation schedule. In addition, these children should be receiving counseling and other necessary treatment as a result of the abuse they have received. Many times, abused children need to have the parenting plan, custody, and visitation schedule specially tailored for them, often in graduated steps.

VI. RECOGNIZING AND APPLYING SPECIAL NEEDS TO DIVORCE CASES

Children with special needs require better-educated lawyers and judges than do typical children. Lawyers and judges involved in cases concerning special needs children should educate themselves on the medical issues relevant to the child's particular special need. Failure to command at least a basic familiarity with these medical issues will result in the child's special needs going unaddressed, by the very people who are in the best position to act in the best interest of the child. That is, after all, the standard in *any* case involving a child—the best interest of the child.

63. *Id.*
64. *Id.*
65. *Id.*
66. *Id.*
67. *Id.*

CHAPTER 3

How Special Needs Can Affect a Child in a Divorce Case

Children with special needs can react in ways that are very different from typical children.[1] They can also react in different degrees as compared to typical children.[2] Divorce is hard on the parents.[3] It is also hard on the children[4]—some say it is hardest on the children.[5] Family stress negatively affects a child's health.[6] Divorce poses a higher psychiatric risk on children.[7] Children whose parents are separated, divorced, or widowed rather than married have a higher rate of eating disorders.[8] Divorce and household discord are considered adverse childhood experiences that have a "strong graded relationship" to the risk of drug use from early adolescence to adulthood.[9] Parental divorce is associated with a higher rate of incidents and accidents, injuries, and illness in

1. Perryman, H. (2005). Parental reaction to the disabled child: Implications for family courts. *Family Court Review*, *43*(4), 596–606.

2. Ball, S. (2002, December). Children with special needs in divorce. Colorado Springs, CO: Author (Sunni Ball, Domestic Relations Program Manager, CASA of Colorado Springs, 701 S. Cascade Ave, Colorado Springs 80903).

3. Tanner, J. Lane, Committee on Psychosocial Aspects of Child and Family Health. (2002). Parental separation and divorce: Can we provide an ounce of prevention? *Pediatrics, 110*(5), 1007–1009.

4. Committee on Psychosocial Aspects of Child and Family Health. (1999). American Academy of Pediatrics: The child in court: A subject review. *Pediatrics, 104*(5), 1145–1148.

5. Barham, V., Devlin, R.A., & LaCasse, C. (2000). Are the new child-support guidelines "adequate" or "reasonable"? *Canadian Public Policy—Analyse de Politiques*, *26*(1), 1–15.

6. Wertlieb, D. (2003). Converging trends in family research and pediatrics: Recent findings for the American Academy of Pediatrics Task Force on the Family, Tufts University Center for Children, and the Eliott-Pearson Department of Child Development, Tufts University, Medford, Massachusetts. *Pediatrics*, *111*(6), 1572–1587.

7. Martinez-Gonzalez, M., Gual, P., Lahortiga, F., Alonso, Y., Irala-Estevez, J., & Cervera, S. (2003). Parental factors, mass media influences, and the onset of eating disorders in a prospective population-based cohort. *Pediatrics, 111*(2), 315–320.

8. *Id.*

9. Dube, S., Felitti, V., Dong, M., Chapman, D., Giles, W., & Anda, R. (2003). Childhood abuse, neglect, and household dysfunction and the risk of illicit drug use: The adverse childhood experiences study. *Pediatrics, 111*(3), 564–572.

children.[10] Children whose parents are divorced have an increased rate of teen pregnancy.[11] Medical issues of children are complicated and worsened by parental divorce.[12] Stressful life events, including divorce, have even been associated with decreased adherence to anti-retroviral medications in children and adults with HIV infection.[13]

Now add to the mix **special needs**, and there is a potential powder keg if the people dealing with these children are not educated on the danger areas. Many family lawyers and judges are handling these cases on the fly.[14] "Court professionals [are] largely ignorant of the unique and sensitive care required to competently address the special needs of these children when formulating parenting plans."[15] It has been estimated that millions of American children have a disability.[16] Considering the extremely high divorce rates among families with special needs children, if the courts and lawyers do not very quickly become educated on the issues inherent in handling family court cases involving special needs children, a huge segment of our population will be subject to a gross miscarriage of justice. Because this segment of the population includes some of the most vulnerable people in our society, we owe them a greater duty of care.

I. TREATING CHILDREN WITH SPECIAL NEEDS DURING DIVORCE

Children with special needs should be treated with special consideration during two phases of divorce—during the divorce and after the divorce. Each phase requires different considerations to be addressed. During both stages, a child with special needs often feels that the divorce is his fault—if he was not so much extra work, his parents would not be getting a divorce.[17] These children often hear people say that their parents divorced because one parent could not handle the stress and pressures of raising a special needs child.[18] This unfortunately reinforces their feelings of guilt. Imagine being a child who is already struggling to cope with having cancer or diabetes, and heap on top

---

10. O'Connor, T., Davies, L., Dunn, J., Golding, J., and the ALSPAC Study Team, from the Social Genetic and Developmental Psychiatry Research Centre, Institute of Psychiatry, King's College, London, United Kingdom; and the Institute of Child Health, University of Bristol, Bristol, United Kingdom. (2000). *Pediatrics, 106*(5), 68–78.

11. Hillis, S., Anda, R., Dube, S., Felitti, V., Marchbanks, P., & Marks, J. (2004). The association between adverse childhood experiences and adolescent pregnancy, long-term psychosocial consequences, and fetal death. *Pediatrics, 113*(2), 320–327.

12. Hagan, Jr., J. (2001). Commentary: The new morbidity: Where the rubber hits the road, or the practitioner's guide to the new morbidity. *Pediatrics, 108*(5), 1206–1210.

13. Williams, P., Storm, D., Montepiedra, G., Nichols, S., Kammerer, B., & Sirois, P., et al. for the PACTG (Pediatric AIDS Clinical Trials Group) 219C Team. (2006). Predictors of adherence to antiretroviral medications in children and adolescents with HIV infection. *Pediatrics*, published online November 13, 2006, doi:10.1542/peds.2006-0493. Retrieved December 6, 2006, from http://pediatrics.aappublications.org/cgi/content/full/peds.2006-0493.

14. Saposnek, D. (2005). Editorial preface to special issue of *Family Court Review. Family Court Review, 43*(4), 563–565.

15. *Id.*

16. Agosta, J. (1995). Family support policy brief. Tualatin, OR: National Center for Family Support, Human Services Research Institute.

17. Cohen, G., and Committee on Psychosocial Aspects of Child and Family Health. (2002). Helping children and families deal with divorce and separation. *Pediatrics, 110*(5), 1019–1023.

18. *Id.*

of that the feeling of being responsible for your parents' divorce. You might think that if you were not around, things would be better for everyone concerned. This is just one illustration of how incredibly important it is for all people involved in a divorce involving special needs children to be aware of and sensitive to these issues.

Many otherwise intelligent people have a misconception that a person with a disability is somehow not as bright as others. When addressing a person with a disability, such people often use words that one would use when talking to someone much younger, or they speak very loudly or very slowly. It is as though they think a person is automatically of lesser intelligence just because they have a special need. Someone needs to explain to them that being blind, or being in a wheelchair, or stuttering does not render a person stupid. The people who have this attitude about people with special needs often patronize them, think they cannot possibly have meaningful input in the situation, and believe they are incapable of making decisions about their lives. This behavior must be prevented in divorce cases involving children with special needs. Children who are treated this way become angry, resentful, distrusting of the process, and uncooperative; or they act out (justifiably) in other ways. Children with special needs must be treated with respect and dignity during a divorce.

A. During the Divorce

During the divorce, a special needs child can experience exacerbation of his symptoms.[19] This may include short-term withdrawal, regression, aggression, loss of language ability, loss of social skills, loss of toilet training, emotional outbursts, loss of academic skills, depression, self-injury, hopelessness, suicidal ideation, running away, and even worsened physical condition.[20] Even children without special needs can experience night terrors, bed-wetting, sleepwalking, and other parasomnias during divorce.[21]

B. After the Divorce

After the divorce, a special needs child can experience all of the preceding situations on a long-term or permanent basis, which may eventually result in the child's institutionalization or even death, either from **suicide** or from worsened physical condition. In addition, the parent who is the caregiver may quickly become so exhausted that **institutional care** may be necessary for the child.[22]

In addition to exacerbation of their existing conditions,[23] these families have the additional stressor of decreased standard of living. The standard of living of all parties usually declines after divorce.[24] Further, the mere fact of having a child who is diagnosed

19. Jennings, S. (2005). Autism in children and parents: Unique considerations for family court professionals. *Family Court Review, 43*(4), 582–595.

20. Johnson, B., Grossman, D., Connell, F., & Koepsell, T. (2000). High-risk periods for childhood injury among siblings. *Pediatrics, 105*(3), 562–568.

21. Laberge, L., Tremblay, R., Vitaro, F., & Montplaisir, J. (2000). Development of parasomnias from childhood to early adolescence. *Pediatrics, 106*(1), 67–74.

22. Jennings, *supra* note 19.

23. Kaufman, F., Halvorson, M., & Carpenter, S. (1999). Association between diabetes control and visits to a multidisciplinary pediatric diabetes clinic. *Pediatrics, 103*(5), 948–951.

24. Barham, Devlin, & LaCasse, *supra* note 5.

with a life-threatening illness is considered a dramatic event, capable of precipitating posttraumatic stress disorder (PTSD).[25]

During the divorce, children with special needs may respond in different ways based on their own unique personality and coping abilities, as well as on their particular special need. Realize that many children have more than one special need; for example, they may have mental retardation and autism. Children with **multiple disabilities** will need even more careful following than will children with one special need.

II. IMPACT OF DIVORCE ON SPECIAL NEEDS CHILDREN, BY CATEGORY OF SPECIAL NEED

A. Autism, Developmental Delays

A child with autism or other developmental delays may show no emotions whatsoever during the divorce, which could cause people to mistakenly think she is not "bothered" by the divorce. But the child may be shutting down emotionally inside, may be terrified of what is happening and how it will affect her, and may feel guilty that she caused the divorce. On the other hand, the child might become hyperactive, spin constantly, shriek inconsolably, lose toilet training, and have emotional outbursts that frighten even her. She might lose toilet training, lose progress made in communication, and regress socially.

Running is always a concern when dealing with children with autism. If a child with autism is not watched every waking and sleeping moment of every day, he may wander off, walk right onto a highway, go with total strangers, plunge into a swimming pool or river, or do other things with apparently no sense of the danger to himself. When such children are under stress, these things may be more likely to happen.

Changes in their routine are often difficult for children with autism. During divorce, everyone's life is "turned upside down." Mom or Dad no longer lives at home; a parent and child may have to move out of the house. Mom might have to go to work and put the child in the hands of a caregiver. The child's daily routine may be completely different. Children with autism need consistency and predictability, and divorce can destroy both.

B. Hearing Impairment, Visual Impairment, and Speech or Language Impairment

Children with hearing, visual, or speech or language impairment already have more difficulty participating in a world that is primarily sighted, hearing, and communicates easily. They can quickly become cut off from the process during a divorce. For example, if a hearing-impaired child does not have someone making sure she knows what is being said and what is going on, she will be disconnected from the process and out of the loop. If a visually impaired child does not have someone explaining things that are going on visually, he can also be cut off. A child with speech or language impairment may have difficulty expressing questions and concerns about what is happening to her life. Treat these children with respect and dignity, *make them part of the process*, and listen to their needs, however they express them.

---

25. Stuber, M., Kazak, A., Meeske, K., Barakat, L., Guthrie, D., & Garnier, H., et al. (1997). Predictors of posttraumatic stress symptoms in childhood cancer survivors. *Pediatrics, 100*(6), 958–964.

C. Emotional Disturbance

During the divorce, a child with a preexisting emotional disturbance needs heightened observation and intervention. The underlying emotional disturbance may be greatly accelerated by the added stress of a divorce. The stress may cause the child's body chemistry to shift, in turn causing problems with his medication. Such children can be particularly vulnerable to feelings of guilt, depression, hopelessness, and suicidal ideation. They may regress, become withdrawn, become more aggressive, run away, injure themselves, or even attempt suicide.

D. Mental Retardation, Traumatic Brain Injury

A child with mental retardation or traumatic brain injury may be frightened and confused by what is happening to his life during a divorce. Someone who can communicate well with the child needs to sit down with the child, *tell him repeatedly that it is not his fault*, that no one is angry with him, that *he will not be abandoned*, that both his parents care about him, and that *they will continue to take care of him*. As soon as the living arrangements are worked out, they need to be explained to the child, so he can start adjusting to the idea and rebuilding his structure. Do not assume that children with mental retardation or traumatic brain injury cannot understand these concepts. They understand far more than many people realize. *The problem is usually not the child's ability to understand, but the adult's ability to explain.*

E. Orthopedic Impairments, Other Health Impairments

Children with other special needs may have some of the same responses as the children discussed earlier. Realize that you are dealing with a person who has all the ordinary pressures and challenges of growing up, as well as all the difficulties of handling life with a special need. Imagine being ten years old and having to stick your finger five times a day and get daily shots of insulin to manage your diabetes. Imagine being 13 years old and going through 30 weeks of chemotherapy after you have had major surgery for cancer. Imagine being eight years old and going through the hurdles of one day in an inaccessible world when you were born without arms.

While to us they are a blessing, these children know they are more work than a typical child. When the family breaks up, *these children are going to feel at fault*. A terminally ill child might feel that if she would hurry up and die, her parents would get back together. She may lose the will to fight her illness, or even lose the will to live.

A child with diabetes or renal disease may be emotionally distraught or distracted and forget to take his insulin or other medication, or he may forget and eat something that will make him get sick. His condition could deteriorate, and he could end up in renal failure or diabetic shock/coma. A child who is in intensive physical therapy may lose the motivation to keep trying and may not make as complete a recovery as he otherwise might have.

Another danger to all these children is that during and after the divorce there may not be enough money to pay for all their medications, equipment, therapy, supplements, dietary needs, and other needs. If the primary caregiver parent has to go back to work, increase the hours at work, or take a second job, the child may have longer hours in day care or before and after school child care, receive less time and nurturing from that parent, and be unable to participate in therapy because the parent who used to take her to therapy now has to be at work all day.

Many special needs children end up in residential or institutional care after their parents divorce, simply because the primary caregiver parent has to be at work all day and can no longer take care of the child. *This is a human tragedy.* We must become more perceptive of how our actions and decisions during divorce affect our most vulnerable children.

Our family courts should not be measured by how quickly and efficiently they can process a divorce, but rather by how compassionately and intelligently they achieve a working plan that is sensitive to the needs of the human beings involved.

CHAPTER 4

Why Child Support Guidelines and Standard Visitation Schedules Do Not Meet the Needs of Special Needs Children

Standard child support charts and visitation schedules do not meet the needs of special needs children, short term or long term. This chapter examines why the application of standard child support charts and visitation schedules fails to meet these needs.

I. CHILD SUPPORT CHARTS

A. Short-Term Needs

During the divorce, special needs children may have more needs than they usually do because of the additional stress factors of the divorce.[1] Divorce can affect a special needs child in numerous ways. Divorce can take an already strained and difficult medical situation and turn it into a full-blown crisis. Additional funds may be necessary to cover the additional expenses, besides the usual expenses involved for the child.

1. Preexisting Expenses

Standard child support charts do not address the higher costs inherent in raising a special needs child. Caring for special needs children is more expensive than caring for children without special needs.[2] It has been estimated that health care costs on standard child support charts are only half of the extra cost of caring for a disabled child.[3] The child support charts need to include separate line items for the additional special needs costs, including therapy, equipment, medications, supplements, dietary costs, sensory items, respite care, professionals, modifications to the home environment, and continually changing needs of the child.

---

1. Perryman, H. (2005). Parental reaction to the disabled child: Implications for family courts. *Family Court Review, 43*(4), 596–606.

2. Meyers, M., Lukemeyer, A., & Smeeding, T. (1996). Welfare, and the burden of disability: Caring for special needs of children in poor families. *Income Security Policy Series* (Paper No. 12). Syracuse, NY: Center for Policy Research, Maxwell School of Citizenship and Public Affairs, Syracuse University.

3. *Id.*

Additionally, there are expenditures for transportation to distant hospitals or sources of medical care, extra laundry, babysitting of other siblings while care is being given to the special needs child, and other medical expenses not paid by public or private insurance.[4] Several studies have found that "[f]amilies with disabled children experienced uncovered, out-of-pocket expenses substantially higher than those of families without disabled children."[5]

Although it is difficult to come up with a precise dollar amount for the cost of raising a special needs child, families raising special needs children "face an avalanche of expenses that far outstrip cost projections for a normal healthy child."[6] Special needs children often require extensive services throughout their lifetime,[7] and those services are often not covered by insurance or are limited by government assistance.[8] Many of these children require assistance in daily living activities such as toileting, eating, bathing, grooming, dressing, communicating, mobility, and behavior management.[9]

2. *Therapy*

Special needs children often require one or more types of therapy—physical therapy, speech and/or language therapy, occupational therapy, sensory integration therapy, communication therapy, music therapy, art therapy, therapeutic horsemanship, behavior therapy, group therapy, individual therapy, or socialization therapy, to name a few.[10] These costs are not easy to assess at the time of the divorce, for several reasons:

- A child may not be in a particular type of therapy at the time of the divorce because she has been wait-listed and has not yet been reached.
- A child may not have needed a particular type of therapy at the time of the divorce, but he needs it as his condition improves, worsens, or otherwise changes.
- At the time of the divorce, a child may be in therapy that is covered by public or other funding, then loses the funding due to governmental or administrative budget cuts after the divorce.
- After the divorce, a new method of therapy may be developed, a new program may be established, or a new therapist may move to the area—although they did not exist or were not available in the area at the time of the divorce.
- Sometimes it is necessary to vary the types of therapy a child receives periodically to increase the effectiveness of the therapy.

---

4. *Id.*
5. *Id.*
6. Pabon, A. (2005). Financial planning for special needs children: A review of available information for parents. *Journal of Personal Finance*, *4*(2), 40–49.
7. Sneed, R., May, W., & Stencel, C. (2000). Training of pediatricians in care of physical disabilities in children with special health needs: Results of a two-state survey of practicing pediatricians and national resident training programs. *Pediatrics*, *105*(3), 554–561.
8. Pabon, *supra* note 6.
9. Agosta, J. (1995). Family support policy brief. Tualatin, OR: National Center for Family Support, Human Services Research Institute.
10. Babb, L. Anne, & Laws, R. (1997). Adopting and advocating for the special needs child: A guide for parents and professionals. Westport, CT: Bergin & Garvey.

3. Equipment

Therapy equipment and other equipment necessitated by a child's special needs present costs that are not always constant.[11] As a child grows, he may need larger leg braces or a larger wheelchair. A child whose diabetes is now controlled with pills may at some point need insulin injections. Different therapeutic techniques will require different equipment. To immerse the child in a therapeutic environment, it is often recommended that the parents become trained in the therapy techniques and do additional therapy at home. This therapy almost always requires equipment. Further, therapy tools and other items must be changed on a regular basis to keep the child interested in and enthusiastic about therapy.

4. Medication

For many reasons, medication costs may vary. New drugs are being developed and discovered every day. People are finding "off-label" uses for existing drugs. A change in the child's condition, or even in his age, may require a change in medication.[12] An adverse reaction to medication may require a medication change. Medications should be kept at the houses of both parents, and the pharmacist or doctor must be told the reason for the request of duplicate prescriptions.[13]

5. Supplements

Many parents and health professionals advocate giving special needs children nutritional supplements. These children, who often have compromised or weakened immune systems, need daily multivitamin and multimineral supplements that are superior to the usual grocery store brands many children take.[14] Specific supplements may be given for specific needs.[15] A child who has difficulty sleeping, for example, might be given melatonin. Many children with special needs have chemical inadequacies or imbalances in their bodies, for which supplements are often recommended.[16] Few of these supplements are covered by insurance, and many of them are quite expensive.[17]

6. Dietary Costs

Many children with special needs have to follow special diets.[18] A diabetic child is often on a strict diabetic diet.[19] A kidney patient may be on a strict renal diet. Many special needs children are lactose intolerant or allergic to dairy products and may be allergic to nuts, artificial coloring agents, preservatives, and other additives.[20] For some of these

---

11. *Id.*
12. *Id.*
13. Jennings, S. (2005). Autism in children and parents: Unique considerations for family court professionals. *Family Court Review, 43*(4), 582–595.
14. Babb & Laws, *supra* note 10.
15. *Id.*
16. *Id.*
17. *Id.*
18. *Id.*
19. *Id.*
20. *Id.*

children, more expensive organic food is the best option. Some children cannot eat anything containing wheat or soy products.[21]

Imagine trying to take a child who cannot eat wheat products to a birthday party. The cake is made with flour, which is made from wheat. Your child does not get to eat the birthday cake. The host serves cookies as well. No, your child cannot eat them. He must also decline the cheese pizza being offered, because the crust is made from dough that contains flour.

The daily life of managing what these children can and cannot eat is extremely difficult, and their diet can result in greater costs than those for a child with no dietary restrictions. If you go to the local organic food store and check the prices on the items for people with wheat-free, dairy-free, or sugar-free diets, you will find they are more expensive than the ordinary foods.

7. Sensory Items (Therapy, Different Clothing/Other Items, Take-Along Items)

Children with special needs often have sensory needs unlike those of other children.[22] Besides the specific behaviors listed next, special needs children may exhibit self-injurious behavior, such as self-cutting, head banging, self-biting, and so on. Entire books have been written about the sensory needs these children may have. To give an extremely sketchy outline, a child may have:

- *Touch issues.* A child who is *hyposensitive* to touch may be seemingly unaware of pain, burning, or how objects feel. She may not complain of ear infections, injections, or accidental painful contact. She may bump into walls, people, or furniture and appear to be unaware of it. A child who is *hypersensitive* to touch may have an adverse reaction to certain textures. She may complain that her socks or other clothing hurt. She may not like to walk barefoot outdoors or get dirty or sticky.[23]
- *Movement issues.* The child may crave fast and spinning movement, swinging, rocking, twirling, and merry-go-rounds. She may fidget, move constantly, or enjoy getting into upside-down positions. She may be a daredevil and be seemingly unaware of danger or have little appropriate fear.[24]
- *Body position issues.* The child may slouch, slump, and sprawl. He may display clumsy and inaccurate actions and bump into objects.[25]
- *Sight issues.* The child may become stressed and excited when there is too much to look at, including words, toys, and other children. She may have poor eye contact, be inattentive when drawing or doing desk work, or overreact to bright light—especially flashing, swirling, or moving lights.[26]
- *Sound issues.* The child may become stressed and overexcited when there is too much noise or chaos—too many sources of noise.[27] It is as though he cannot filter out the different sounds or voices, and they are all blaring at him at the same time. He performs best in a quiet, calm environment. He may run out of the room or hide in the pantry

---

21. *Id.*

22. Kranowitz, C. S. (2005). The out-of-sync child: Recognizing and coping with sensory integration dysfunction (2nd ed.). New York: Perigee Trade, Penguin Group.

23. *Id.*

24. *Id.*

25. *Id.*

26. *Id.*

27. *Id.*

when there are too many people being loud in the room. He may cover his ears when it is noisy. The noise from hair dryers, vacuums, sirens, and alarm clocks can cause him to shriek, cover his ears, and run from the room as though he is terrified.[28]

- *Smell issues.* She may object to odors that you do not even notice. Sometimes you will be unable to figure out what she smells. At other times, it will seem as if she could sit in a diaper full of urine and feces and seem not to notice the smell.[29]
- *Taste issues.* He may object to certain temperatures of food and will usually want food to be at room temperature. He probably has a limited repertoire of foods, often accepting only finger foods. Many such children require high-quality nutritional supplements to avoid malnutrition because they will eat only four or five foods—such as rice, bananas, milk, and apples. Many of these children cannot stand to eat creamy-textured food, such as pudding, yogurt, and Jell-O. Such textures cause the child's gag reflex to overreact and he will vomit, even if he wants to eat the food.[30]
- *Vestibular issues.* Vestibular sense provides humans information about the position of our head in relation to the earth's surface, as well as the movement of our body through space and the ability to balance.[31] We receive this information through the inner ear.[32] A child with these issues may need to swing or rock for 20 or 30 minutes at various times during the day in order to calm down, be able to focus, or get energy.[33]
- *Proprioceptive issues.* Proprioceptive sense provides us with information about body position and movement of body parts.[34] We receive this information through stretching and contracting our muscles.[35] For example, in a child with these issues, his brain may "forget" where his left hip is and send him crashing into a wall to send a message to the brain about where his left hip is. At school, he may "ricochet" his way down the hallway, crashing into the lockers on one wall and then the lockers on the opposite wall.[36]
- *Sensorimotor issues.* This child may have difficulty with fine motor skills. He may be delayed in eating with a spoon or fork, in tying his shoes, in getting himself dressed, or in writing or drawing. He may have difficulty with motor planning and have difficulty in walking through a room without running into furniture or people.[37]
- *Bilateral coordination issues.* This child may be unable to do jumping jacks, swimming, skipping, or other activities involving coordinating the use of both the right and left sides of her body.[38]

8. Respite Care

The primary caregiver parent is often on duty 24-7 with a special needs child.[39] Often, they must place alarms on the doors to let them know if the child has run. Sometimes a child will shriek constantly whenever the primary caregiver parent is out of sight, which can make taking a shower or doing laundry an absolute nightmare. Yet, errands must

---

28. *Id.*
29. *Id.*
30. *Id.*
31. *Id.* at 54.
32. *Id.*
33. *Id.*
34. *Id.*
35. *Id.*
36. *Id.*
37. *Id.*
38. *Id.*
39. Perryman, *supra* note 1.

still be run, chores completed, yard work done. To accomplish some of these things, the parent must retain additional child care.

An allowance should be made for additional child care (respite care) in the regular child support amount. The amount allowed should *not* be for the cheapest teenage babysitter. Special needs children require specialized, trained people who do not work for teenage babysitter wages.

In addition, being the primary caregiver parent is physically and mentally exhausting.[40] It is like being the head nurse in the ICU 24 hours a day, seven days a week. If we tried to have such a nurse work for years on end without ever being able to go home and get a good night's sleep or have a day off, she would burn out very soon. Her health would suffer and so would patient care. Primary caregiver parents often go for *years* without a good night's sleep or a day off.[41] The child support amount should allow for respite care, especially in cases in which the other parent does not actively participate in the child's hands-on, regular daily care.

9. Professionals

Necessary professionals involved in the care of a special needs child can include specialty physicians, physical therapists, occupational therapists, psychotherapists, social skills therapists, behavioral specialists, medical assessors, support group facilitators, tutors, parent-training teachers, and special education lawyers.[42]

10. Modifications to the Home Environment

As mentioned earlier, sometimes parents of special needs children must set alarms on all the doors, day and night, to let them know if the child has left the house and wandered off. Sometimes this happens in the middle of the night, during winter, or at other times that present a greater-than-usual danger to such a child.

These children often have seemingly no sense of danger. Locks must be put on the oven so they will not get burned and on the toilets so they will not stick their head in and drown. Bookcases, appliances, and heavy furniture must be bolted to the walls so the child will not pull it down on top of herself in case she climbs on it. Cushioning blocks may need to be installed semi-permanently on the corners of fireplaces and walls in case the child crashes into them.

Different types of lighting may be necessary. If therapy is done in the home, modifications will be necessary to create a therapeutic environment that is devoid of distractions and objects that cause sensory distress to the child. To create this environment may require having the basement finished or a room or two remodeled.

11. Changes in the Child's Needs

The needs of these children are constantly changing. Sometimes they change very rapidly. In the short term, all of the areas just discussed must be continually monitored and adapted to meet the child's changing needs. If the child is making progress, the primary caregiver

40. Taylor, N., Wall, S., Liebow, H., Sabatino, C., Timberlake, E., & Farber, M. (2005). Mother and soldier: Raising a child with a disability in a low-income military family. *Exceptional Children, 72*(1), 83–99.

41. Lawson, K. L. (2001). Contemplating selective reproduction: The subjective appraisal of parenting a child with a disability. *Journal of Reproductive and Infant Psychology, 19*(1), 73–82.

42. Jennings, *supra* note 13.

parent must be able to move the child on to the next stage of therapy. This may require additional training, equipment, or other items. Just as you would not make progress in your physical fitness if you never varied or increased your workouts, a child with special needs will plateau and stop making progress if her therapies are never varied or increased.

12. Costs Caused by the Divorce

Besides all the preexisting costs just discussed, the child may need more therapy, counseling, or medication to deal with the additional stress and regression caused by the divorce.

B. Long-Term Needs

After the divorce, events and situations will occur over the long term and will affect the amount of child support necessitated by the child's special needs. The parent who is the primary caregiver frequently faces barriers to employment and to advances in career, due to the increased burden of the daily care of the special needs child as well as to the unpredictable nature of having to deal with unexpected medical, emotional, and other crises in the child's life.[43] Therefore, the primary caregiver parent will have less opportunity to earn income to support herself, the special needs child, and any other children in the home as well.[44] Primary caregivers spend a median of four hours and 42 minutes per day in caring for severely disabled children; some primary caregivers spend up to 20 hours per day caring for their disabled children.[45] In addition to the extra burden of caring for children with special needs, many primary caregivers are unable to enter the workforce or be employed full-time as a result of problems relating to the availability and cost of special needs child care.[46]

Developments in the child's condition can also affect the need for child support. A child with cancer, for example, may be in remission at the time of the divorce and then have a relapse of the cancer a few months or years later. A child with an emotional disturbance may be holding his own until he hits puberty and then spin out of control. A child with asthma may eventually outgrow the asthma, although we now know that not all children do. A child's allergies or diabetes may worsen over time. A child with kidney or liver disease or leukemia may find a match for an organ donor or a bone marrow transplant.

Families raising children with special needs often devote every waking moment and every dollar they have in trying to meet their child's needs. They do not have the extra time or money to spend going to court and hiring lawyers to frequently modify child support amounts when there have been changes in the costs of the child's needs. *The courts should develop an informal process that addresses this issue so these families can focus on the much more important job of raising their children.*

There can be language in the child support chart for the child support to increase informally—within the limitation of a certain percentage, without requiring a formal court procedure—by having the parents complete a form documenting the change and mailing it to the court. Perhaps a *better solution* would be for the family courts to have a *special*

43. Meyers, Lukemeyer, & Smeeding, *supra* note 2.
44. *Id.*
45. *Id.*
46. *Id.*

needs coordinator who would sit as an informal and quick tribunal for such matters, especially when the parents do not agree on the payment of the additional expenses. When you consider all the children who have special needs and the extremely high divorce rates among their families, the special needs coordinator would be a very busy person.

There is a huge social price to pay when families with disabled children do not have sufficient resources. The hardship imposed on these families in addition to the burden of dealing with a disability itself is almost incomprehensible. A study was performed on families with special needs children: nearly two-thirds had incomes at or below the poverty line.[47] In the study, the researchers looked at the effect of disability in terms of actual hardship to the family.[48] "The fraction of the families reporting that children went hungry in prior months more than doubled for those with special needs child(ren); reports of adults going hungry were 16 to 24 percentage points higher."[49] The study also found evidence that families with disabled children had more evictions, utility shutoffs, and homelessness.[50] For many families who are already low income, having a special needs child pushes them from the level of merely low income to the level of deep poverty—at or below 75 percent of poverty-level income.[51] When child support is not paid or is inadequate, mothers and children often have turned to welfare (public assistance).[52]

II. VISITATION SCHEDULES

Standard visitation schedules are often grossly inappropriate for special needs children, for many reasons.

A. Noncustodial Parent

The noncustodial parent may not have the training and may not be willing to learn how to properly care for the child. Often the parent's refusal to devote themselves to the care the child needs contributed to the divorce.[53] These issues can include

- following the proper diet for a child with diabetes;
- lifting, feeding, toileting, and bathing and dressing a wheelchair-bound child;
- dealing with medication issues and potential urgent care issues with a terminally ill child;
- signing or communicating in another manner with a child who has hearing impairment;
- understanding and responding appropriately to a child with an emotional disturbance;
- modifying their new home environment for the therapeutic, safety, sensory, and other needs of the child;
- spending the necessary hours doing the therapy with the child that would be done if the child were at home with the primary caregiver parent;

---

47. *Id.*

48. *Id.*

49. *Id.*

50. *Id.*

51. Lukemeyer, A., Meyers, M., & Smeeding, T. (1996). Expensive children in poor families: Out-of-pocket expenditures for the care of disabled and chronically ill children and welfare reform. *Income Security Policy Series* (Paper No. 17). Syracuse, NY: Center for Policy Research, Maxwell School of Citizenship and Public Affairs, Syracuse University.

52. Katz, S. (1994). Historical perspective and current trends in the legal process of divorce. *The Future of Children—Children and Divorce*, *4*(1), 44–62.

53. Perryman, *supra* note 1.

- taking the child to therapy and treatments; and
- consistently and reliably giving the child her medications.

1. Child's Schedule

Often special needs children have very structured lives.[54] They follow a regimented schedule that needs to be done essentially the same way every day.[55] Many times the necessary equipment is all located at the primary caregiver parent's house, because it is just too expensive to buy all the necessary equipment for two households after a divorce. These children often do not handle transitions well, and they need consistency and predictability in their daily lives and schedules.[56]

When a child has developmental delays, *her custody arrangements should be based upon her developmental age rather than on her chronological age.*[57] The cookie-cutter parenting plans employed by many family courts will result in a special needs child with the developmental age of a three-year-old being treated as a 12- or 15-year-old and could have catastrophic results.

To properly assess the levels of impairment and strengths of each special needs child, family courts should use psychological and medical reports as well as psychoeducational assessments, report cards, individualized educational plans (IEPs), 504 Plans,[58] and detailed information from the child's teachers.[59] (See footnote 58 for an explanation of IEPs and 504 Plans.) The court should also consider input from the special needs child's parents and typical siblings.[60] If necessary, a child psychologist should be utilized by the court.[61] Other professionals whose input could be of great benefit to family courts in these cases include guardians ad litem (but only if trained in special needs), therapists, special masters, parenting coaches, or coordinators.[62] Although some may object that certain evaluators may fail to meet the high standard of reliability expected for expert evidence, they should nonetheless be allowed to express opinions as to best interests of the special needs children.[63]

---

54. Jennings, *supra* note 13; Perryman, *supra* note 1.

55. Perryman, *supra* note 1.

56. Jennings, *supra* note 13; Perryman, *supra* note 1.

57. Jennings, *supra* note 13.

58. An IEP is a legal document, mandated by the IDEA, that controls the procedural requirements. It is more involved than a 504 Plan. An IEP is required for students with disabilities who require specialized instruction. A 504 Plan is a written plan required for students with disabilities needing only reasonable accommodation. It is less involved than an IEP. An excellent explanation may be found in *A Parent's Guide to Special Education*, by L. Wilmhurst & A. W. Brue (Amacom, 2005). See also "IEPs vs. 504 Plans," and the entire Sevier County Special Education website. Retrieved September 10, 2008, from https://www.sevier.org/site/default.aspx?PageType=2&PageModuleInstanceID=486&ViewID=838b13a1-2ccb-4c74-83cb-0b9f098d6937&RenderLoc=0&FlexDataID=7938. Additional helpful materials include the Learning Disabilities OnLine website, http://www.LDonline.org (especially the materials on accommodations and modifications) and the Cleveland Heights Teachers Union website materials on 504 Plan Frequently Asked Questions, http://www.chtu.org. Both retrieved September 10, 2008.

59. *Id.*

60. *Id.*

61. *Id.*

62. *Id.*

63. Bala, N. (2005). Tippins and Wittman asked the wrong question: Evaluators may not be "experts," but they can express best interests opinions. *Family Court Review, 43*(4), 554–562.

PROVIDING FOR A SPECIAL NEEDS CHILD

- psychological and medical records
- psychoeducational assessments
- report cards
- individualized educational plans (IEPs) and 504 Plans
- detailed information from teachers
- input from child's parents
- input from child's siblings
- child psychologist
- guardian ad litem
- special needs coordinator

It is often better to have the special needs child sleep at the primary caregiver's home every weeknight and at the noncustodial parent's house only on alternate weekends.[64] Even then, it may be better for the child to have fewer overnights or no overnights.[65]

Sometimes the visitation consists of the noncustodial parent coming to the house of the primary caregiver and participating in the child's evening activities, especially if the child's necessary equipment is located at the primary caregiver's house.[66] Obviously, this arrangement can be awkward for divorced or divorcing parents and for any significant others who may be involved (new spouses, etc.). Even though this situation is somewhat difficult for the parents, the most important factor should be the *needs and best interests* of the special needs child. An awkward situation for a parent is better than putting the child into an inappropriate setting, having to haul all their necessary equipment and supplies, and turning the child's structure upside down. When people have a special needs child, their expectations should be different than those of parents of typical children.

It is important to not forget the needs of non–special needs siblings. Siblings of special needs children are often overlooked in family law cases. Their lives are already being stressed because their families are going through the experience of divorce. Even before the divorce, much of their parents' time and energy was taken up by caring for the special needs sibling. A good parenting plan will provide for *one-on-one time* of the non–special needs siblings with their parents.[67]

The best parenting plans will address the safety and unique needs of the special needs child and properly deal with the needs of typical siblings.[68]

64. Jennings, *supra* note 13; Perryman, *supra* note 1.
65. Jennings, *supra* note 13.
66. *Id.*
67. *Id.*
68. Perryman, *supra* note 1.

B. Environmental Modifications

The home environment of a special needs child must be modified at both parents' homes to meet the child's special needs. A child with severe food allergies could have a fatal reaction to certain foods. All such food must be removed from both households. A child with asthma and or pet allergies or other allergies must be in a home environment at both households that is appropriate for their special needs (i.e., no pets, no smoking, etc.). All required medications should be kept at both households. This includes inhalers, testing kits for the diabetic child, and all other medically necessary items. The doctors and pharmacists should be told the reason for the duplicate prescriptions and duplicate items. If possible, all necessary equipment should be maintained at both households.

For the numerous reasons just discussed, the existing child support guidelines and visitation schedules (parenting plans) do not meet the needs of special needs children. Legislation must be enacted that specifically addresses the issues of child support and visitation schedules (parenting plans) for special needs children when their families are going through divorce, paternity, and other family court cases. Courts need to implement policies and procedures to ensure that the unique needs of these families with special needs children are met.

CHAPTER 5

Legislation, Case Law, and Parenting Plans

I. LEGISLATION

There is great need for legislation is this area. The existing federal legislation protects special needs children only in the areas of health care and education. While health care and education are both necessary, *no federal legislation exists that protects special needs children when their families are going through a divorce, paternity, or other family law case.* The state legislation that exists in the area of family law is virtually silent on the issue of special needs children. Lawyers and judges desperately need to have legislation to guide them in handling these cases. Due to the paucity of legislation in this area, there is a corresponding lack of legal treatises and professional articles to guide lawyers and judges.

Until the last decade or so, little to nothing was published on this topic in the professional literature as guidance, so divorce lawyers and judges have had to struggle to find out how to accurately and effectively identify and manage these cases.[1]

The best approach would be federal legislation that could then be adopted by the state legislatures. The advantages of this approach are twofold:

1. *Uniformity*—one body of legislation that would be consistent throughout the country. This uniformity would prevent the problems of
   - Inconsistent results from one state to another
   - Forum shopping—people choosing one state over another based on one state's version of special needs family law legislation or based on that state's lack of special needs family law legislation
2. *Timeliness*—there is desperate need for legislation *now*. It would be much quicker to have federal legislation enacted and then adopted by the states than to wait for 50 different states to draft 50 different bodies of legislation whenever the states get around to doing so.

---

1. Brown, C., Goodman, S., & Kupper, L. (2003). The unplanned journey: When you learn that your child has a disability. *News Digest 20* (3rd ed.).

The number of special needs children is increasing; therefore, it is more important than ever that we enact legislation to help these families when they traverse the family court system.[2] The divorce rate in special needs families is 85 to 90 percent.[3] Existing legislation does not adequately address the issues inherent in family law cases involving special needs children. If our legislatures do not act quickly, we will have a crisis of national proportions on our hands.

The vast majority of families with a special needs child will go through a divorce. When these families go through the family court process with the existing grossly inadequate legislation, many of these families end up in stark poverty as a result.[4] In addition, serious harm can occur to the special needs child whose family has gone through the family court process utilizing the existing inadequate legislation. The special needs child can experience an exacerbation of his symptoms.[5] These may include withdrawal, regression, aggression, loss of language ability, loss of social skills, loss of toilet training, emotional outbursts, loss of academic skills, depression, self-injury, hopelessness, suicidal ideation, running away, and even worsened physical condition.[6] This exacerbation of symptoms may eventually result in institutionalization of the child because the single parent is no longer able to care for the child adequately on her own.[7] The worsened symptoms can also result in the death of the special needs child, either from suicide or from worsened physical condition.[8] When the parent who is the caregiver does not have her unique needs addressed adequately by the family courts, she may have to make the heartbreaking decision to institutionalize her special needs child due to sheer exhaustion or abject poverty.[9]

A. Federal Law

Legislation exists that addresses the health care issues and the education issues as they relate to people with special needs; however, legislation needs to be adopted that addresses the family law issues for people with special needs. The following legislation addresses health care issues and education issues of people with special needs.

1. Health Care Issues

Title V of the Social Security Act (42 U.S.C. Chapter 7, subchapter V, §§ 701–710 (1989)) requires child health professionals to provide early identification of children

2. Newacheck, P., Strickland, B., Shonkoff, J., Perrin, J., McPherson, M., & McManus, M., et al. (1998). An epidemiologic profile of children with special health care needs. *Pediatrics, 102*(1), 117–123.

3. Kraus, M. (2005). Planning is important even when life doesn't go the way we plan. *Family Court Review, 43*(4), 607–611.

4. Barham, V., Devlin, R. A., & LaCasse, C. (2000). Are the new child-support guidelines "adequate" or "reasonable"? *Canadian Public Policy-Analyse de Politiques, 26*(1), 1–15.

5. Jennings, S. (2005). Autism in children and parents: Unique considerations for family court professionals. *Family Court Review, 43*(4), 582–595.

6. Johnson, B., Grossman, D., Connell, F., & Koepsell, T. (2000). High-risk periods for childhood injury among siblings. *Pediatrics, 105*(3), 562–568.

7. Jennings, S. (2005). Autism in children and parents: Unique considerations for family court professionals. *Family Court Review, 43*(4), 582–595.

8. *Id.*

9. *Id.*

with disabilities.[10] Title V authorizes grants-in-aid to states for health programs for mothers and children (Title V, Part 1), which includes crippled children (Title V, Part 2) and welfare services for children (Title V, Part 3).[11] Title V of the Social Security Act was passed in the 1930s.[12] In the 1940s, the Emergency Maternity Infant Care program provided free and complete maternity and infant health care for wives and infants of certain servicemen.[13] In the 1980s, the Maternal and Child Health Services Block Grant unified seven separate health care programs into one program of formula grants to states administered by a federal special projects authority.[14] In the 1990s, the Healthy Start program and the Child Health Improvement Act targeted the issues of uninsured children and infant mortality.[15]

There are public benefit programs that can provide monthly cash payments or pay for medical expenses of a disabled child. Supplemental Security Income (SSI) is a federal Social Security program that does not require a child to have worked or paid Social Security taxes in order to be eligible for payments. It provides monthly payments for food and shelter if the child is disabled and falls below certain levels of "countable" assets and income.[16]

2. Educational Issues

The Individuals with Disabilities Education Improvement Act (IDEA) of 1997, amended in 2004 (Pub. L. No. 108–446), is intended to ensure that all children with disabilities receive a free appropriate public education, with specially designed instruction provided at no cost to the parents, tailored to meet the individual needs of a child with a disability.[17] IDEA was built upon the framework of the Education for All Handicapped Children Act (EAHCA), passed in 1975, which gave children with disabilities the right to a free appropriate public education in the least restrictive environment.[18] This legislation was passed in response to a grave concern that many disabled children in our country were not having their needs met in our public education system.[19] "At that time, Congress estimated that more than half the nation's children with disabilities

---

10. Council on Children with Disabilities, Section on Developmental Behavioral Pediatrics, Bright Futures Steering Committee and Medical Home Initiatives for Children with Special Needs Project Advisory Committee. (2006). Identifying infants and young children with developmental disorders in the medical home: An algorithm for developmental surveillance and screening. *Pediatrics, 118*(1), 405–420.

11. van Dyck, P. (2003). A history of child health equity legislation in the united states. *Pediatrics, 112*(3), 727–730.

12. *Id.*

13. *Id.*

14. *Id.*

15. *Id.*

16. Courtney, Richard A. (2005, November). Getting it all together: Essential legal and financial planning for children with special needs. *EP Magazine.*

17. Karger, J., for the National Center on Accessing the General Curriculum (NCAC). (n.d.). Access to the general curriculum for students with disabilities: A discussion of the interrelationship between IDEA '97 and NCLB (a Policy Paper for Educators and Families). Washington, DC: U.S. Department of Education, Office of Special Education Programs; National Center for Homeless Education (NCHE) at SERVE. (n.d.). Individuals with Disabilities Education Improvement Act (IDEA) of 2004 Provisions for Children and Youth with Disabilities Who Experience Homelessness. Greensboro, NC: NCHE, P.O. Box 5367.

18. *Id.*

19. Karger, *supra* note 17.

were not receiving appropriate educational services and that one million children with disabilities were being completely excluded from the public school system (20 U.S.C. § 1400 (c)(2)(B)–(C))."[20] The massive numbers of special needs children whose needs are not being met in the family law system demands appropriate legislation in this area.

B. State Law

All 50 states have statutes that deal with divorce, yet few of them have legislation that specifically addresses the unique issues inherent in family law cases involving children with special needs. The rates of childhood disability are increasing.[21] Washington state has a child support worksheet that allows for deviation from the standard child support calculation for "special needs of disabled children." The worksheet is found at the end of this chapter.

Of the remaining states, some of the state divorce statutes contain general provisions that allow the judge to deviate from standard results when there are special circumstances, extraordinary medical expenses, or other unusual facts. Quite a few states do not even give a nod to deviating from standard results for special needs. The divorce laws of the 50 states may be found as follows:

- Alabama—Title 30, Chapter 2
- Alaska—Title 25, Chapter 24
- Arizona—Chapter 3
- Arkansas—Title 9, Subtitle 2, § 12
- California—Part 3
- Colorado—Title 14, Article 10 (Statute # 14-10-106)
- Connecticut—Title 46, Chapter 810, §§ 46-13 to 46-31
- Delaware—Title 13, Chapter 15
- Florida—Title 6, Chapter 61
- Georgia—§§ 19-4-1 through 19-6-47
- Hawaii—Chapter 580
- Idaho—§§ 32-501 through 32-901
- Illinois—Chapter 750
- Indiana—Title 31, Article 15
- Iowa—Chapter 598, §§ 1–42
- Kansas—Chapter 23
- Kentucky—Chapter 403
- Louisiana—Civil Code, §§ 101 to 103
- Maine—Title 19, Chapter 13
- Maryland—§§ 8-101 through 8-213
- Massachusetts—Chapter 208
- Michigan—Chapter 552
- Minnesota—Chapter 518
- Mississippi—Title 93, Chapter 5
- Missouri—Chapter 452
- Montana—Title 40, Chapter 4
- Nebraska—Chapter 42, §§ 42-344 through 42-381

20. *Id.*

21. Seal, P., & Ireland, M. (2005). Addressing transition to adult health care for adolescents with special health care needs. *Pediatrics, 115*(6), 1607–1612.

- Nevada—Chapter 125
- New Hampshire—Title 43, Chapter 458
- New Jersey—Title 2A, §§ 34-2 through 34-6
- New Mexico—Chapter 40, Article 4
- New York—Chapter 14, Article 10-12
- North Carolina—Chapter 50
- North Dakota—Chapter 14-05
- Ohio—Title 31, Chapter 31-05
- Oklahoma—43-134
- Oregon—Title 11, Chapter 107
- Pennsylvania—Title 23, Part 3
- Rhode Island—Chapter 15, §§ 15-5-1 through 15-5-29
- South Carolina—Title 20, Chapter 3
- South Dakota—Title 25, Chapter 4
- Tennessee—Title 36, Chapter 4
- Texas—Title 1, Chapter 6 (Family Law)
- Utah—Title 30, Chapter 3
- Vermont—Title 15, Chapter 11
- Virginia—Title 20, Chapter 6
- Washington—Title 26, Chapter 9
- West Virginia—Chapter 48, Article 2
- Wisconsin—Chapter 767
- Wyoming—Title 20, Chapter 2
- District of Columbia—Title 16, Chapter 9[22]

Legislation is needed in many aspects of divorce law:

- Custody determinations
- Visitation schedules and terms
- Calculation of child support
- Calculation of maintenance (alimony)
- Determination of property distribution
- Length of term of child support
- Length of term of maintenance (alimony)
- Legal custody
- Education
- Payment of expenses based on special needs
- Appointment of guardian ad litem
- Counseling
- Special orders unique to specific cases

Court forms should be changed to alert the court to the existence of the issue of special needs beginning at the time of filing. Special needs should be noted and/or addressed in the following documents/forms:

- Civil Cover Filing Sheet
- Petition
- Answer
- Interrogatories

22. Legal Information Institute. Retrieved October 1, 2005, from https://www.law.cornell.edu/wex/table_divorce_old.

- Financial Filings (e.g., Statement of Income and Expenses)
- Motion for Appointment of Guardian ad Litem
- Parenting Plan/Custody Schedule
- Settlement Agreement
- Decree of Dissolution

Lawyers should alter their office forms to address the issues inherent in handling cases involving children with special needs. They should note the existence of special needs in these areas:

- Initial Intake Interview Questionnaire
- Client Information Sheet
- List of contacts (should include all doctors, therapists, etc.)
- Client file should have a separate section for Special Needs. This section should include
    1. A complete medical/psychiatric history of the child
    2. The child's medical records
    3. Psychiatric records
    4. School records
    5. Therapy records
    6. IEPs (Individual Educational Plans) and 504 Plans[23]
    7. All doctors and therapists and other medical professionals with all their contact information and affiliation information
    8. The child's current daily schedule and therapy plan in detail
    9. A summary and then a thorough narrative of the child's special needs and how these needs impact the child's daily life
    10. An itemization and explanation of the costs involved in or caused by the child's special needs
    11. The impact caring for the child has had on the primary caregiver parent's career and retirement account(s)
    12. A chronological account of the child's special needs, describing when and how they were diagnosed
    13. A narrative of each parent's involvement in the child's care
    14. A discussion of how the parents suggest handling issues of visitation during and after divorce
    15. A discussion of how the parents suggest handling the issue of child support during and after divorce
    16. A discussion of how the parents suggest handling the issue of additional costs during and after divorce

23. An IEP is a legal document, mandated by IDEA, that controls the procedural requirements. It is more involved than a 504 Plan. An IEP is required for students with disabilities who require specialized instruction. A 504 Plan is a written plan required for students with disabilities needing only reasonable accommodation. It is less involved than an IEP. An excellent explanation may be found in L. Wilmhurst & A. W. Brue, *A Parent's Guide to Special Education* (Amacom, 2005). See also "IEPs vs. 504 Plans," and the entire Sevier County Special Education website. Retrieved July 18, 2022, https://www.sevier.org/site/default.aspx?PageType=2&PageModuleInstanceID=486&ViewID=838b13a1-2ccb-4c74-83cb-0b9f098d6937&RenderLoc=0&FlexDataID=7938. Additional helpful materials include the Learning Disabilities OnLine website, http://www.LDonline.org (especially the materials on accommodations and modifications) and the Cleveland Heights Teachers Union website materials on 504 Plan Frequently Asked Questions, http://www.chtu.org. Both retrieved September 10, 2008.

17. A discussion of how the parents suggest handling the issue of maintenance (alimony) during and after divorce
18. A discussion of how the parents suggest handling the issue of retirement account distribution
19. A discussion of how the parents suggest handling the issue of property distribution
20. A discussion of how the parents suggest handling the issue of modification of any of the terms related to the special needs of the child after the divorce
21. A discussion of how the parents suggest handling the issue of resolving disputes after the divorce
22. Proposed documents (child support chart, parenting plan, settlement agreement) to reflect these unique terms

II. CASE LAW

In the years since the first edition of this book was published, there has been a great deal of litigation in our family courts dealing with the unique issues that face families with special needs children and parents when they separate, divorce, and seek modifications of their original decrees. In the first edition, we analyzed case law dealing with the education of special needs children, applying the federal legislation appropriate to that issue; federal laws addressing the rights of disabled people to be free from discrimination in housing, employment, and education; and ensuring children with disabilities have the same opportunities for participation, independent living, and economic self-sufficiency as their nondisabled peers. This federal legislation requires special services be provided at no cost when these services are required to address the child's individual learning needs, and when the child's individual needs will not be met by standard public education.[24] This legal theory could be applied to special needs family law cases. Special needs children should have the same opportunities in the family court system for participation, independent living, and economic self-sufficiency as their nondisabled peers. Special services should be provided when the child's individual needs will not be met by standard family court practices and standard family law legislation.

Within the arena of the family law cases, there is case law involving increased amounts or later termination of child support due to the greater costs inherent in raising children with special needs, *but the decisions are all made on a case-by-case basis, rather than upon specific case law.*[25] Further, the courts are precluded from awarding child support for a disabled child beyond the age of majority if prohibited by state statute. The court in *Hendricks v. Sanks*, 143 N.C. App. 544, 545 S.E.2d 779 (2001), allowed child support to continue for a limited time past the age of 18 for a child with Down syndrome—but only to the age of 20, which was the age for termination of child support for a nondisabled child in mainstream education under North Carolina law. Some courts

24. Wilmhurst & Brue, *supra* note 23, at 13–14.

25. Favrow v. Vargas (Conn. 1992), 222 Conn. 699; 610 A.2d 1267; C.E.S. v. D.D.S. (E.D. Mo. 1990), 783 S.W.2d 458; *In re* Marriage of Swanson (Mont. 1986), 220 Mont. 490, 716 P.2d 1276; Hendricks v. Sanks (N.C. App. 2001), 143 N.C. App. 544, 545 S.E.2d 779; Greer v. Greer (N.C. App. 1991), 101 N.C. App. 351, 399 S.E.2d 399.

around the United States have held their state statutes do not impose a parental duty to support a disabled adult child.[26]

Other states, however, have drafted provisions in their state statutes that protect disabled children beyond the age of 18. Under Missouri law, a child who is "physically or mentally incapacitated from supporting himself and insolvent and unmarried" may be eligible for court-ordered parental child support beyond the age of 18.[27] Other states address this issue indirectly by defining a "child" or "minor child" as including disabled children of any age who are not able to support themselves.[28]

It is usually within the discretion of the family court judge to decide if it is appropriate to deviate from standard child support amounts based upon a showing of greater costs for raising a child with special needs.[29] There is case law in which the courts determined visitation based upon the needs of the child; but again, *these decisions are all made on a case-by-case basis rather than upon specific statute.*[30] It is within the discretion of the family court judge to decide if it is appropriate to deviate from standard child custody and visitation plans based on a showing of such deviation being in the best interests of a child with special needs.[31]

As states begin to pass legislation specifically addressing the unique needs of children with special needs in divorce cases, expect a great deal of litigation to interpret this legislation. We as a public are learning so much about special needs so quickly that this area will be the subject of much confrontation. The numbers of special needs children are increasing every year.[32] The divorce rates among families with special needs children are astronomical. *State legislatures would be wise to set in place a logical plan to deal with this situation.* A good first step would be to pass legislation to address the situation proactively, rather than wait for it to reach crisis proportions and then react under great stress. The state legislatures should adopt legislation that is consistent and

---

26. *See* Smith v. Smith, 447 N.W.2d 715, 716 (Mich. 1989); Meyers v. Meyers, 383 N.W.2d 784, 789 (Neb. 1986); Beiter v. Beiter, 539 N.Y.S.2d 271, 272–73 (1989); Day v. Gatewood, No. 02*A01-9805-CV-00141, 1999 Tenn. App. LEXIS 285, at 11* (Apr. 30, 1999) cited in Jeffrey W. Childers, *Recent Development: Hendricks v. Sanks: One Small Step for the Continued Parental Support of Disabled Children beyond the Age of Majority in North Carolina*, 80(6) N.C.L. REV. 2106, 2108–09 (2002).

27. MO. ANN. STAT. 452.340(4) (West Supp. 2002).

28. *See, e.g.*, NEV. REV. STAT. ANN. 125B.200(2)(c) (Michie 2001); MINN. STAT. ANN. 518.54(2) (West 1990); UTAH CODE ANN. 78-45-2(6)(c) (Supp. 2001); and OHIO REV. CODE ANN. 3109.01 (Anderson 2000) cited in Childers, *supra* note 26, at 2108–09.

29. *Id.*

30. *In re* Marriage of Melville (1st App. Dist., 2004), 122 Cal. App. 4th 601; 18 Cal. Rptr. 3d 685; Cole v. Cole (Fla. 5th DCA 1988), 530 So.2d 467; Stricklin v. Stricklin (Fla. 5th DCA 1980), 383 So.2d 1183; In the Interest of K.M. (Ga. App. 2003), 260 Ga. App. 635, 580 S.E.2d 636; Cousens v. Pittman (Ga. App. 2004), 266 Ga. App. 387, 597 S.E.2d 486; *In re* Marriage of Evans (Ill. 4th DCA 1992), 229 Ill. App. 3d 932, 595 N.E.2d 237; Winkler v. Winkler (Ind. 5th DCA 1997), 689 N.E.2d 447; Rodgers v. Knauff (*In re* N.A.K.) (Minn. 2002), 649 N.W.2d 166; Riley v. Amundsen (*In re* N.G.H.) (Mont. 2004), 322 Mont. 20, 92 P.3d 1215; *In re* Custody of D.M.G. (Mont. 1998), 287 Mont. 120, 951 P.2d 1377; Knoll v. Waters (NY 3d A.D. 2003), 305 A.D.2d 741, 760 N.Y.S.2d 245; Deyo v. Deyo (NY 3d A.D. 1997), 240 A.D.2d 781, 658 N.Y.S.2d 153.

31. *Id.*

32. Williams, T., Schone, E., Archibald, M., & Thompson, J. (2004). A national assessment of children with special health care needs: Prevalence of special needs and use of health care services among children in the military health system. *Pediatrics, 114*(2), 384–393.

relatively uniform from state to state, to avoid having parents move around the country in an attempt to "forum shop."

In recent years, some parents have tried to reduce the amount of their child support obligation by using proposed special needs trusts and adoption subsidies to offset the child support obligation. Chapter 10 of this book discusses the various issues of special needs trusts and children with special needs, including child support.

In *Tluzek v. Tluzek*,[33] the husband wanted the court to allow him to pay less child support by using the monthly adoption subsidy the state of Florida paid for their special needs children to offset his child support obligation. The court denied his request as being contrary to the expressed intent of Fla. Stat. § 409.166 Children within the Child Welfare System; Adoption Assistance Program.[34] That statute includes developmental disabilities, physical handicaps, and emotional handicaps within its definition of "special needs child." The special needs child and the adoptive family can receive adoption assistance from the state that can include financial assistance and services, like a maintenance subsidy. Also, the state might provide medical and Medicaid assistance for the child.

The purpose of the Florida adoption subsidy statute is to help the adoptive parents provide the extra care that a special needs child requires. It can be more challenging to find people willing to adopt children who have special needs and are in the custody of the state, so the special needs subsidy encourages the adoption of these children.

The court in *Tluzek* instructed that, when adoptive parents who receive a special needs adoption subsidy divorce, the courts should first calculate the child support obligation of the parents and then award each parent a proportionate share of the monthly subsidy separate from the child support obligation. The portion of the subsidy for each parent should be consistent with their time-sharing proportions. The court stated that the subsidy should not be a credit against or an offset of child support because doing so would take away the benefit of the subsidy for meeting the special needs of the child. The court also said that courts are allowed to deviate from the standard child support calculations and order a party to pay more than the minimum child support amount based on the costs associated with the child's disability.

Courts across America are now deviating upward from their state child support guidelines to meet the increased costs of raising children with special needs. In *Halim v. El-Alayli*,[35] the court in Tennessee awarded an amount greater than the Tennessee Child Support Guidelines for a special needs child with severe autism.

Another victory for families with special needs children is that some courts are now holding that a parent's obligation to pay child support does not terminate automatically when the child turns 18 and graduates from high school if the child is disabled. In *Guthrie v. Guthrie*,[36] the court said that the duty of a parent to support a child who has a mental or physical disability and needs support does not cease at the time of reaching majority. In *Guthrie*, the state statute that automatically terminated the obligation to pay child support at the age of 18 or when the child should have graduated from high school,

---

33. Tluzek v. Tluzek, 179 So.3d 455 (C.A. 5th Dist. 2015).

34. http://www.leg.state.fl.us/statutes/index.cfm?App_mode=Display_Statute&Search_String=&URL=0400-0499/0409/Sections/0409.166.html.

35. Halim v. El-Alayli, 2017 Tenn. App. LEXIS 270, 2017 WL 1534963 (C.A. Nashville 2017).

36. Guthrie v. Guthrie, 2015 Ark. App. 108 (C.A. Arkansas, Div. One 2015).

whichever date is later, made no exception for disabled children. Nonetheless, the court affirmed the obligation of a parent to continue to support a disabled adult child.

There have been quite a few cases that have wrestled with the unique challenges of custody and visitation issues in family law cases involving families with special needs. Some courts are taking the time to evaluate these disputes based on the facts of each case, rather than using a cookie-cutter standard parenting plan. Every judge who has the courage to do what these families need in the best interest of the children with special needs contributes a stone to the foundation of precedent on which tomorrow's judges can base their decisions.

In *A.L.-S v. B.S.*,[37] the court dealt with the issue of how to handle custody and visitation schedules when the parents have one child with special needs and one child without special needs. The court awarded sole legal custody of both children to one parent and sole physical custody of the child without special needs to that parent. The court ordered shared physical custody of the child with special needs on an equal time basis.

Sometimes, a parent lives in denial of a child's special needs. In *Whitehead v. Myers (In the Interest of D.W.)*,[38] the court held that the parents of two children with developmental disabilities were not fit to care for those children because the parents denied that the children had significant special needs and, as such, lacked the ability to meet their needs. The court awarded permanent custody of the children to the grandparents, who had been raising the children and taking the children for their needed medical care, assessments, therapies, and educational services after the parents failed to do so.

The court in *Matter of Razdan v. Mendoza-Pautrat*[39] modified and limited the noncustodial parent's visitation to accommodate the therapy schedule of the child with special needs. The parents had four children, one of whom received regular therapy for his special needs. The noncustodial parent had visitation of the children on alternate weekends. The court crafted a visitation schedule that accommodated the child's therapy so that the child would not miss out on therapy on those alternate weekends.

In *McCarthy v. Adams*,[40] the appellate court affirmed the decision of the trial court denying the noncustodial parent's request to increase that parent's limited award of custody for purposes of visitation. The child, born in 2015, has autism and receives counseling and in-home therapy sessions. He attends special education classes and has an in-classroom aid. Since the parents divorced in 2019, the father has only exercised supervised visitation of the child in the mother's home on Sundays from 10:00 am until 12:30 pm. Father asked the court to increase his visitation time. Mother has provided all of the childcare, scheduled all of the child's evaluations, made all the arrangements for the child's therapy, made all the educational and health care decisions, and performed all of the parental duties since the divorce.

Father claimed that Mother "caused" the child's autism by, in the father's opinion, not offering the child enough opportunities for socialization and that, if the child lived

37. A.L.-S. v. B.S., 2016 Pa. Dist & Cnty. Dec LEXIS 3384, Common Pleas Court of Lawrence County, Pennsylvania, No. 10487 of 2014, C.A. (2016).

38. Whitehead v. Myers (In the Interest of D.W.), 716 S.E.2d 785, 311 Ga. App. 680 (C.A. Georgia 2011).

39. Razdan v. Mendoza-Pautrat, 137 A.D.3d 1149, 27 N.Y.S.3d 641 (2016).

40. McCarthy v. Adams, 2022 Pa. Super. Unpub. LEXIS 8 , 2022 WL 17149, Superior Court of Pennsylvania, No. 768 WDA 2021 (2022). NON-PRECEDENTIAL DECISION—SEE SUPERIOR COURT I.O.P. 65.37.

with the father, he could cure the child's autism. Father also testified that Mother's multiple sclerosis (MS) makes him concerned for her ability to parent.

The trial court found that there was no evidence to indicate that the mother's medical condition hampered her ability to parent the child. The trial court justified its decision to continue the supervised visits because the father was incapable of caring for the child's special needs because of his lack of insight concerning the child's special needs and the father's inappropriate behavior during his visits. The appellate court affirmed the decision of the trial court.

A. Standard Child Support Chart

In most states, the standard child support chart includes no specific provisions for special needs. Many of the expenses involved in raising a child with special needs do not fall within the "extraordinary medical expenses" category of a standard child support chart. Usually, these extraordinary medical expenses are limited to co-pays, deductibles, and uncovered out-of-pocket direct medical expenses of medication, doctor visits, and hospitalizations only, and not for the numerous additional expenses of properly raising a child with special needs (therapy, counseling, palliative care, over-the-counter medications and supplies, special diet/nutritional needs, special shoes/orthotics/clothing, individualized supplements, and so on.) Many lawyers and judges are unaware of the numerous costs involved in raising a child with special needs and will not know to include them in "other extraordinary expenses." Having some of these things itemized on the chart itself will help make people aware of these expenses. Standard charts also do not provide for child care for respite. They allow only for child care that is work related. It is essential to provide for **respite care** (child care that makes it possible for the primary caregiver parent to run errands and attend to other necessary functions and activities that are not possible while caring for the special needs child) for the primary caregiver parent. The special needs Child Support Chart that follows itemizes many of the additional expenses of properly raising a child with special needs, including respite care. The special needs Child Support Chart is a standard Missouri child support chart to which the line itemization has been added.

CHILD SUPPORT CHART

In the Circuit Court of __________ County, Missouri

Case No. _______________—Division _______

In re the Marriage of: ____

Form 14SN CHILD SUPPORT AMOUNT CALCULATION WORKSHEET FOR USE IN SPECIAL NEEDS CASES

CHILDREN	DATE OF BIRTH	CHILDREN	DATE OF BIRTH
Name		Name	

	Parent Receiving Support	Parent Paying Support	Combined
1. MONTHLY GROSS INCOME	$	$	
a. Court-ordered maintenance being received	$	$	
2. ADJUSTMENTS (per month)	($)	($)	
a. Other court or administratively ordered child support being paid			
b. Court-ordered maintenance being paid	($)	($)	
c. Support obligation for other children in parent's primary physical custody	($)	($)	
3. ADJUSTED MONTHLY GROSS INCOME (sum of lines 1 and 1a, minus lines 2a, 2b, and 2c)	$	$	$
4. PROPORTIONATE SHARE OF COMBINED ADJUSTED MONTHLY GROSS INCOME (each parent's line 3 income divided by combined line 3 income)	%	%	
5. BASIC CHILD SUPPORT AMOUNT (from support chart using combined line 3 income)			$
6. ADDITIONAL CHILD-REARING COSTS (per month)			
a. Reasonable work-related child care costs of the parent receiving support, less any child care tax credit	$		

b. Reasonable work-related child care costs of the parent paying support		$	
c. Health insurance costs for the children who are subjects of this proceeding	$	$	
d. Uninsured extraordinary medical costs (agreed by parents or ordered by court)	$	$	
e. Other extraordinary child rearing costs (agreed by parents or ordered by court)	$	$	
f. Special needs expenses and costs: therapy equipment medications supplements dietary costs sensory items respite care other reasonable items			
7. TOTAL ADDITIONAL CHILD SUPPORT COSTS (sum of lines 6a, 6b, 6c, 6d, 6e, and 6f)	$	$	$
8. TOTAL COMBINED CHILD SUPPORT COSTS (sum of line 5 and combined line 7)			$
9. EACH PARENT'S SUPPORT OBLIGATION (multiply line 8 by each parent's line 4)	$	$	
10. CREDIT FOR ADDITIONAL CHILD-REARING COSTS (line 7 of parent paying support)		$	
11. ADJUSTMENTS FOR A PORTION OF THE AMOUNTS OF EXPENDED DURING PERIODS OF OVERNIGHT VISITATION OR CUSTODY (multiply line 5 by 0.22%)		$	
12. ADJUSTMENT FOR RESPITE CARE AND OTHER EXPENSES IF VISITATION IS NOT REGULARLY EXERCISED			
13. PRESUMED CHILD SUPPORT AMOUNT (line 9 minus line 10 and 11 plus line 12)		**($)**	
PREPARED BY: Attorney for			
EXHIBIT # __________			

B. Standard Parenting Plan

A standard parenting plan (visitation schedule) follows. It was developed by the Missouri Bar. It contains a few specific provisions for special needs, and the few "special needs" provisions actually deal with supervised visitation, not with children with special needs.

STANDARD PARENTING PLAN

____

Judge:	Case No.:
Father:	Mother:
Home Address:	Home Address:
Home Phone:	Home Phone:
Work Phone:	Work Phone:

PROPOSED PARENTING PLAN OF:

[ ] Petitioner   [ ] Respondent   [ ] Both Parties   [ ] Court-Ordered Plan (Court Use Only)

[ ] Temporary Order & Judgment   [ ] Final Judgment

The following children were born to or adopted by the parties:

CHILDREN NAMES   **DATES OF BIRTH**

CUSTODY

[ ] Mother and Father shall have joint legal custody and joint physical custody of all children.
[ ] Mother and Father shall have joint legal custody and [ ] Mother [ ] Father shall have sole physical custody of all children.
[ ] Mother [ ] Father shall have sole legal custody and Mother and Father shall have joint physical custody of all children.
[ ] Mother [ ] Father shall have sole legal custody and sole physical custody of all children.
[ ] Third Party, _______________, shall have sole legal and sole physical custody of all children.

PRIMARY RESIDENCE OF CHILDREN FOR MAILING AND EDUCATIONAL PURPOSES:

[ ] Mother [ ] Father [ ] at the above address.

PARENTING TIME

[ ] OPTION A: COURT-APPROVED PARENTING TIME "SCHEDULE J" WHICH IS AS FOLLOWS:

THE NONCUSTODIAL PARENT SHALL HAVE REGULAR PERIODS OF VISITATION AND CUSTODY OF THE MINOR CHILDREN. IN THE EVENT THAT THE PARENTS CANNOT AGREE ON SPECIFIC PERIODS, THEN THE MINIMUM SCHEDULE SHALL BE AS FOLLOWS:

1. **Weekend.** Every other weekend beginning at 6:00 PM on Friday through 6:00 PM on Sunday. The first such weekend shall be on the second weekend following the date of the Judgment and Decree.
2. **Weekday.** If the parents live within a 50-mile radius of each other: one evening each week from 6:00 PM on Wednesday until 6:00 PM on Thursday, with the noncustodial parent being responsible for all transportation to and from school and/or day care.
3. **Holidays and Special Days.**
   a. Holiday and special day custody shall be from 9:00 AM until 6:00 PM and shall prevail over weekend, weekday, and summer vacation except for Easter, Memorial Day, Labor Day, and Thanksgiving, when visitation shall include the entire weekend from 6:00 PM Friday through 6:00 PM Monday, with Thanksgiving being from 9:00 AM Thanksgiving Day through 6:00 PM Sunday.
   b. Mother shall have the minor children on her birthday and on Mother's Day of each year.
   c. Father shall have the minor children on his birthday and on Father's Day of each year.
   d. The noncustodial parent shall have custody of the minor children in odd-numbered years on Easter, Fourth of July, and each child's birthday, and in even-numbered years on Memorial Day, Labor Day, and Thanksgiving.
4. **Christmas Vacation.** For the Christmas season following the implementation of the most recent Judgment and Decree, the noncustodial parent shall have the minor children from 9:00 AM on December 25th through 9:00 AM on December 31st. The next Christmas season, the noncustodial parent shall have the minor children from 6:00 PM the day the children's school Christmas vacation begins through 9:00 AM on December 25th and from 9:00 AM on December 31st through 9:00 AM the day prior to the day children's school Christmas vacation ends. Thereafter, during each Christmas season, the noncustodial parent's custody shall rotate between the above groups of dates.
5. **Summer Vacation.** The noncustodial parent shall have the minor children each summer beginning three days after school ends for a two-week period. At the end of this two-week period, the custodial parent shall have the minor children for two weeks. The parents shall alternate in a like manner until three days before school begins, at which time the children will be returned to the custodial parent. There shall be no weekend or weekday visitation during the summer.

For preschool children, the date for commencement and termination of Christmas and Summer visitation shall be based upon the public school calendar for the district in which the child primarily resides.

[ ] **OPTION B: PARENTING TIME "SCHEDULE J" WHICH IS MODIFIED AS FOLLOWS:**

[ ] **OPTION C: PARENTING TIME AS PER ATTACHED SCHEDULE EXCHANGES**

[ ] When school is in session:

Exchanges of all children from Mother to Father shall occur at:
[ ] Residence of Mother [ ] Residence of Father [ ] School
[ ] Other Location ______

Exchanges of all children from Father to Mother shall occur at:
[ ] Residence of Mother [ ] Residence of Father [ ] School
[ ] Other Location ______
[ ] When school is not in session or if all children are not school age:

Exchange of all children from Mother to Father shall occur at:
[ ] Residence of Mother [ ] Residence of Father
[ ] Other Location ______

Exchange of all children from Father to Mother shall occur at:
[ ] Residence of Mother [ ] Residence of Father
[ ] Other Location ______
[ ] If an exchange occurs at a location other than a parent's residence, the parent scheduled to have time with the children shall pick up and return the children to the specified location, and the other parent shall be responsible for ensuring the children are at the specified location for pickup, unless other arrangements are described.

TRANSPORTATION

Transportation arrangements for all children for all scheduled parenting times, including weekdays, weekends, holidays, and vacation times, shall be as follows:

[ ] Father shall be responsible for transportation of the children at the beginning of the visit. Mother shall be responsible for transportation of the children at the end of the visit.

[ ] Mother and Father shall share responsibility for all transportation of the children, including cost, as follows:

[ ] Extraordinary Transportation Costs (bus, taxi, train, airfare) shall be the responsibility of:

[ ] Mother [ ] Father [ ] Shared % Mother % Father

CHANGES

The parents' schedules and commitments may require occasional changes in the parenting time schedule. Parents shall attempt to agree on any changes, but the parent receiving a request for a change shall have the final decision on whether the change shall occur.

The parent making the request may make such request
[ ] in person [ ] by phone [ ] in writing to the other parent [ ] other.

The request for change shall be made no later than
[ ] 24 hours [ ] one week [ ] two weeks [ ] other prior to the date of the requested change.

The parent receiving the request shall respond no later than
[ ] 24 hours [ ] one week [ ] two weeks [ ] other after receiving the requested change.

The response to the request may be made
[ ] in person [ ] by phone [ ] in writing to the other parent [ ] other.
[ ] Any parent requesting a change of schedule shall be responsible for any additional child care or transportation costs resulting from the change.

Mother and Father shall cooperate to allow the children to meet their school and social commitments.

TELEPHONE CONTACTS

Father shall have access to all children by telephone during the following times: 9:00 AM to 9:00 PM with the following restrictions: no phone calls after 9:00 PM.

SPECIAL NEEDS (If applicable)

Provide this information *only* if there are special needs, such as supervised visits, supervised exchanges, or other restrictions necessary to ensure the safety and well-being of all children.

[ ] Mother [ ] Father shall have supervised visits with the children.
How often visits will be held:

Length of visits:
Visits shall be supervised by a
[ ] mutually agreed upon third party [ ] professional/agency.

Name:

Location:

Exchanges of all children shall be supervised by a
[ ] mutually agreed upon third party [ ] professional agency or person. Specify agency or person:
for beginning of visit:
for end of visit:
State the reasons for the restrictions listed in "a" or "c":
Other restrictions:

RELOCATION

Absent exigent circumstances as determined by a court with jurisdiction, you, as a party to this action, are ordered to notify, in writing by certified mail, return receipt requested, and at least sixty days prior to the proposed relocation, each party to this action of any proposed relocation of the principal residence of the children, including the following information: (1) the intended new residence, including the specific address and mailing address, if known, and if not known, the city; (2) the home telephone number of the new residence, if known; (3) the date of the intended move or proposed relocation; (4) a brief statement of the specific reasons for the proposed relocation of the children; and (5) a proposal for a revised schedule of custody or visitation with the children. Your obligation to provide this information to each party continues as long as you or any other party by virtue of this order is entitled to custody of a child covered by this order. Your failure to obey the order of this court regarding the proposed relocation may result in further litigation to enforce such order, including contempt of court. In addition, your failure to notify a party of a relocation of the child may be considered in a proceeding to modify custody or visitation with the children. Reasonable costs and attorney fees shall be assessed against you if you fail to give the required notice.

DECISION-MAKING

Parents should attempt to share responsibility for making all major decisions regarding each child. If not shared, explain the reason and which parent will be responsible for the decision. Include how decisions will be made and information shared on all aspects of the children's lives, including but not necessarily limited to:

Decision-Making Rights and Responsibilities	**Shared; If Not, Reason Why**	**Person Responsible Mother or Father**
Education (what school the child will attend, entry into special classes)	Shared	
Medical (medical procedures needed, medications to be taken, mental health treatment decisions)	Shared	
Dental (procedures needed, including orthodontics)	Shared	
Selection of health care Providers (doctor, hospital, therapist, and psychiatrists)	Shared	
Child care providers when with Mother	Shared	

Decision-Making Rights and Responsibilities	Shared; If Not, Reason Why	Person Responsible Mother or Father
Child care providers when with Father	Shared	
Extracurricular activities (what the child will participate in when these activities involve each person's parenting time)	Shared	
Religious upbringing	Shared	

COMMUNICATION

Parents need to communicate information to each other concerning the children's needs and performances in different areas, including educational and medical information, and the children's activities.

[ ] Each parent shall inform the other parent as soon as possible of all school, sporting, and other special activity notices and cooperate in the children's consistent attendance at such events.

[ ] Each parent shall always keep the other parent informed of his or her actual residence address, mailing address if different, home and work telephone numbers, and any changes within 30 days of such change occurring.

[ ] Neither parent shall say or do anything in the presence or hearing of the children that would in any way diminish the children's love or affection for the other parent and shall not allow others to do so.

[ ] All court-related and financial communications between the parents shall occur at a time when the children are not present and, therefore, shall not occur at times of exchanges of the children or during telephone visits with the children.

[ ] Neither parent shall schedule activities for the children during the other parent's scheduled parenting time without the other parent's prior agreement.

DISPUTE RESOLUTION

[ ] Parents shall attempt to resolve any matters on which they disagree or that involve interpreting the parenting plan through the following alternative dispute resolution process prior to any court action:

[ ] Counseling by
[ ] Mediation by
[ ] Other:
The cost of this process shall be allocated between the parties as follows:
[ ] % Mother; % Father
[ ] based on each party's proportional share of income
[ ] as determined in the dispute resolution process
The process shall be started by notifying the other party by:
[ ] written request [ ] certified mail [ ] other

[ ] All matters on which the parents disagree or that involve interpreting the parenting plan and for which the court has authority to act shall be resolved through appropriate court action.

CHILD SUPPORT AND OTHER EXPENSES

As set forth in the most recent judgment and order of the Court.

______________________________	______________________________
PETITIONER	RESPONDENT
______________________________	______________________________
Date	Date
______________________________	______________________________
ATTORNEY FOR PETITIONER	ATTORNEY FOR RESPONDENT
______________________________	______________________________
Date	Date

While the preceding parenting plan, developed by the Missouri Bar Association, does a good job of addressing many important issues and details, it needs to contain specific provisions to address the unique issues inherent in handling divorces in families with special needs children. A proposed parenting plan for use in special needs cases follows.

IN THE FAMILY COURT OF THE COUNTY OF ____________________
STATE OF ____________________

In Re the Marriage of:	)	
	)	
____________________,	)	
______________,	)	
Petitioner,	)	
vs.	)	Case No. ____________________
____________________,	)	Division: _______
______________,	)	
Respondent.	)	

CONSENT PARENTING PLAN FOR SPECIAL NEEDS

For purposes of this Parenting Plan, "Minor Children" refers to CHILD ONE, born Month, Day, Year, and CHILD TWO, born Month, Day, Year, either collectively, or either child separately, as is appropriate.

Mother and Father shall have joint legal custody, and Father shall have sole physical custody of said minor children.

Father's residence shall be designated as the primary residence of the minor children for mailing and educational purposes.

CUSTODY
PARENTING TIME SCHEDULE

Due to the special needs of the children, the standard visitation schedule is not in the best interests of the children. The girls are 12-year-old twins. One of the children, CHILD TWO, has cerebral palsy. She receives intensive therapy for many hours every week, and ,by necessity, her life is extremely structured.

The two most important aspects of this Parenting Plan are

- The best interests of the children and
- Cooperation of the parents.

CUSTODY, VISITATION, AND RESIDENTIAL TIME FOR EACH CHILD WITH EACH PARENT SHALL BE AT SUCH TIMES AS THE PARTIES SHALL AGREE. The parties are strongly encouraged to work together cooperatively and flexibly to reach by amicable agreement such custody, visitation, and residential times as shall be in the best interests of the children and keeping in mind their special needs. In the event the parties cannot agree, Mother shall have custody, visitation, or residential time as set forth below; and Father shall have all other time as his custody, visitation, or residential time.

EACH PARENT IS STRONGLY ENCOURAGED TO PUT THE CHILDREN FIRST AND TO MAKE EVERY REASONABLE EFFORT TO MEET THE UNIQUE NEEDS OF THE SPECIAL NEEDS CHILD(REN). Each parent is strongly encouraged to take time every week to spend one-on-one time with the special needs child and to spend one-on-one time with the non–special needs child.

WEEKDAY VISITATION

Mother may come to Father's house to visit the children during the evenings whenever her schedule permits, as long as the parties shall so agree. In the event the parties cannot agree upon the night or nights of this visitation, Mother shall visit the children at Father's house or pick them up at Father's house on Wednesday evenings. Mother shall visit/pick up children at 6:00 PM and return them to Father's house by 7:15 PM, when she is welcome to participate in their bedtime routine, which usually lasts until 8:00 PM. Mother may extend this weekday visitation to overnight visitation. In the event the parties agree upon overnight visitation during the week, Mother shall either return the children to Father's house the next morning or take them to their morning activity, as agreed to by the parties.

WEEKENDS

The children are involved in many activities due to their special needs. These activities require great flexibility and cooperation by the parents regarding the weekend visitation. The general goal is that Mother shall have the children for approximately half of the weekends, although this will often not be every other weekend. The parties shall frequently consult each other regarding the scheduled activities and arrange the weekend visitation around the schedules and best interests of the children. If the parties cannot agree, Mother shall have visitation of the children every other weekend beginning at 6:00 PM on Friday through and ending at 6:00 PM on Sunday, beginning the weekend following the date of the judgment. If either parent's holiday weekend, as set forth below, conflicts with this, then the parent losing their regular weekend shall receive the other parent's next regular weekend to thereafter be followed by the original schedule so that each would have two consecutive weekends.

SUMMER

The children attend summer school for six weeks every year. This usually runs from June through August. There is a week or two between the regular school year letting out and the start of summer school, and there is a week or two between the end of summer school and the beginning of the next school year. During these weeks, the girls usually attend a special needs summer day camp. It is important for the girls to attend summer school. If they are registered for summer school but do not attend consistently, they will not be eligible to attend in subsequent years.

Mother may exercise periods of summer visitation during the summer regardless of whether it is during the weeks of summer school, as long as she shall take the children to summer school if her time periods fall during those weeks.

Since these arrangements must be made well in advance, Mother shall notify Father of her choice of option in writing by March 1st every year.

Mother may have liberal summer visitation as the parties shall agree. In the event the parties cannot agree, subject to the above provisions, Mother shall have three weeks each summer (to be divided into three 7-consecutive day periods) to coincide with the children's school summer vacation. Mother may select the first week of this summer vacation by notifying Father of same (each notification herein to be in writing) by February 1st of each year, one week may then be excluded by Father by February 15th and then the next week may be selected by Mother by March lst; one more week may then be excluded by Father by March 15th, and the final week may be selected by Mother by April 1st. Father's excluded weeks shall prevail over Mother's weekend and weekday periods set forth above.

HOLIDAYS AND SPECIAL DAYS

1. Holiday and special day custody shall prevail over weekend, weekday, and summer vacation set forth above. Birthday periods shall not prevail when in conflict with other Holidays and Special Days.
2. Mother shall have the minor children on her birthday and on Mother's Day of each year from 9:00 AM to 9:00 PM; plus "Holiday Group A" in even-numbered years and "Holiday Group B" in odd-numbered years.
3. Father shall have the minor children on his birthday and on Father's Day of each year from 9:00 AM to 9:00 PM; plus "Holiday Group A" in odd-numbered years and "Holiday Group B" in even-numbered years.
4. Mother and Father are encouraged to communicate to attempt to arrange a combined event/activity for the children's birthday. In the event they cannot agree, the following provisions regarding the children's birthday shall apply.
5. Due to the serious special needs of the children, the conditions stated in the above paragraphs concerning WEEKDAY, WEEKEND, and SUMMER visitation shall apply to HOLIDAY GROUPS A & B.

HOLIDAY GROUP A

1. PRESIDENT'S DAY/WASHINGTON'S BIRTHDAY (OBSERVED) weekend from 5:00 PM the Friday prior to 8:00 AM the following Tuesday.
2. A period of 7 (seven) days during the children's school Spring break, the exact days to be selected and notice given in writing to the other parent by February lst.
3. INDEPENDENCE DAY—If July 4th falls on a (a) Tuesday, Wednesday, or Thursday from 5:00 PM on July 3rd until 9:00 AM on July 5th (b) Friday or Saturday from 5:00 PM on the Thursday before until 9:00 AM on the following Monday, (c) Sunday or Monday from 5:00 PM on the Friday before until 9:00 AM on the following Tuesday.
4. HALLOWEEN (October 31st) night from 4:00 PM until 9:00 AM the following day.
5. CHRISTMAS VACATION from December 25th beginning at 10:00 AM through 9:00 AM on December 31st.
6. Each child's birthday from 9:00 AM until 9:00 AM the following day.

HOLIDAY GROUP B

1. MARTIN LUTHER KING weekend from 5:00 PM the Friday prior through 8:00 AM the following Tuesday.
2. MEMORIAL DAY weekend from 5:00 PM the Friday prior through 8:00 AM the following Tuesday.
3. LABOR DAY weekend from 5:00 PM the Friday prior through 8:00 AM the following Tuesday.
4. THANKSGIVING weekend from 5:00 PM the Wednesday prior through 8:00 AM the following Monday.
5. CHRISTMAS VACATION from 5:00 PM the day the children's school Christmas vacation begins through 10:00 AM on December 25th and December 31st beginning at 9:00 AM through 8:00 AM the day the children's school Christmas vacation ends.
6. The day prior to each child's birthday beginning at 9:00 AM through 9:00 AM the day of the birthday.

The serious special needs of the children requires that Mother and Father be far more cooperative and flexible than the parents of children without special needs.

EXCHANGES

[X] When school is in session:

Exchanges of all children from Mother to Father shall occur at:

[ ] Residence of Mother [X] Residence of Father [ ] School

[ ] Other Location—Parents currently reside at same location, exchanges not applicable.

Exchanges of all children from Father to Mother shall occur at:
[ ] Residence of Mother [X] Residence of Father [ ] School
[ ] Other Location
[ ] When school is not in session or if all children are not school age:

Exchange of all children from Mother to Father shall occur at:
[ ] Residence of Mother [X] Residence of Father
[ ] Other Location

Exchange of all children from Father to Mother shall occur at:
[ ] Residence of Mother [X] Residence of Father
[ ] Other Location
[ ] If an exchange occurs at a location other than a parent's residence, the parent scheduled to have time with the children shall pick up and return the children to the specified location and the other parent shall be responsible for assuring the children are at the specified location for pick up, unless other arrangements are described.

TRANSPORTATION

Transportation arrangements for all children for all scheduled parenting times, including weekdays, weekends, holidays, and vacation times, shall be as follows:

[X] Mother shall be responsible for transportation of the children at the beginning of the visit. Mother shall be responsible for transportation of the children at the end of the visit.

Mother and Father shall share responsibility for all transportation of the children, including cost, as follows:

[ ] Extraordinary Transportation Costs (bus, taxi, train, airfare) shall be the responsibility of Mother [ ] Father [ ] Shared % Mother % Father

CHANGES

The parents' schedules and commitments may require occasional changes in the parenting time schedule. Parents shall attempt to agree on any changes, but the parent receiving a request for a change shall have the final decision on whether the change shall occur.

The parent making the request may make such request
[X] in person [X] by phone [X] in writing to the other parent [X] other—email

The request for change shall be made no later than:
[ ] 24 hours [X] one week [ ] two weeks [ ] other—prior to the date of the requested change.

The parent receiving the request shall respond no later than:
24 hours [ ] one week [ ] two weeks [X] other—72 hours
after receiving the requested change.

The response to the request may be made

[X] in person [X] by phone [X] in writing to the other parent [X] other—e-mail

Any parent requesting a change of schedule shall be responsible for any additional child care or transportation costs resulting from the change.

Mother and Father shall cooperate to allow the children to meet their therapeutic, school, and social commitments.

TELEPHONE CONTACTS

Each parent shall have reasonable access to all children by telephone during any period in which the children are with the other parent, unless otherwise specified.

RELOCATION

Absent exigent circumstances as determined by a court with jurisdiction, you, as a party to this action, are ordered to notify, in writing by certified mail, return receipt requested, and at least sixty days prior to the proposed relocation, each party to this action of any proposed relocation of the principal residence of the children, including the following information: (1) the intended new residence, including the specific address and mailing address, if known, and if not known, the city; (2) the home telephone number of the new residence, if known; (3) the date of the intended move or proposed relocation; (4) a brief statement of the specific reasons for the proposed relocation of the children; and (5) a proposal for a revised schedule of custody or visitation with the children. Your obligation to provide this information to each party continues as long as you or any other party by virtue of this order is entitled to custody of a child covered by this order. Your failure to obey the order of this Court regarding the proposed relocation may result in further litigation to enforce such order, including contempt of court. In addition, your failure to notify a party of a relocation of the child may be considered in a proceeding to modify custody or visitation with the children. Reasonable costs and attorney fees shall be assessed against you if you fail to give the required notice.

LEGAL CUSTODY

Legal Custody: The parties shall agree before making any final decisions on issues affecting the growth and development of the children, including, but not limited to, choice of religious upbringing; choice of child care provider; choice of school; course of study; special tutoring; extracurricular activities including but not limited to music, art, dance, and other cultural lessons or activities and gymnastics or other athletic activities; choice of camp or other comparable summer activity; nonemergency medical and dental treatment; psychological, psychiatric, or like treatment or counseling; the choice of particular health care providers; the extent of any travel away from home; part- or full-time employment; purchase or operation of a motor vehicle; contraception and sex education; and decisions relating to actual or potential litigation on behalf of the children. However, each parent may make decisions regarding the day-to-day care and control of the children and in emergencies affecting the health and safety of the children while the children are residing with him or her. The parents shall endeavor, whenever reasonable, to be consistent in such day-to-day decisions.

Communication: Each parent shall ensure that the other parent is provided with copies of all communications or information received from a child's school, and if a second copy of the communication is not provided by the school shall make a copy for the other parent. Each parent shall notify the other of any activity such as school conferences, programs, sporting and other special events, etc., where parents are invited to attend; and each shall encourage and welcome the presence of the other.

Children Not Involved in Court or Financial Communications: The parties shall not talk about adult issues, parenting matters, financial issues, and other court-related topics when the children are present. Such discussions shall not be had during custody exchanges of the children or during telephone visits. The children shall not be used to carry such messages, written communication, or child support payments between the parents.

Medical Care Information: Each parent shall have the authority to seek any emergency medical treatment for the children when in his or her custody. Each shall advise the other of any medical emergency or serious illness or injury suffered by the minor children as soon as possible after learning of the same and shall give the other parent details of the emergency, injury, or illness and the name and telephone numbers of all treating doctors. Each parent shall inform the other before any routine medical care, treatment, or examination by a health care provider including said provider's name and telephone number. Each party shall direct all doctors involved in the care and treatment of the minor children to give the other parent all information regarding any injury or illness and the medical treatment or examination, if requested. For purposes of this paragraph, a serious injury or illness is one that requires a child (1) to be confined to home for more than 48 hours; or (2) to be admitted to, or treated at, a hospital or surgical facility; or (3) to receive any type of general anesthesia or invasive surgical procedure or test.

Child Care Provider: If both parents will need to use a child care provider during periods of custody or visitation, they shall use the same child care provider, unless the distances between their residences or places of employment make the use of the same child care provider unreasonable.

Access to Records: Each parent shall be entitled to immediate access from the other or from a third party to records and information pertaining to the children, including, but not limited to, medical, dental, health, child care, school or educational records; and each shall take whatever steps are necessary to ensure that the other parent has such access.

Activities Not to Conflict with Custody or Visitation: The parties shall enroll the children in activities, particularly outside of school, that, to the extent possible, are scheduled at times and places that avoid interruption and disruption of the custody or visitation time of the other party unless consented to by that parent. The special needs of the children require far greater cooperation and flexibility by the parents than is required of the parents of children without special needs.

Resolution of Disputes: If the parties fail to agree on the interpretation of the Parenting Plan, or are unable to agree upon a final decision on issues affecting the growth and development or health and safety of the children, they shall submit the dispute to a mutually agreed-upon Special Needs Coordinator who shall hear and arbitrate the issue. In the event they are not able to agree on a Special Needs Coordinator, they shall each select a Special Needs Coordinator from the list of approved Special Needs Coordinators maintained by the ___________ County Family Court, and the two Special Needs Coordinators shall determine who shall arbitrate the case. The Special Needs Coordinator shall be a quick and informal tribunal to arbitrate issues that may arise in the future, including but not limited to increasing or decreasing child support; changes in therapy, treatment, education, custody, and/or visitation; and issues relating to expenses.

CHILD SUPPORT AND OTHER EXPENSES

Due to the special needs of the child(ren), the application of Standard Child Support Guidelines would be inappropriate and/or unjust. The initial amount of child support shall be $_________ per month, payable by Mother to Father. This amount shall be modifiable. This is the base amount, which DOES include the current amount for nutritional supplements/regimens, and DOES NOT include additional support for therapy, activities, camps, or other expenses necessitated by their special needs. Parents shall pay for these additional items based upon their proportional share of income. Parents acknowledge that future nutritional supplements/regimens may involve an increased cost, and parents agree to pay such increased cost based upon their proportional income.

Child support shall terminate for CHILD TWO in accordance with § _______ [Statutes of state of _______________].

The Parties recognize that due to the special needs of CHILD ONE, child support may not terminate at age 18 or at any particular age and may continue if the child is physically or mentally incapacitated from supporting herself and insolvent and unmarried as per § _______ [Statutes of state of _______________].

In addition, each party will continue to contribute to child support as long as they are able to provide child support.

The child support shall be paid 50% on the 1st and 50% on the 15th day of each month.

HEALTH CARE COSTS

The children are currently covered by _______________ medical insurance through Father's employer. Both parents shall cooperate to keep the children covered under this insurance or under another plan. In the event it becomes appropriate to obtain other health insurance for the children, the parents shall pay the expense of such coverage based upon their proportionate share of income. Both parents shall cooperate to provide insurance ID cards to the other parent as applicable, and to complete all forms required by the coverage.

Unless both parties have agreed to use a health care provider that is not covered by the health benefit plan, if a parent incurs an expense to a health care provider that is not covered by the health benefit plan that would have been covered, or covered at a more favorable rate, if a provider included in the plan had been used, then that parent shall pay seventy-five percent (75%) and the other parent twenty-five percent (25%) of the uncovered expenses.

"Health expenses" shall be defined in accordance with Internal Revenue Code (1987) § 213 "Medical, Dental, etc., Expenses" or any other section enacted in replacement, in addition or in substitution thereof, and/or any Internal Revenue Regulation including, but not limited to, § 1.213-1 or any relevant Regulation enacted in replacement, in addition or in substitution thereof, or any relevant Treasury Decision, Regulation, or any Revenue Ruling defining those types or kinds of medical costs that are deductible under the Internal Revenue Code; and shall also include orthodontia and optical care (including, but not limited to, prescription eyeglasses or contact lenses and eye examinations conducted by an optician, optometrist, or ophthalmologist), treatment, and appliances. Psychological and counseling expenses shall be paid as the parties agree, or absent agreement to the extent they are included as "Health Expenses" defined above or are determined by the child's case manager to be in the best interests of the child.

All health expenses incurred on behalf of the children and not paid by the health benefit plan shall be paid based upon each parent's proportionate share of income. The health expenses covered by this paragraph are not limited to just the usual medical, dental, orthodontic, optical, and psychological expenses of children without special needs. Due to the special needs of the children, they have and are expected to continue to have extraordinary medical, therapeutic, and other expenses that shall be paid by the parents based upon proportionate share of income, in addition to the base amount of child support.

The Parties recognize that due to the special needs of CHILD ONE, payment of health care costs may not terminate at age 18 or at any particular age and may continue if the child is physically or mentally incapacitated from supporting herself and insolvent and unmarried as per § _______ [Statutes of state of _______________].

In addition, each party will continue to contribute to health care as long as they are able to provide health care.

FOR EACH CHILD WITH SPECIAL NEEDS, ATTACH AN EXHIBIT CONTAINING A SUMMARY OF:

[ ] Diagnosis
[ ] Doctors, therapists, and other professionals
[ ] Child's current daily schedule and routine
[ ] Child's current therapy plan
[ ] Summary of how special needs affect the child's daily life
[ ] Itemization and explanation of the costs involved in or caused by the special needs
[ ] Who is the primary caregiver of the child
[ ] Primary caregiver's daily schedule
[ ] Statement as to the impact of transitions and schedule changes on the child
[ ] List of equipment and special items needed by the child the location of such items
[ ] Suggested physical custody arrangement
[ ] Suggested legal custody arrangement
[ ] Suggested visitation—daily, weekly, weekends, holidays, summers, and special days

EDUCATION AND EXTRAORDINARY EXPENSES

Due to the special needs of the children, they currently incur and are expected to continue to incur extraordinary educational and other expenses. These shall be paid by the parties based upon their proportionate share of income. If the parties cannot agree on the extraordinary expenses for education, therapy, activities, equipment, supplements, and/or other items, the parties agree to pay (based upon their proportionate share of income) for the items determined by the child's/children's Special Needs Coordinator to be in the best interest of the child/children.

____________________ ____________________

Petitioner Respondent

____________________ ____________________

Attorney for Petitioner Attorney for Respondent

[Adapted from Special Needs Parenting Plan, coauthored with Kieran Coyne, attorney in St. Louis, Missouri.]

The Washington State Child Support worksheet follows. It includes special needs as a reason to deviate from the standard amount of child support.

Washington Practice Series™
Methods of Practice
Kelly Kunsch FNa
Part II. Domestic Relations
Chapter 21. Dissolution of Marriage
Robert K. Ricketts FNb, Lisa A. Wolfard FNc

§ 21.38 Order of Child Support

SUPERIOR COURT OF WASHINGTON
COUNTY OF

		)	
		)	
In re:		)	NO.
		)	
		)	ORDER OF CHILD
		)	SUPPORT
	Petitioner	)	(ORS)
and		)	
	Respondent.	)	

I. JUDGMENT SUMMARY

[ ] Does not apply because no attorney's fees or back support has been ordered.
[ ] The judgment summary:
A. Judgment Creditor ______________________________
B. Judgment Debtor ________________________________
C. Principal judgment amount (back support) $ _____________
from _______________ (Date) to __________________ (Date).
D. Interest to date of Judgment $ _____________
E. Attorney's fees $ _____________
F. Costs $ _____________
G. Other recovery amount $ _____________
H. Principal judgment shall bear interest at _________% per annum.
I. Attorney's fees, costs, and other recovery amounts shall bear interest at __________% per annum.
J. Attorney for Judgment Creditor ____________________
K. Attorney for Judgment Debtor ______________________
L. Other:

II. BASIS

2.1 TYPE OF PROCEDING
This order is entered pursuant to:
[ ] a decree of dissolution, legal separation, or a declaration of invalidity.
[ ] an order determining parentage.

[ ] an order for modification of child support.
[ ] a hearing for temporary child support.
[ ] an order of adjustment.
[ ] an order for modification of a custody decree or parenting plan.
[ ] other:

2.2 CHILD SUPPORT WORKSHEET
The child support worksheet which has been approved by the court is attached to this order and is incorporated by reference or has been initialed and filed separately and is incorporated by reference.

2.3 OTHER:

III. ORDER

IT IS ORDERED that:
3.1 CHILDREN FOR WHOM SUPPORT IS REQUIRED

Soc. Sec. Number	Name	Date of Birth
______________	______________	____________
______________	______________	____________
______________	______________	____________
______________	______________	____________

3.2 PERSON PAYING SUPPORT (OBLIGOR)
Name:
Address:
Soc. Sec. Number:
Employer and Address:
[ ] Monthly Net Income: $___________
[ ] The income of the obligor is imputed at $__________ because:
  [ ] the obligor's income is unknown.
  [ ] the obligor is voluntarily unemployed.
  [ ] the obligor is voluntarily underemployed.
  [ ] other:

3.3 PERSON RECEIVING SUPPORT (OBLIGEE)
Name:
Address:
Soc. Sec. Number:
Employer and Address:
[ ] Monthly Net Income: $___________
[ ] The income of the obligee is imputed at $__________ because:
  [ ] the obligee's income is unknown.
  [ ] the obligee is voluntarily unemployed.
  [ ] the obligee is voluntarily underemployed.
  [ ] other:

The parent receiving support may be required to submit an accounting of how the support is being spent to benefit the child.

3.4 TRANSFER PAYMENT

[ ] The obligor parent shall pay $________ per month.

[ ] The obligor parents shall pay the following amounts per month for the following children:

Amount	Name	
________________	__________________	$__________
________________	__________________	$__________
________________	__________________	$__________
________________	__________________	$__________
TOTAL MONTHLY AMOUNT		$__________

[ ] If one of the children changes age brackets or terminates support, child support shall be as follows

[ ] Other:

3.5 STANDARD CALCULATION

$____________________ per month. (See Worksheet line 15.)

3.6 REASONS FOR DEVIATION FROM STANDARD CALCULATION.

[ ] The child support amount ordered in paragraph 3.4 does not deviate from the standard calculation.

[ ] The child support amount ordered in paragraph 3.4 deviates from the standard calculation for the following reasons:

- [ ] Income of a new spouse of the parent requesting a deviation for other reasons;
- [ ] Income of other adults in the household of the parent requesting deviation for other reasons;
- [ ] Child support actually paid or received for other children from other relationships;
- [ ] Gifts;
- [ ] Prizes;
- [ ] Possession of wealth;
- [ ] Extraordinary income of a child;
- [ ] Tax planning which results in greater benefit to the children;
- [ ] A nonrecurring source of income;
- [ ] Payment would reduce the parent's income level below the DSHS need standard for one person;
- [ ] Extraordinary debt not voluntarily incurred;
- [ ] A significant disparity in the living costs of the parents due to conditions beyond their control;
- [ ] Special needs of disabled children;
- [ ] Special medical, educational, or psychological needs of the children;

[ ] The child spends a significant amount of time with the parent who is obligated to make a support transfer payment. The deviation does not result in insufficient funds in the receiving parent's household to meet the basic needs of the child. The child does not receive public assistance;
[ ] Children from other relationships;
[ ] Costs incurred or anticipated to be incurred by the parents in compliance with court-ordered reunification efforts or under a voluntary placement agreement with an agency supervising the child;
[ ] Other:

The factual basis for these reasons is as follows:

3.7 REASONS WHY REQUEST FOR DEVIATION WAS DENIED
[ ] Does not apply.
[ ] The deviation sought by the [ ] obligor [ ] obligee was denied because:
[ ] no good reason exists to justify deviation.
[ ] other:

3.8 STARTING DATE AND DAY TO BE PAID
Starting Date:
Day(s) of the month support is due:

3.9 INCREMENTAL PAYMENTS
[ ] Does not apply.
[ ] This is a modification of child support. Pursuant to RCW 26.09.170(8)(c), the obligation has been modified by more than thirty percent and the change would cause significant hardship. The increase in the child support obligation set forth in Paragraph 3.4 shall be implemented in two equal increments, one at the time of this order and the second on ________________ (Date), six months from the entry of this order.

3.10 HOW SUPPORT PAYMENTS SHALL BE MADE
[ ] The Office of Support Enforcement provides support enforcement services for this case (this includes welfare cases, cases in which a parent has requested services from OSE, and cases in which a parent signs the application for services from OSE on bottom of the support order). Support payments shall be made to:
Washington State Support Registry
P.O. Box 9009
Olympia, WA 98507
[ ] The Office of Support Enforcement does not provide support enforcement services for this case. Support payments shall be made to:
[ ] ____________________
____
____
[ ] Washington State Support Registry
P.O. Box 9009
Olympia, WA 98507
(OSE will process payments but will not take any collection action.)

When payments are to be made to the Support Registry, each party shall notify the Washington State Support Registry of any change in residence address. A party required to make payments to the Washington State Support Registry will not receive credit for a payment made to any other party or entity. The obligor parent shall notify the registry of the name and address of his or her current employer, whether he or she has access to health insurance coverage at reasonable cost and, if so, the health insurance policy information.

3.11 WAGE WITHHOLDING ACTION

A notice of payroll deduction may be issued or other income withholding under Chapter 26.18 RCW or Chapter 74.20A RCW may be taken, without further notice to the obligor parent at any time after entry of this order unless an alternative provision is made below:

If the court orders immediate wage withholding in a case where OSE does not provide support enforcement services, a mandatory wage assignment under Chap. 26.18 RCW must be entered and support payments must be made to the Support Registry.

[ ] Wage withholding, by notice of payroll deduction or other income withholding action under Chapter 26.18 RCW or Chapter 74.20A RCW, without further notice to the obligor, is delayed until a payment is past due, because:

[ ] The parties have reached a written agreement which the court approves that provides for an alternate arrangement.

[ ] The Office of Support Enforcement provides support enforcement services for this case [see 3.10] and there is good cause as stated below under "Good Cause"] not to require immediate income withholding which is in the best interests of the child and, in modification cases, previously ordered child support has been timely paid:

[ ] The Office of Support Enforcement does not provide support enforcement services for this case [see 3.10] and there is good cause [as stated below under "Good Cause"] not to require immediate income withholding:

Good Cause: ____

____

3.12 TERMINATION OF SUPPORT

Support shall be paid:

[ ] provided that this is a temporary order, until a subsequent child support order is entered by the court.

[ ] until the child(ren) reach(es) the age of 18, except as otherwise provided below in Paragraph 3.13.

[ ] until the child(ren) reach(es) the age of 18 or as long as the child(ren) remain(s) enrolled in high school, whichever occurs last, except as otherwise provided below in Paragraph 3.13.

[ ] after the age of 18 for ____________________ (Name) who is a dependent adult child, until the child is capable of self-support and the necessity for support ceases.

[ ] until the obligation for post-secondary support set forth in Paragraph 3.13 begins for the child(ren).

[ ] other:

3.13 POST SECONDARY EDUCATIONAL SUPPORT

[ ] No post-secondary educational support shall be required.

[ ] The right to petition for post-secondary support is reserved provided that the right is exercised before support terminates as set forth in Paragraph 3.12.

[ ] The parents shall pay for the post-secondary educational support of the child(ren). Post-secondary support provisions will be decided by agreement or by the court.

[ ] Other:

3.14 PAYMENT FOR EXPENSES NOT INCLUDED IN THE TRANSFER PAYMENT

[ ] Does not apply because all payments, except medical, are included in the transfer payment.

[ ] The mother shall pay ________% and the father _________% (each parent's proportional share of income from the Child Support Schedule Worksheet, line 6) of the following expenses incurred on behalf of the children listed in Paragraph 3.1:

  [ ] day care
  [ ] educational expenses
  [ ] long-distance transportation expenses
  [ ] other:

[ ] Payments shall be made to

  [ ] the provider of the service
  [ ] the parent receiving the transfer payment.

[ ] The obligor shall pay the following amounts each month the expense is incurred on behalf of the children listed in Paragraph 3.1:

  [ ] day care: $___________ payable to the [ ] day care provider [ ] other parent;
  [ ] educational expenses: $___________ payable to the [ ] educational provider [ ] other parent;
  [ ] long distance transportation: $___________ payable to the [ ] transportation provider [ ] other parent.
  [ ] other:

3.15 PERIODIC ADJUSTMENT

[ ] Does not apply.

[ ] Child support shall be adjusted periodically as follows:

[ ] Other:

3.16 INCOME TAX EXEMPTIONS

[ ] Does not apply.

[ ] Tax exemptions for the children shall be allocated as follows:

[ ] The parents shall sign the federal income tax dependency exemption waiver.

[ ] Other:

3.17 MEDICAL INSURANCE

[ ] Health insurance coverage for the child(ren) listed in Paragraph 3.1 shall be provided by the [ ] mother [ ] father [ ] both parents if coverage that can be extended to cover the child(ren) is or becomes available through employment or is union

related and the cost of such coverage does not exceed $___________ (25 percent of the obligated parent's basic child support obligation).

[ ] Health insurance coverage shall be provided as set forth above by the [ ] mother [ ] father [ ] both parents, even if the cost of such coverage exceeds 25 percent of the obligated parent's basic child support obligation.

[ ] The reasons for not ordering the [ ] mother [ ] father to provide health insurance coverage for the child(ren) are

The parent(s) shall maintain health insurance coverage, if available for the children listed in Paragraph 3.1, until further order of the court or until health insurance is no longer available through the parents' employer or union and no conversion privileges exist to continue coverage following termination of employment.

A parent who is required under this order to provide health insurance coverage is liable for any covered health care costs for which that parent receives direct payment from an insurer.

A parent who is required under this order to provide health insurance coverage shall provide proof of such coverage is available or not available within twenty days of the entry of this order or within twenty days of the date such coverage becomes available, to:

If proof of such health insurance coverage is available or not available is not provided within twenty days the obligee or the Department of Social and Health Services may seek direct enforcement of the coverage through the obligor's employer or union without further notice to the obligor as provided under Chapter 26.18 RCW.

3.18 EXTRAORDINARY HEALTH CARE EXPENSES

The OBLIGOR shall pay ___________% of extraordinary health care expenses (the obligor's proportional share of income from the Child Support Schedule Worksheet, line 6), if monthly medical expenses exceed $___________ (5% of the basic support obligation from Worksheet line 5).

3.19 BACK CHILD SUPPORT

[ ] Back child support is not addressed in this order.

[ ] The obligee parent is awarded a judgment against the obligor parent in the amount of $_________ for back child support for the period from _____________ (Date) to _____________ (Date).

[ ] Other:

3.20 BACK INTEREST

[ ] Back interest is not address in this order.

[ ] The obligee parent is awarded a judgment against the obligor parent in the amount of $___________ for back interest for the period from ___________ (Date) to _____________ (Date).

[ ] Other:

3.2 OTHER

Dated: ______________________________

____

Judge/Commissioner
Presented by:
Approved for entry:
Notice of presentation waived:

Signature	Signature
Print or Type Name	Print or Type Name

[ ] I apply for full support enforcement services from the DSHS Office of Support Enforcement.

Signature of Party

[ ] Approved for entry in Public Assistance cases, notice of presentation waived.

Assistant Attorney General

Print or Type Name
Library References:
C.J.S. Divorce § 669–671, 673–683, 700–705, 708.
West's Key No. Digests, Divorce 308

a. Seattle University School of Law, Member of the Washington Bar.

b. Robert K. Ricketts is a member of the Washington State Bar Association and is in private practice in Tacoma. He gratefully acknowledges the assistance of Professor Sheldon Frankel of the University of Puget Sound School of Law for his authorship of sections 21.15 through 21.19.

c. Lisa A. Wolfard is a partner at the law firm of Short, Cressman & Burgess in Seattle.

CHAPTER 6

Model Child Support Chart, Parenting Plan, and Modification

The following models are intended to aid state legislatures in adopting uniform child support charts, parenting plans, and modifications when handling cases involving special needs children. They include specific provisions necessary to adequately address the unique needs of families with special needs children going through the family court process.

MODEL CHILD SUPPORT CHART FOR USE IN SPECIAL NEEDS CASES

In re the Marriage of: ____

Form 14SN CHILD SUPPORT AMOUNT CALCULATION WORKSHEET

CHILDREN	DATE OF BIRTH	CHILDREN	DATE OF BIRTH
Name		Name	

	Parent Receiving Support	Parent Paying Support	Combined
1. MONTHLY GROSS INCOME	$	$	
a. Court-ordered maintenance being received	$	$	
2. ADJUSTMENTS (per month)	($)	($)	
a. Other court or administratively ordered child support being paid			
b. Court-ordered maintenance being paid	($)	($)	
c. Support obligation for other children in parent's primary physical custody	($)	($)	
3. ADJUSTED MONTHLY GROSS INCOME (sum of lines 1 and 1a, minus lines 2a, 2b, and 2c)	$	$	$
4. PROPORTIONATE SHARE OF COMBINED ADJUSTED MONTHLY GROSS INCOME (each parent's line 3 income divided by combined line 3 income)	%	%	
5. BASIC CHILD SUPPORT AMOUNT (from support chart using combined line 3 income)			$
6. ADDITIONAL CHILD-REARING COSTS (per month)	$		
a. Reasonable work-related child care costs of the parent receiving support, less any child care tax credit			
b. Reasonable work-related child care costs of the parent paying support		$	
c. Health insurance costs for the children who are subjects of this proceeding	$	$	

d. Uninsured extraordinary medical costs (agreed by parents or ordered by court)	$	$	
e. Other extraordinary child-rearing costs (agreed by parents or ordered by court)	$	$	
f. Special needs expenses and costs: therapy equipment medications supplements dietary costs sensory items respite care other reasonable items			
7. TOTAL ADDITIONAL CHILD SUPPORT COSTS (sum of lines 6a, 6b, 6c, 6d, and 6e)	$	$	$
8. TOTAL COMBINED CHILD SUPPORT COSTS (sum of line 5 and combined line 7)			$
9. EACH PARENT'S SUPPORT OBLIGATION (multiply line 8 by each parent's line 4)	$	$	
10. CREDIT FOR ADDITIONAL CHILD-REARING COSTS (line 7 of parent paying support)		$	
11. ADJUSTMENTS FOR A PORTION OF THE AMOUNTS OF EXPENDED DURING PERIODS OF OVERNIGHT VISITATION OR CUSTODY (multiply line 5 by 0.22%)		$	
12. PRESUMED CHILD SUPPORT AMOUNT (line 9 minus line 10 and 11 plus line 12)		**($)**	
PREPARED BY: Attorney for			
EXHIBIT # __________			

MODEL PARENTING PLAN FOR USE IN SPECIAL NEEDS CASES

IN THE FAMILY COURT OF THE COUNTY OF ____________
STATE OF ______________

In Re the Marriage of:	)	
	)	
____________________,	)	
______________,	)	
Petitioner,	)	
vs.	)	Case No. __________________
____________________,	)	Division: _______
______________,	)	
Respondent.	)	

CONSENT PARENTING PLAN FOR SPECIAL NEEDS

For purposes of this Parenting Plan, "Minor Children" refers to CHILD ONE, born Month, Day, Year, and CHILD TWO, born Month, Day, Year, either collectively, or either child separately, as is appropriate.

Mother and Father shall have joint legal custody, and Father shall have sole physical custody of said minor children.

Father's residence shall be designated as the primary residence of the minor children for mailing and educational purposes.

CUSTODY PARENTING TIME SCHEDULE

Due to the special needs of the children, the standard visitation schedule is not in the best interests of the children. The girls are 12-year-old twins. One of the children, CHILD ONE, has cerebral palsy. She receives intensive therapy for many hours every week, and, by necessity, her life is extremely structured.

The two most important aspects of this Parenting Plan are

- The best interests of the children and
- Cooperation of the parents.

CUSTODY, VISITATION, AND RESIDENTIAL TIME FOR EACH CHILD WITH EACH PARENT SHALL BE AT SUCH TIMES AS THE PARTIES SHALL AGREE. The parties are strongly encouraged to work together cooperatively and flexibly to reach by amicable agreement such custody, visitation, and residential times as shall be in the best interests of the children and keeping in mind their special needs. In the event the parties cannot agree, Mother shall have custody, visitation, or residential time as set forth below; and Father shall have all other time as his custody, visitation, or residential time.

EACH PARENT IS STRONGLY ENCOURAGED TO PUT THE CHILDREN FIRST AND TO MAKE EVERY REASONABLE EFFORT TO MEET THE UNIQUE NEEDS OF THE SPECIAL NEEDS CHILD(REN). Each parent is strongly encouraged to take time every week to spend one-on-one time with the special needs child and to spend one-on-one time with the non–special needs child.

WEEKDAY VISITATION

Mother may come to Father's house to visit the children during the evenings whenever her schedule permits, as long as the parties shall so agree. In the event the parties cannot agree upon the night or nights of this visitation, Mother shall visit the children at Father's house or pick them up at Father's house on Wednesday evenings. Mother shall visit/pick up children at 6:00 PM and return them to Father's house by 7:15 PM, when she is welcome to participate in their bedtime routine, which usually lasts until 8:00 PM. Mother may extend this weekday visitation to overnight visitation. In the event the parties agree upon overnight visitation during the week, Mother shall either return the children to Father's house the next morning or take them to their morning activity, as agreed to by the parties.

WEEKENDS

The children are involved in many activities due to their special needs. These activities require great flexibility and cooperation by the parents regarding the weekend visitation. The general goal is that Mother shall have the children for approximately half of the weekends, although this will often not be every other weekend. The parties shall frequently consult each other regarding the scheduled activities and arrange the weekend visitation around the schedules and best interests of the children. If the parties cannot agree, Mother shall have visitation of the children every other weekend beginning at 6:00 PM on Friday through and ending at 6:00 PM on Sunday, beginning the weekend following the date of the judgment. If either parent's holiday weekend, as set forth below, conflicts with this, then the parent losing their regular weekend shall receive the other parent's next regular weekend to thereafter be followed by the original schedule so that each would have two consecutive weekends.

SUMMER

The children attend summer school for six weeks every year. This usually runs from June through August. There is a week or two between the regular school year letting out and the start of summer school, and there is a week or two between the end of summer school and the beginning of the next school year. During these weeks, the girls usually attend a special needs summer day camp. It is important for the girls to attend summer school. If they are registered for summer school but do not attend consistently, they will not be eligible to attend in subsequent years.

Mother may exercise periods of summer visitation during the summer regardless of whether it is during the weeks of summer school, as long as she shall take the children to summer school if her time periods fall during those weeks.

Since these arrangements must be made well in advance, Mother shall notify Father of her choice of option in writing by March 1st every year.

Mother may have liberal summer visitation as the parties shall agree. In the event the parties cannot agree, subject to the above provisions, Mother shall have three weeks each summer (to be divided into three seven-consecutive-day periods) to coincide with the children's school summer vacation. Mother may select the first week of this summer vacation by notifying Father of same (each notification herein to be in writing) by February 1st of each year, one week may then be excluded by Father by February 15th and then the next week may be selected by Mother by March lst, one more week may then be excluded by Father by March 15th, the final week may be selected by Mother by April lst. Father's excluded weeks shall prevail over Mother's weekend and weekday periods set forth above.

HOLIDAYS AND SPECIAL DAYS

1. Holiday and special day custody shall prevail over weekend, weekday, and summer vacation set forth above. Birthday periods shall not prevail when in conflict with other Holidays and Special Days.
2. Mother shall have the minor children on her birthday and on Mother's Day of each year from 9:00 AM to 9:00 PM; plus "Holiday Group A" in even-numbered years and "Holiday Group B" in odd-numbered years.
3. Father shall have the minor children on his birthday and on Father's Day of each year from 9:00 AM to 9:00 PM; plus "Holiday Group A" in odd-numbered years and "Holiday Group B" in even-numbered years.
4. Mother and Father are encouraged to communicate to attempt to arrange a combined event/activity for the children's birthday. In the event they cannot agree, the following provisions regarding the children's birthday shall apply.
5. Due to the serious special needs of the children, the conditions stated in the above paragraphs concerning WEEKDAY, WEEKEND, and SUMMER visitation shall apply to HOLIDAY GROUPS A & B.

HOLIDAY GROUP A

1. PRESIDENT'S DAY/WASHINGTON'S BIRTHDAY (OBSERVED) weekend from 5:00 PM the Friday prior to 8:00 AM the following Tuesday.
2. A period of 7 (seven) days during the children's school spring break, the exact days to be selected and notice given in writing to the other parent by February lst.
3. INDEPENDENCE DAY — If July 4th falls on: (a) Tuesday, Wednesday, or Thursday from 5:00 PM on July 3rd until 9:00 AM on July 5th, (b) Friday or Saturday from 5:00 PM on the Thursday before until 9:00 AM on the following Monday, (c) Sunday or Monday from 5:00 PM on the Friday before until 9:00 AM on the following Tuesday.
4. HALLOWEEN (October 31st) night from 4:00 PM until 9:00 AM the following day.
5. CHRISTMAS VACATION from December 25th beginning at 10:00 AM through 9:00 AM on December 31st.
6. Each child's birthday from 9:00 AM until 9:00 AM the following day.

HOLIDAY GROUP B

1. MARTIN LUTHER KING weekend from 5:00 PM the Friday prior through 8:00 AM the following Tuesday.
2. MEMORIAL DAY weekend from 5:00 PM the Friday prior through 8:00 AM the following Tuesday.
3. LABOR DAY weekend from 5:00 PM the Friday prior through 8:00 AM the following Tuesday.
4. THANKSGIVING weekend from 5:00 PM the Wednesday prior through 8:00 AM the following Monday.
5. CHRISTMAS VACATION from 5:00 PM the day the children's school Christmas vacation begins through 10:00 AM on December 25th and December 31st beginning at 9:00 AM through 8:00 AM the day the children's school Christmas vacation ends.
6. The day prior to each child's birthday beginning at 9:00 AM through 9:00 AM the day of the birthday.

The serious special needs of the children requires that Mother and Father be far more cooperative and flexible than the parents of children without special needs.

EXCHANGES

[X] When school is in session:
Exchanges of all children from Mother to Father shall occur at:
[ ] Residence of Mother [X] Residence of Father [ ] School
[ ] Other Location—Parents currently reside at same location; exchanges not applicable.

Exchanges of all children from Father to Mother shall occur at:
[ ] Residence of Mother [X] Residence of Father [ ] School
[ ] Other Location

[ ] When school is not in session or if all children are not school age:
Exchange of all children from Mother to Father shall occur at:
[ ] Residence of Mother [X] Residence of Father
[ ] Other Location

Exchange of all children from Father to Mother shall occur at:
[ ] Residence of Mother [X] Residence of Father
[ ] Other Location

[ ] If an exchange occurs at a location other than a parent's residence, the parent scheduled to have time with the children shall pick up and return the children to the specified location and the other parent shall be responsible for assuring the children are at the specified location for pick up, unless other arrangements are described.

TRANSPORTATION

Transportation arrangements for all children for all scheduled parenting time(s) including weekdays, weekends, holidays, and vacation times shall be as follows:

[X] Mother shall be responsible for transportation of the children at the beginning of the visit. Mother shall be responsible for transportation of the children at the end of the visit.

Mother and Father shall share responsibility for all transportation of the children, including cost, as follows:

[ ] Extraordinary transportation costs (bus, taxi, train, airfare) shall be the responsibility of [ ] Mother [ ] Father [ ] Shared % Mother % Father

CHANGES

The parents' schedules and commitments may require occasional changes in the parenting time schedule. Parents shall attempt to agree on any changes, but the parent receiving a request for a change shall have the final decision on whether the change shall occur.

The parent making the request may make such request
[X] in person [X] by phone [X] in writing to the other parent [X] other—email

The request for change shall be made no later than:
[ ] 24 hours [X] one week [ ] two weeks [ ] other—prior to the date of the requested change.

The parent receiving the request shall respond no later than:
[ ] 24 hours [ ] one week [ ] two weeks [X] other—72 hours after receiving the requested change.

The response to the request may be made
[X] in person [X] by phone [X] in writing to the other parent [X] other—email

Any parent requesting a change of schedule shall be responsible for any additional child care or transportation costs resulting from the change.

Mother and Father shall cooperate to allow the children to meet their therapeutic, school, and social commitments.

TELEPHONE CONTACTS

Each parent shall have reasonable access to all children by telephone during any period in which the children are with the other parent, unless otherwise specified.

RELOCATION

Absent exigent circumstances as determined by a court with jurisdiction, you, as a party to this action, are ordered to notify, in writing by certified mail, return receipt requested, and at least 60 days prior to the proposed relocation, each party to this action of any proposed relocation of the principal residence of the children, including the following information: (1) the intended new residence, including the specific address and mailing address, if known, and if not known, the city; (2) the home telephone number of the new residence, if known; (3) the date of the intended move or proposed relocation; (4) a brief statement of the specific reasons for the proposed relocation of the children;

and (5) a proposal for a revised schedule of custody or visitation with the children. Your obligation to provide this information to each party continues as long as you or any other party by virtue of this order is entitled to custody of a child covered by this order. Your failure to obey the order of this court regarding the proposed relocation may result in further litigation to enforce such order, including contempt of court. In addition, your failure to notify a party of a relocation of the child may be considered in a proceeding to modify custody or visitation with the children. Reasonable costs and attorney fees shall be assessed against you if you fail to give the required notice.

LEGAL CUSTODY

Legal Custody: The parties shall agree before making any final decisions on issues affecting the growth and development of the children including, but not limited to, choice of religious upbringing; choice of child care provider; choice of school; course of study; special tutoring; extracurricular activities including, but not limited to, music, art, dance, and other cultural lessons or activities and gymnastics or other athletic activities; choice of camp or other comparable summer activity; nonemergency medical and dental treatment; psychological, psychiatric, or like treatment or counseling; the choice of particular health care providers; the extent of any travel away from home; part or full-time employment; purchase or operation of a motor vehicle; contraception and sex education; and decisions relating to actual or potential litigation on behalf of the children. However, each parent may make decisions regarding the day-to-day care and control of the children and in emergencies affecting the health and safety of the children while the children are residing with him or her. The parents shall endeavor, whenever reasonable, to be consistent in such day-to-day decisions.

Communication: Each parent shall ensure that the other parent is provided with copies of all communications or information received from a child's school, and if a second copy of the communication is not provided by the school shall make a copy for the other parent. Each parent shall notify the other of any activity such as school conferences, programs, sporting, and other special events, etc., where parents are invited to attend; and each shall encourage and welcome the presence of the other.

Children Not Involved in Court or Financial Communications: The parties shall not talk about adult issues, parenting matters, financial issues, and other court-related topics when the children are present. Such discussions shall not be had during custody exchanges of the children or during telephone visits. The children shall not be used to carry such messages, written communication, or child support payments between the parents.

Medical Care Information: Each parent shall have the authority to seek any emergency medical treatment for the children when in his or her custody. Each shall advise the other of any medical emergency or serious illness or injury suffered by the minor children as soon as possible after learning of the same and shall give the other parent details of the emergency, injury, or illness and the name and telephone numbers of all treating doctors. Each parent shall inform the other before any routine medical care, treatment, or examination by a health care provider including said provider's name and telephone number. Each party shall direct all doctors involved in the care and treatment of the minor children to give the other parent all information regarding any injury or illness and the medical treatment or examination, if requested. For purposes of this paragraph, a serious injury or illness is one that requires a child (1) to be confined to home for more than 48 hours; or (2) to be admitted to, or treated at, a hospital or surgical facility; or (3) to receive any type of general anesthesia or invasive surgical procedure or test.

Child Care Provider: If both parents will need to use a child care provider during periods of custody or visitation, they shall use the same child care provider, unless the distances between their residences or places of employment make the use of the same child care provider unreasonable.

Access to Records: Each parent shall be entitled to immediate access from the other or from a third party to records and information pertaining to the children including, but not limited to, medical, dental, health, child care, school or educational records; and each shall take whatever steps are necessary to ensure that the other parent has such access.

Activities Not to Conflict with Custody or Visitation: The parties shall enroll the children in activities, particularly outside of school, that, to the extent possible, are scheduled at times and places that avoid interruption and disruption of the custody or visitation time of the other party unless consented to by that parent. The special needs of the children require far greater cooperation and flexibility by the parents than is required of the parents of children without special needs.

Resolution of Disputes: If the parties fail to agree on the interpretation of the Parenting Plan, or are unable to agree upon a final decision on issues affecting the growth and development or health and safety of the children, they shall submit the dispute to a mutually agreed-upon Special Needs Coordinator who shall hear and arbitrate the issue. In the event they are not able to agree on a Special Needs Coordinator, they shall each select a Special Needs Coordinator from the list of approved Special Needs Coordinators maintained by the ___________ County Family Court, and the two Special Needs Coordinators shall determine who shall arbitrate the case. The Special Needs Coordinator shall be a quick and informal tribunal to arbitrate issues that may arise in the future including, but not limited to, increasing or decreasing child support; changes in therapy, treatment, education, custody, and/or visitation; and issues relating to expenses.

CHILD SUPPORT AND OTHER EXPENSES

Due to the special needs of the children, the application of Standard Child Support Guidelines would be inappropriate and/or unjust. The initial amount of child support shall be $_________ per month, payable by Mother to Father. This amount shall be modifiable. This is the base amount, which DOES include the current amount for nutritional supplements/regimens, and DOES NOT include additional support for therapy, activities, camps, or other expenses necessitated by their special needs. Parents shall pay for these additional items based upon their proportional share of income. Parents acknowledge that future nutritional supplements/regimens may involve an increased cost, and parents agree to pay such increased cost based upon their proportional income.

Child support shall terminate for CHILD TWO in accordance with § _______ [Statutes of state of _______________].

The Parties recognize that due to the special needs of CHILD ONE, child support may not terminate at age 18 or at any particular age and may continue if the child is physically or mentally incapacitated from supporting herself and insolvent and unmarried as per § _______ [Statutes of state of _______________].

In addition, each party will continue to contribute to child support as long as they are able to provide child support.

The child support shall be paid 50% on the 1st and 50% on the 15th day of each month.

HEALTH CARE COSTS

The children are currently covered by _______________ medical insurance through Father's employer. Both parents shall cooperate to keep the children covered under this insurance or under another plan. In the event it becomes appropriate to obtain other health insurance for the children, the parents shall pay the expense of such coverage based upon their proportionate share of income. Both parents shall cooperate to provide insurance ID cards to the other parent as applicable, and to complete all forms required by the coverage.

Unless both parties have agreed to use a health care provider that is not covered by the health benefit plan, if a parent incurs an expense to a health care provider that is not covered by the health benefit plan that would have been covered, or covered at a more favorable rate, if a provider included in the plan had been used, then that parent shall pay seventy-five percent (75%) and the other parent twenty-five percent (25%) of the uncovered expenses.

"Health expenses" shall be defined in accordance with Internal Revenue Code (1987) § 213 "Medical, Dental, etc., Expenses" or any other section enacted in replacement, in addition or in substitution thereof, and/or any Internal Revenue Regulation including, but not limited to, § 1.213-1 or any relevant Regulation enacted in replacement, in addition or in substitution thereof, or any relevant Treasury Decision, Regulation, or any Revenue Ruling defining those types or kinds of medical costs that are deductible under the Internal Revenue Code; and shall also include orthodontia and optical care (including, but not limited to, prescription eyeglasses or contact lenses and eye examinations conducted by an optician, optometrist, or ophthalmologist), treatment, and appliances. Psychological and counseling expenses shall be paid as the parties agree, or absent agreement to the extent they are included as "Health Expenses" defined above or are determined by the child's case manager to be in the best interests of the child.

All health expenses incurred on behalf of the children and not paid by the health benefit plan shall be paid based upon each parent's proportionate share of income. The health expenses covered by this paragraph are not limited to just the usual medical, dental, orthodontic, optical, and psychological expenses of children without special needs. Due to the special needs of the children, they have and are expected to continue to have extraordinary medical, therapeutic, and other expenses that shall be paid by the parents based upon proportionate share of income, in addition to the base amount of child support.

The Parties recognize that due to the special needs of CHILD ONE, payment of health care costs may not terminate at age 18 or at any particular age and may continue if the child is physically or mentally incapacitated from supporting herself and insolvent and unmarried as per § _______ [Statutes of state of _______________].

In addition, each party will continue to contribute to health care as long as they are able to provide health care.

FOR EACH CHILD WITH SPECIAL NEEDS, ATTACH AN EXHIBIT CONTAINING A SUMMARY OF:

[ ] Diagnosis
[ ] Doctors, therapists, and other professionals
[ ] Child's current daily schedule and routine
[ ] Child's current therapy plan
[ ] Summary of how special needs affect the child's daily life
[ ] Itemization and explanation of the costs involved in or caused by the special needs
[ ] Who is the primary caregiver of the child
[ ] Primary caregiver's daily schedule
[ ] Statement as to the impact of transitions and schedule changes on the child
[ ] List of equipment and special items needed by the child and the location of such items
[ ] Suggested physical custody arrangement
[ ] Suggested legal custody arrangement
[ ] Suggested visitation—daily, weekly, weekends, holidays, summers, and special days

EDUCATION AND EXTRAORDINARY EXPENSES

Due to the special needs of the children, they currently incur and are expected to continue to incur extraordinary educational and other expenses. These shall be paid by the parties based upon their proportionate share of income. If the parties cannot agree on the extraordinary expenses for education, therapy, activities, equipment, supplements, and/or other items, the parties agree to pay (based upon their proportionate share of income) for the items determined by the child's/children's Special Needs Coordinator to be in the best interest of the child/children.

________________________	________________________
Petitioner	Respondent
________________________	________________________
Attorney for Petitioner	Attorney for Respondent

[Adapted from Special Needs Parenting Plan, coauthored with Kieran Coyne, attorney in St. Louis, Missouri.]

MODEL MODIFICATION FOR USE IN SPECIAL NEEDS CASES

CONSENT MODIFICATION—SPECIAL NEEDS

The parties hereby agree to modify the terms of the original Decree of Dissolution entered by this Court on ____________________, 20__, in the following respects:

1. ____
2. ____
3. ____

This Consent Modification is based upon the following facts:

1. ____
2. ____
3. ____

This Consent Modification shall be in effect until:

_____ Further Order of this Court.
_____ The date of ______________________________.
_____ The occurrence of ______________________________ event.

All other provisions of the original Decree of Dissolution entered in this case on ______________________________, 20___, shall continue in full force and effect.

______________________ ______________________
Petitioner Respondent

______________________ ______________________
Petitioner's Attorney Respondent's Attorney

Dated this _____ day of ________________________________, 20___.

SO ORDERED:

____

CHAPTER 7

Maintenance and Property Distribution in Special Needs Cases

In determining the issues of property distribution and maintenance (alimony), lawyers and judges must look at additional factors in cases involving special needs children. For several reasons, the usual approach to maintenance and property distribution does not achieve a fair or just result when applied to cases involving special needs children.

I. MAINTENANCE

Often, the primary caregiver parent is unable to devote the time and attention to her career she otherwise would, were she not caring for a special needs child.[1] Managing the care of a special needs child can be a full-time job.[2] Managing the doctor appointments, therapy, researching to find additional resources and treatment options, securing and maintaining funding for the child's expenses, and doing the additional work necessary to provide daily care of a special needs child all take a great deal of time and attention.[3]

Special needs children average three times as many sick days and school absence days as other children.[4] They also have more doctor visits.[5] It can be difficult, if not impossible, to keep a job when you are frequently spending time taking your child to doctor appointments, taking your child to therapy, scheduling appointments for your child, dealing with concerns of therapists, and responding to crisis after crisis.[6] Dealing with these unpredictable crises places a psychological burden on the family of special needs children.[7] With a special needs child, at least one parent has to be on call 24 hours

1. Lee, S., Oh, G., Hartmann, H., & Gault, B. (2004). The impact of disabilities on mothers' work participation: Examining differences between single and married mothers. Washington, DC: Institute for Women's Policy Research.

2. Hornby, G. (2005). Fathers' views of the effects on their families of children with Down's syndrome. *Journal of Child and Family Studies*, *4*(1), 103–117.

3. *Id.*

4. Newacheck, P.W., Strickland, B., Shonkoff, J.P., Perrin, J.M., McPherson, M., & McManus, M., Lauver, C., Fox, H., & Arango, P. (1998). An epidemiologic profile of children with special health care needs. *Pediatrics*, *102*(1), 117–123.

5. Scal, P. (2002). Transition for youth with chronic conditions: Primary care physicians' approaches. *Pediatrics*, *110*(6), 1315–1321.

6. Lee et al., *supra* note 1.

7. Ganz, M., & Tendulkar, S. (2006). Mental health care services for children with special care needs and their family members: Prevalence and correlates of unmet needs. *Pediatrics*, *117*(6), 2138–2148.

a day, seven days a week. Schools, therapists, and others who work with a special needs child require that someone be designated as the primary contact person, and that person must be readily accessible whenever the child is not physically with them. All of this stress will take its toll on the parents.[8]

Often, special needs children are sick more frequently than other children.[9] When special needs children are sick, the parent who is the primary caregiver often must stay home with them. That parent must also pick up the child when something goes wrong, whether at school, day care, or therapy. The primary caregiver parent may have to miss a lot of time from his job in responding to these needs of the child.[10] Few employers will tolerate an employee who is unreliable, unpredictable, and frequently absent—even though it is for a very good reason. Even when these children are not acutely ill, many of them have major limitations in the areas of mobility, self-care, communication, and/or learning.[11] On a day-to-day basis, the multiple treatment needs of special needs children can be very time-consuming for the caregiving parent.[12]

Many primary caregiver parents are thus unable to work full-time or even part-time, depending on the magnitude of the child's needs and the particular circumstances of the case.[13] If the parent's career is not adaptable to reduced hours and unpredictable schedule, the parent may be unable to work at all. A flight attendant, for example, cannot do her job of being on flights all around the country if she must be available to get her child from school or therapy at a moment's notice. Taking care of dependent children decreases the amount caregivers can work as well as decreasing the chance of remarriage.[14]

The physical and emotional exhaustion take a toll on the primary caregiver parent.[15] The critical illness of a child has long-lasting effects in the family and on child behavior.[16] Taking care of a special needs child is a full-time job in itself, and a tough one.[17] *Many people cannot do it.* If the primary caregiver parent has other children to care for, does all the cooking, cleaning, laundry, grocery shopping, errands, and numerous other things necessary to maintain the home, there is simply no time or energy left to hold down an outside job. Often the primary caregiver parent is also doing therapy with the

8. Tavormina, J., Boll, T., Dunn, N., Luscomb, R., & Taylor, J. (1981). Psychosocial effects on parents of raising a physically handicapped child. *Journal of Abnormal Child Psychology, 9*(1), 121–131.

9. Newacheck et al., *supra* note 4.

10. Lee, et al., *supra* note 1.

11. Msall, M., Avery, R., Tremont, M., Lima, J., Rogers, M., & Hogan, D. (2003). Functional disability and school activity limitations in 41,300 school-age children: Relationship to medical impairments. *Pediatrics, 111*(3), 548–553.

12. Committee on Children with Disabilities. (1999). Care coordination: Integrating health and related systems of care for children with special health care needs. *Pediatrics, 104*(4), 978–981.

13. Lee et al., *supra* note 1.

14. Sheehan, G., & Fehlberg, B. (2000, Autumn). Families, and divorce and family law, Australian Institute of Family Studies. *Family Matters, 55*, 4–9.

15. *Id.*

16. Rautava, P., Lehtonen, L., Helenius, H., & Sillanpää, M. (2003). Effect of newborn hospitalization on family and child behavior: A 12-year follow-up study. *Pediatrics, 111*(2), 277–283.

17. Van Hoven, M. (2004). Letter to the editor regarding "Compassion or opportunism?" *Pediatrics, 114*(3), 896–897; Silverman, W. (2004). Commentary: Compassion or Opportunism? *Pediatrics, 113*(2), 402–403.

child at home. There are simply not enough hours in the day to add an outside job to the full-time job or two this person is already doing.

In addition, it can be difficult or cost prohibitive to obtain appropriate child care for a special needs child.[18] This factor can also make it impractical for the caregiving parent to have a full-time job outside the house.[19] Thus, based on the bare numbers, a case that does not look like a maintenance case may be one in which maintenance should be awarded to the primary caregiver parent.

II. PROPERTY DISTRIBUTION

The primary caregiver parent may also need a larger than ordinary proportion of the marital assets, for the reasons just discussed as well as because he or she has a limited opportunity to replace existing items when they wear out. The primary caregiver parent who is devoting most of his waking hours to the care of a special needs child does not have the opportunity to walk away from the situation eight hours a day, earn a full-time income, advance in his career, and replace the items awarded to him in the divorce when those items break or wear out. The other parent has the freedom to focus on her career, earn a living, and provide for herself. She has much greater future economic opportunity.

III. RETIREMENT ACCOUNTS

The primary caregiver parent often suffers over the long term because after the divorce she is precluded from contributing to a retirement account, as she would if she were the other parent. Usually pensions and retirement accounts are divided at the time of the divorce by determining how much was put into the account and how much accumulated in the account during the marriage. If the primary caregiver parent will be ineligible to contribute to a retirement account because she is taking care of the special needs child and thus not employed enough hours or not employed at all, she will be penalized financially and may be destitute in her old age.

The courts should view the primary caregiver parent's role in taking care of the special needs child as a job equal to that of the other parent, and they should develop a formula for assigning future retirement contributions of the other parent to the retirement account of the primary caregiver parent. If caring for the special needs child is considered a job, which is in a sense a joint venture with the other parent—since they did make or adopt this child together—then it follows logically that future contributions to retirement accounts should be distributed to both joint venturers. Marriage is an economic partnership in which there is a shared enterprise.[20] It logically follows that the special needs child, who is the product of such marriage, is the subject matter of a joint venture, economic partnership, or shared enterprise.

---

18. Lee et al., *supra* note 1.

19. *Id.*

20. Katz, S. (1994). Historical perspective and current trends in the legal process of divorce. *The Future of Children—Children and Divorce*, *4*(1), 44–62.

IV. CAREER ADVANCEMENT

There should also be financial contribution because when the primary caregiver parent is primarily devoted to the care of the special needs child, he will not have the same career advancement as he would if he were not so devoting his time. The other parent is able to focus on her career, be a dedicated employee or professional, and advance in her career. The primary caregiver parent's career will not follow the same path, due to his care of the special needs child. When deciding property distribution in cases involving special needs children, the lawyers and judges should also consider this factor.

In summary, cases involving special needs children may be appropriate for the award of maintenance to the primary caregiver parent because managing the care of the special needs child often results in unemployment, underemployment, or unstable employment of the primary caregiver parent. The primary caregiver parent is also more likely to suffer from physical exhaustion from the massive nonstop work of caring for a special needs child. Primary caregivers are less likely to remarry, thereby reducing the likelihood of another source of income or financial stability. Obtaining appropriate child care for a special needs child can be difficult and cost prohibitive. Further, primary caregiver parents may need a larger than ordinary proportion of marital assets because of their decreased economic opportunity. Primary caregiver parents also may need a greater than ordinary proportion of retirement accounts set aside to them, and it may be appropriate to develop a formula assigning future retirement account contributions to both parents.

CHAPTER 8

Roles of the Parties

In divorces involving special needs children, there are several parties who each have a role. Their duties and responsibilities are greater than in the typical divorce case. The parties are

- the special needs child
- the custodial parent
- the noncustodial parent
- the attorneys of the parents
- the judge
- the guardian ad litem
- other professionals—educators, medical professionals, therapists, and service providers

I. RIGHTS OF THE PARTIES

A. Special Needs Child

What are their rights? A special needs child has the right to have her unique issues and needs recognized, understood, and considered an important factor by the legal professionals. She has the right to be treated with dignity and respect. She has the right of input into what happens to her—indeed, where appropriate, to participate and be part of the process of decision-making. Many of these children are wise beyond their years and can contribute at a level one would not expect in a child of their age. Some of them are more like adults in the bodies of children, perhaps due to the serious nature of the medical struggles they have faced.

B. Custodial Parent (Primary Caregiver Parent)

The **custodial parent (primary caregiver parent)** has the right to be recognized as an expert on his or her child and should be more actively involved in the process of determining the details of the outcome than one might be in a standard case. There should be a rebuttable presumption that the custodial parent is the best authority on the child's daily schedule, individual needs, and issues and on how custody and visitation terms will affect the child.

C. Noncustodial Parent (Non–primary Caregiver Parent)

The **noncustodial parent (non–primary caregiver parent)** should be treated as the next-best person to contribute those details about the child, unless shown otherwise. It is tempting sometimes to judge noncustodial parents harshly because they are not devoting themselves to the care of their special needs child. Sometimes this is warranted, but not always. Some parents make a thoughtful determination of the person who would be best suited to take care of the child, and of the person who would be best suited to bring in the income to pay for the child's needs. Both jobs are essential. Then again, there are the parents who emotionally abandon the child and just want out of the situation because they are too selfish to devote themselves to the special needs child at the level required.[1] Even in this situation they are still, at least biologically, the parent of the child and should have some voice. Of course, such parents will have far more credibility with the courts if they take courses and educate themselves on their child's particular special needs and medical condition.[2]

D. Lawyers

The lawyers have the right to an opportunity to present creative solutions to the court and have them considered with an open mind. Cookie-cutter approaches do not work, and they are not in the best interests of special needs children. They live "outside the box," and we need to think "outside the box" to find solutions that are appropriate for them.

E. Judge

The judge has the right to find creative solutions to the unique problems presented by divorces involving special needs children, and to be given great deference in these decisions by the appellate courts. Often special needs cases are high-conflict cases.[3] The parents may be battling against each other, either out of a sincere disagreement as to the child's condition and/or needs[4] or due to one parent being committed to the child's best interest and the other parent being committed to his or her own interests.[5] Whatever the underlying cause, in high-conflict cases, the judge should be allowed to use a professional intermediary, such as a special needs coordinator, special master, parent coach, or parenting coordinator.[6] Such professional intermediary would handle many of the details, disputes, and day-to-day interactions between the parents—high-maintenance aspects that have become a huge burden on our family courts. Contentious divorces can result in psychological maltreatment of the child by the parent, which results in harm to the child.[7] This has both short- and long-term negative effects on the child and gives the child the message that he is unwanted, unloved, and worthless.[8] High-conflict divorcing

1. Tanner, J. Lane, the Committee on Psychosocial Aspects of Child and Family Health. (2002). Parental separation and divorce: Can we provide an ounce of prevention? *Pediatrics, 110*(5), 1007–1009.

2. Jennings, S. (2005). Autism in children and parents: Unique considerations for family court professionals. *Family Court Review, 43*(4), 582–595.

3. *Id.*

4. Stein, M., Diller, L., & Resnikoff, R. (2001). ADHD, divorce, and parental disagreement about the diagnosis and treatment. *Journal of Developmental & Behavioral Pediatrics, 107*(4), 867–872.

5. Jennings, *supra* note 2.

6. *Id.*

7. Kairys, S., Johnson, C., & the Committee on Child Abuse and Neglect. (2002). The psychological maltreatment of children—technical report. *Pediatrics, 109*(4), 68–76.

8. *Id.*

families also put the children at risk for various kinds of developmental difficulties[9] and cause the children to have emotional and behavioral maladjustment.[10]

F. Guardian ad Litem/Special Needs Coordinator

The guardian ad litem (GAL)/special needs coordinator has the right to dig deeper and get far more information and detail than usual to formulate the best plan for the special needs child. The guardian ad litem/special needs coordinator also has the right to come up with creative solutions to the issues of the particular case.

G. Other Professionals

Other professionals have a right to be heard by the court when they have concerns to express or information that should be heard by the court. These professionals have the right to be treated as experts in their field, even when it is a field with which the court has little familiarity. Developments in the various types of special needs treatments are happening so rapidly that courts cannot rely only upon information on outdated treatment options.

II. RESPONSIBILITIES OF THE PARTIES

A. Special Needs Child

The special needs child has the responsibility to make a reasonable effort to cooperate with the other parties as they struggle to achieve a good result. The special needs child also has the responsibility to try to approach the new situation with a good attitude and a spirit of cooperation.

B. Parents

The custodial parent and noncustodial parent (primary caregiver parent and non-primary caregiver parent) have duties to bring the necessary information and experts to the attention of their lawyers, to facilitate the lawyer in obtaining releases and records, and to have reasonable expectations. They also have the responsibilities to set aside their differences and put the needs of the child first, and to try in good faith to make the arrangement work.

C. Lawyers

The lawyers (including the GAL/special needs coordinator) have greater responsibility in cases involving special needs children. It is a specialty within a specialty. If the lawyer does not have at least a basic understanding of the child's particular special needs, she should educate herself on the subject. She should also make sure she has thorough information in her client file on the details of this particular child's situation. She should compile the information she needs to have in her client files when handling divorces involving special needs children.

---

9. Roseby, V., & Johnston, J. (1998). Children of Armageddon: Common developmental threats in high conflict divorcing families. *Childhood Adolescent Psychiatry*, *7*(2), 295–309.

10. Johnston, J. (1994). High-conflict divorce: The future of children. *Children & Divorce*, *4*(1) 165–182.

PRACTICE TIP

Checklist for Client File Contents
In addition to the usual items contained in a divorce client file, a lawyer handling a divorce case involving special needs should have the following items:

1. Medical reports, test results, diagnoses
2. Evaluations
3. Treatment plans
4. Therapy plans
5. Medication plans
6. Child's safety plans for home, school, and away
7. Medical bills
8. Documentation of all costs
9. IEPs (Individualized Education Plans) and 504 Plans, current and previous[11]
10. Information on every treating professional
11. Copies of articles or book excerpts providing basic information on child's particular condition
12. Detailed therapy and treatment schedule
13. Detailed daily schedule
14. Documentation for all pertinent items

D. Judge

The judge also has a greater responsibility in deciding cases involving special needs children. If the judge does not have a basic understanding of the child's particular special needs, he should educate himself. How can he rule that a plan is in the best interests of a child if he does not know what the child's special needs involve? The judge should make sure the lawyers are giving sufficient attention to the child's special needs and that they are not merely applying a standard form to a case where the child's special needs demand deviation from the norm. The judge also has a duty to listen with an open mind to proposed terms or arrangements that are creatively designed to meet the unique special needs of a particular child.

E. Other Professionals

The other professionals have a responsibility to cooperate with the legal professionals and be fair to both parents, even when they may have strong feelings about the case.

11. An IEP is a legal document, mandated by the IDEA, that controls the procedural requirements. It is more involved than a 504 Plan. An IEP is required for students with disabilities who require specialized instruction. A 504 Plan is a written plan required for students with disabilities needing only reasonable accommodation. It is less involved than an IEP. An excellent explanation may be found in *A Parent's Guide to Special Education*, by L. Wilmhurst & A. W. Brue (Amacom, 2005). *See also* "IEPs vs. 504 Plans," and the entire Sevier County Special Education website. Retrieved July 15, 2022, from https://www.sevier.org/site/default.aspx?PageType=2&PageModuleInstanceID=486&ViewID=838b13a1-2ccb-4c74-83cb-0b9f098d6937&RenderLoc=0&FlexDataID=7938. Additional helpful materials include the Learning Disabilities OnLine website, http://www.LDonline.org (especially the materials on accommodations and modifications) and the Cleveland Heights Teachers Union website materials on 504 Plan Frequently Asked Questions, http://www.chtu.org. Both retrieved July 5, 2022.

Their strong feelings can be expressed, but they should not present information in a blatantly biased or one-sided manner.

III. PARTICIPATION

All parties need to participate at a higher level of cooperation and open-mindedness than would ordinarily be found in divorce cases. Releases should be freely given, without the necessity of a court order or even formal discovery process. The parents need to be able to work together for years, perhaps for the rest of the child's life, to raise the special needs child. If the divorce is a bitter, high-conflict experience, it will damage the parents' ability to work together in the future. The lawyers need to make every reasonable effort to handle this type of case in a much more cooperative, even cordial manner if at all possible. If the GAL determines that the input of the child would be both appropriate and helpful, the child should be allowed to give that input. Everyone involved in the process needs to work together to help these families.[12]

If all the parties in family law cases involving special needs children receive their rights as discussed in this chapter, they will all have an investment in the process and will try harder to make the end result work. If all the parties fully perform their responsibilities, the unique needs of the special needs child will be met; all parties will have a voice and will be treated with dignity and respect; and, most importantly, the family courts will have properly administered justice for some of their most vulnerable constituents.

---

12. Birenbaum, A., & Cohen, H. (1993). On the importance of helping families: Policy implications from a national study. *Mental Retardation, 31*(2), 67–74.

CHAPTER 9

Special Considerations in Special Needs Family Law Cases

Special needs children whose families are going through divorce will require particular attention to their unique issues in areas of child support, custody, maintenance, and property distribution. Other issues, however, can greatly affect the successful implementation of any court order or parenting plan. These issues are

- Individualized Education Plans (IEPs), 504 Plans,[1] and therapy plans
- Behavior of special needs children as it relates to school and law enforcement
- Religion
- Parents with special needs
- Planning for a crisis
- Using technology to facilitate co-parenting

I. INDIVIDUALIZED EDUCATION PLANS (IEPS) AND 504 PLANS

The Individuals with Disabilities in Education Act (IDEA) and section 504 of the Rehabilitation Act of 1973 provide that each eligible child is guaranteed a free appropriate public education designed to address his or her unique means.[2] Inclusion has long been considered a positive thing, both for children with disabilities and for typical children.[3] This is true even though teachers of students with learning disabilities, behavioral

1. An IEP is a legal document, mandated by IDEA, that controls the procedural requirements. It is more involved than a 504 Plan. An IEP is required for students with disabilities who require specialized instruction. A 504 Plan is a written plan required for students with disabilities needing only reasonable accommodation. It is less involved than an IEP. An excellent explanation may be found in *A Parent's Guide to Special Education*, by L. Wilmhurst & A. W. Brue (Amacom, 2005). *See also* "IEPs vs. 504 Plans," and the entire Sevier County Special Education website. Retrieved July 15, 2022, from https://www.sevier.org/site/default.aspx?PageType=2&PageModuleInstanceID=486&ViewID=838b13a1-2ccb-4c74-83cb-0b9f098d6937&RenderLoc=0&FlexDataID=7938. Additional helpful materials include the Learning Disabilities OnLine website, http://www.LDonline.org (especially the materials on accommodations and modifications) and the Cleveland Heights Teachers Union website materials on 504 Plan Frequently Asked Questions, http://www.chtu.org. Both retrieved July 5, 2022.

2. Des Jardins, C. (1993). How to advocate for your special needs child. *Psychology Today, 18*(4), 15–16; Dalton, M. A. (2002). Education rights and the special needs child. *Child and Adolescent Psychiatry Clin. N. Am., 11*(4), 859–868.

3. Pearson, V., Lo, E., Chui, E., & Wong, D. (2003). A heart to learn and care? Teachers' responses toward special needs children in mainstream schools in Hong Kong. *Disability & Society, 18*(4), 489–508.

problems, and/or physical difficulties experience more problems in maintaining classroom discipline, have a greater workload, and struggle to manage the differing academic standards of special needs children and typical children.[4]

When a child has a condition qualifying him for modifications that require specialized instruction at school, the school district often calls together the child's parents, teachers, and therapists so they can devise a plan tailored to meet the individual needs of the child in the educational setting.[5] This group of people is referred to as the "IEP team."[6] The plan they devise and write for the individual child is called an IEP, or Individualized Educational Plan.[7] The plan should contain many things, including

- results of testing performed on the child
- recommendations
- areas of strengths and weakness
- input from the parents, teachers, and therapists
- measurable goals to accomplish during the school year
- modifications deemed necessary for the child at school, on testing, class work, seating, assistance, communication, therapies, and many other areas[8]

A 504 Plan is usually written by a committee, which should include the student (if appropriate), his or her parents/guardians, teacher, school counselor, and the school's 504 coordinator.[9] The 504 coordinator is usually a person who is not a special educator (assistant principal or guidance counselor, for example), but special educators often advise the 504 committee. The 504 Plans involve such things as seat assignment within the classroom, allowing a diabetic child to eat in the classroom, going to the nurse for administration of medication, modification of testing time limits, and moving a child from special education to regular education placement.[10]

A well-written IEP or 504 Plan will contain many details about how the child's special needs affect her, at least in the school environment.[11] This information can be very helpful to the court in getting a thorough picture of the individual child and how her special needs affect her daily life. In turn, when the IEP or 504 Plan is written, any provisions of the court order that would affect the effectiveness and implementation of the IEP or 504 Plan should be brought to the attention of the IEP team or 504 committee. If all the parties cooperate and openly communicate with each other, the child will achieve greater success. The parents should be willing to share information from one forum

4. *Id.*

5. Dalton, *supra* note 2.

6. *Id.*

7. *Id.*

8. *Id.*

9. Wilmhurst & Brue, *supra* note 1, at 13–14. American Management Association (New York, NY: Amacom). *See also* "IEPs vs. 504 Plans," and the entire Sevier County Special Education website. Retrieved July 15, 2022, from https://www.sevier.org/site/default.aspx?PageType=2&PageModuleInstanceID=486&ViewID=838b13a1-2ccb-4c74-83cb-0b9f098d6937&RenderLoc=0&FlexDataID=7938. Additional helpful materials include the Learning Disabilities OnLine website, http://www.LDonline.org (especially the materials on accommodations and modifications) and the Cleveland Heights Teachers Union website materials on 504 Plan Frequently Asked Questions, http://www.chtu.org. Both retrieved July 5, 2022.

10. Cleveland Heights Teachers Union website materials on 504 Plan Frequently Asked Questions. Retrieved July 5, 2022, at http://www.chtu.org.

11. *Id.*

with the others. Therapists outside of school should be given a copy of the child's IEP or 504 Plan so they can coordinate their therapy with that done at school. This avoids conflicting goals, conflicting methodology, and duplication. The lawyers should have a copy of the IEPs, 504 Plans, and therapy plans for special needs children when handling divorces in order to have a more complete picture of the special needs child.

II. BEHAVIOR—SCHOOL AND CRIMINAL JUSTICE SYSTEM

Lawyers with expertise in the area of special needs are frequently called by parents of special needs children to help in times of crisis, when their special needs child has gotten in trouble at school or with the law because of behavior related to his or her special needs. When people who are unaware of a child's condition or who do not have a basic understanding of the particular special needs that the child is dealing with, they can misunderstand or misinterpret the child's behavior as something it is not.[12] For example, a child with autism might look like any other child. If this child is walking down the hallway, is spoken to by a school official, and either does not respond or makes an odd noise because she is nonverbal, it could be misinterpreted as disrespectful or bad behavior. If this child is at a store and is startled by something, she might run out of the store and end up being chased, tackled to the ground, and arrested under suspicion of shoplifting. Individuals with mental or emotional disabilities are especially vulnerable to having negative experiences with law enforcement.[13] People with developmental disorders are seven times more likely than other people to come into contact with police, and their behavior in these situations is not always understood as socially appropriate.[14]

Some courts have applied Title II of the Americans with Disabilities Act (ADA) to cases that involve interactions between individuals with mental or emotional disabilities and encounters with law enforcement personnel. However, multiple courts have refused to recognize that law enforcement agencies should require or provide training to their officers on how to recognize behaviors that are common with certain special needs like autism and how to interact peacefully with individuals whose disabilities caused them to behave differently from neurotypical people during encounters with the police.

In *Leibel v. City of Buckeye*,[15] the court acknowledged that the complaint contained "plausible allegations that [the officer] acted improperly (by arresting C.L. without probable cause, using excessive force, violating the ADA, and committing battery)." In this case, a 14-year-old with autism was playing in a public park in Buckeye, Arizona, and "stimming" with a piece of string. His caregiver had stepped away for a few minutes. Stimming is common behavior in people with developmental disabilities, and involves holding an object at a particular angle, moving the item repetitively, or similar conduct to cope with sensory issues.

Although the 14-year-old child was not causing any harm to himself or anyone else, a police officer approached and misinterpreted the boy's actions as being under the influence

---

12. Bryan, T., Pearl, R., & Herzog, A. (1989). Learning disabled adolescents' vulnerability to crime: Attitudes, anxieties, experiences. *Learning Disabilities Research, 5*(1), 51–60.

13. *Id.*

14. Debbaudt, D. (2002). *Autism, advocates, and law enforcement professionals: Recognizing and reducing risk situations for people with autism spectrum disorders.* London: Jessica Kingsley Publishers.

15. Leibel v. City of Buckeye, 364 F. Supp. 3d 1027, 1045 (Ariz. 2019).

of illegal drugs. When the officer asked what he was doing, the boy explained that he was stimming, and showed the officer the piece of string. As the officer continued to question him, the child turned to leave, at which time the officer handcuffed the boy, slammed him against a tree, wrestled him to the ground, and pinned the child with the officer's full body weight. The boy screamed that he needed help and could not breathe.

The caregiver returned at that time and told the officer that the boy had autism. She explained the boy's stimming behavior, but the officer continued to pin the boy to the ground with his full weight, even though the caregiver told the police officer that the boy's hand was turning white. The officer did not get off of the child until another officer arrived. The boy suffered significant physical injuries to his face, back, arms, and ankle and had to have surgery to repair the ankle injury and numerous other medical procedures. He also suffered emotional damage.

This case is but one example of the harm that can be inflicted on people with special needs when law enforcement officers do not receive training on how to recognize the sometimes atypical conduct of people with special needs and how to interact with them peacefully. Some people with special needs are charged with resisting arrest, assaulting a police officer, or other crimes because of the behaviors caused by their disability.

Lawyers who deal with divorces involving special needs children need to be aware that the families may well call you when such crises arise. Your files from the divorce contain information that can be vital in getting these types of situations resolved. Try to calmly and patiently educate the persons involved about the special needs of the child, and why the child acted the way he did. At school, he should not, in general, be punished for behavior arising from his disability. In the criminal justice setting, the child's special needs can often be used as a defense to criminal charges or as a basis for a dismissal of charges.

PRACTICE TIP

It is important for lawyers to truly understand the nature of the special needs of these children. You cannot explain their behavior to someone else if you do not understand it.

III. RELIGION

Under the best of circumstances, religion can be a tremendous source of conflict. Throughout human history, millions of people have died over religious differences. When a family is going through a divorce and there are differences in religion, it can turn into the fight of the century. Deeply held convictions can make people intractable and resistant to compromise. Religious issues can refer to any of four situations:

1. Mother observes one faith and Father observes a different faith.
2. One parent observes a faith and the other parent does not observe any faith.
3. The parents observe the same general faith, but to varying degrees or in different ways.
4. One or more of the parents' religious practices could cause harm to the child.

When there are religious issues during a divorce involving special needs children, the special needs of the child must be given great weight. If, for example, the child has a severe wheat allergy and the Communion service involves the child eating a wafer that contains wheat, modifications should be made in the religious observances in the best interest of the child.

Sometimes parents refuse all medical treatment, therapies, and medications for their special needs child based upon religious beliefs. In a situation like this, the local family services department should be contacted for the welfare of the child to be investigated. If this situation arises in the context of a divorce, the judge and GAL/special needs coordinator should be made aware of the situation as soon as the lawyers learn of it, as long as confidentiality rules and state's rules are followed.

Generally, after divorce, the child can attend religious services with the parent with whom she is staying or visiting at the time of such religious service. If the custody and visitation arrangement is modified for the special needs of the child, such that one parent seldom has physical custody of the child during the time of their religious services, the visitation schedule should provide clearly delineated opportunities for that parent to either take the child to their religious services or to observe with the child in another setting. The parents must realize that the best interests of the special needs child are served when the parents work together in a spirit of cooperation.

Another issue that must be considered is the child's right to some spiritual development. A child may have some disabilities, but that does not mean she does not have the capacity to wonder about the same things the rest of us do: Where did we come from? Why are we here? Where are we going? Is there life after death? Perhaps even more than typical children, children with disabilities need to be given the freedom to explore their spirituality.[16]

When the issues of Individualized Educational Plans (IEPs), 504 Plans, law enforcement, and religion are given their proper attention, the attorneys can craft a parenting plan that will work better for the family with the special needs child. As attorneys and judges become more aware of these issues, they can better meet the unique needs of families with special needs children as they go through the family courts.

IV. PARENTS WITH SPECIAL NEEDS

Although the focus of this book is on divorces involving children with special needs, if you practice much divorce law, you will come across cases involving parents with special needs. Sometimes, a parent will have the same physical or mental health issue as the child, or a related condition. That circumstance might be a benefit, in that the parent can understand what the child is going through and offer some insights for the benefit of the court and the other parent. On the other hand, the condition itself might be one that complicates the parenting issues.

Just as often, a parent will have a special need that none of the children have. The condition might not be hereditary. You might need to draft specially tailored terms to the parenting plan or create a safety plan. For example, if a parent who cannot drive because of a seizure disorder, you will need to address transportation issues for purposes of visitation. Also, when there are very young children, infants and toddlers, in the family, and a parent has a medical condition that could create a medical emergency without warning, a

16. Pridmore, P., & Pridmore, J. (2004). Promoting the spiritual development of sick children. *International Journal of Children's Spirituality*, *9*(1), 21–38.

safety plan could be necessary. In situations like these, the court might want to appoint a professional who does not represent any of the parties to offer guidance to the court on the special needs and draft a proposed visitation plan and safety plan.

In the tragic situation in which a parent receives a terminal diagnosis, the party should exercise exquisite care and thoughtfulness when crafting the visitation plan. You do not want to deny children the opportunity to build memories with their dying parent. The children will never get the opportunity to go back and make those memories. It could be useful to get ongoing psychological intervention for both parents and the children to help them cope with the situation.

Sometimes it can be appropriate to increase a parent's time with the children when they do not are not expected to live very long. When done correctly, this can be a benefit for both the ill parent and the children. Guidance from a psychologist can help to create the ground rules for what is within the range of age appropriateness for the children psychologically.

One should be prepared, however, for the possibility of the parent's condition going into remission. The practice of medicine is more an art than a science in situations like this. The party should strive to be flexible and cooperative if this outcome happens. The remission could be brief, like a few months, or it could go on for years. One should not be too quick to cut back on the special needs parent's visitation during a period of remission, for two reasons. One, when the parent feels better during remission, they can often do more activities with the children, which will be good for the children emotionally when their parent becomes ill again. Two, being less generous with the visitation schedule of the parent with the medical condition because of going into a remission is like punishing the person for not dying.

The fact that a parent has an illness, severe injury, or another special need does not make them less of a parent. In the past, some courts have restricted visitation of parents with special needs out of a mistaken assumption that doing so is in the best interest of the children. That approach teaches children that parents with special needs are "less than" other parents. Also, that approach teaches children that parents with special needs do not deserve custody or visitation of their children. Those are not lessons we want to teach the next generation.

When a parent has a special need that could impact any of the terms of custody or visitation, the divorce papers should address that situation directly. Just as children with special needs should be evaluated on an individual basis when the family goes through the divorce, it is also inappropriate to gloss over a parent's special needs and use a cookie-cutter schedule of parenting time.

V. PLANNING FOR A CRISIS

The COVID-19 global pandemic disrupted the lives of millions of people. Life as we knew it came to a screeching halt with very little warning. We all learned many skills we otherwise would not have had to learn, like working remotely and scavenging local shops and online shopping for basic necessities.

People with special needs experienced great disruption. They could not get needed medical services or supplies. While many people went out of control over trying to find toilet paper, families with special needs had to figure out what to do when they could not buy syringes for their children with diabetes, alcohol pads to safely give their children injections, and medications their children needed but that were not in stock because some people bought out all the supplies and hoarded them.

Schedules got turned upside-down. Since many people with special needs do best with a predictable routine, the sudden changes to their daily lives created extreme anxiety and panic. Getting through a typical day in the pre-COVID-19 world took all of their coping skills, so surviving the unpredictability and frequent changes of the pandemic pushed many people in the special needs community to the breaking point.

Some children with special needs became nonverbal, lost toileting skills, and even needed assistance they had not previously required to perform routine tasks of everyday life like dressing and eating. Many children lost progress they had worked for years to attain because they missed therapy for months.

Schools struggled to educate mainstream children remotely. For children with communication, processing, behavioral, attention, and other challenges, remote learning was an exercise in futility. There were hearing-impaired children who did not receive captioning of their classroom lectures, so they could not know what the teacher was saying. Children with low vision or blindness received printed assignments they could not see.

Class teleconference sessions often used software that was not compatible with the specialized software that many children with special needs require to enlarge the written material so they can see it or read it aloud. Children living with intellectual impairments were frequently left behind in the classroom teleconference sessions because there were no aides assisting them as they used to have present in the physical classroom. The very children who had the greatest needs received the least instruction in many instances.

Some children did not receive their annual IEP (Individual Education Plan) meetings for a year or two, which meant that they did not receive special education services. Those who did have an IEP in place often did not have the access to the technology that they needed to participate in meaningful therapy sessions.

Parents did not always agree on what to do when child care and schools shut down. Sometimes, one parent provided the lion's share of the child care for months on end and had to work remotely while managing their child's special needs 24/7 and without additional child support to help pay for the increased costs that resulted from the other parent not taking care of the child for their usual amount of parenting time.

Some parents insisted on exercising their usual schedule even when doing so exposed a medically fragile child to another person in that parent's household who had COVID. Many parents did not agree on whether they or the child should receive the COVID-19 vaccine when it became available. Some parents were at odds about wearing masks, physical distancing, washing hands, sanitizing items, and traveling.

Parents filed motions for contempt and motions to modify the child support or custody plan, but the courts were closed for long blocks of time. When the courts started holding hearings again, many of them were held remotely using teleconferencing programs and civil cases often took a back seat to the criminal case backlog.

One thing the COVID-19 pandemic taught us is that all divorcing parents, but especially divorced families with special needs, need to provide in their divorce papers a detailed plan for how to deal with the many types of fall-out that can result when there is a crisis like a global pandemic. If we believe the people who hold themselves out as experts, COVID-19 will not be the last pandemic.

VI. USING TECHNOLOGY TO FACILITATE CO-PARENTING

For quite a few years, there have been apps available that can facilitate co-parenting. Some judges require divorcing parents to use these apps in high-conflict divorces. Some of the functions of these apps include:

- The parents can communicate with each other without having to actually talk on the phone or in person, thereby reducing the likelihood of a confrontation.
- Parents can notify each other when they are running late to pick up or drop off the child.
- They can let each other know about school conferences, sports practices and games, doctor appointments, and other events.
- The app can keep a record of all the communications that the judge can access if there are disputes between the party, like allegations that one parent failed to keep the other informed or was verbally abusive.

Technology like these apps could be highly useful to help people co-parent when they have a special needs child or if one of the parents has a special need. We do not identify specific apps here because technology changes quickly.

Family law attorneys will want to request that language governing the use of a particular app and the admissibility in court of the data from the app be made a part of the divorce papers. You might want to talk to the judge on a given case about which app to use, because some judges prefer one app over another.

CHAPTER 10

Estate Planning for Families with Special Needs

Just as anyone who gets divorced needs to revisit their estate planning documents and revise them or create new ones, families with special needs should do so as well. These families have unique issues to address in addition to the usual goals of estate planning.[1] This chapter offers suggestions about how to approach this situation and discuss special needs trusts, guardianships, and conservatorships.

The estate planner needs to determine:

- Who has special needs in the family. Sometimes, there are multiple children with special needs or a parent and a child with special needs.
- The type and severity of the special needs
- The individual's current legal capacity
- The prognosis for the person's condition
- Any government assistance the individual currently receives or anticipates needing in the future
- The goals the family has that they wish to accomplish through estate planning documents

When there is only one person in the family who has special needs, the job of estate planning is simpler. Whether the personal with the physical or mental health challenge is a parent or a child, there are fewer moving parts than in a situation in which you need to plan for multiple people with special needs. There are more "what if" questions the estate planner needs to ask when there is more than one person needing specialized estate planning.

Performing estate planning for a family with special needs is a sophisticated process. A best practice recommendation is to refer the family to an attorney whose practice focuses on estate planning to handle the work. Special needs trusts have different rules for their formation and administration than other trusts. If something goes wrong in either aspect, the disabled parent or child could lose their eligibility for Medicaid or other public assistance programs, which could leave them without the medical care and other services they so desperately require.

1. Pabon, A. (2005). Financial planning for special needs children: A review of available information for parents. *Journal of Personal Finance*, *4*(2), 40–49.

I. SPECIAL NEEDS TRUSTS

One common mistake people make in estate planning for families with special needs is to assume that setting up a special needs trust will convince the court to terminate a parent's obligation to pay child support. Using a special needs trust in this manner could cause significant problems for the child.

In *J.B. v. W.B.*,[2] the Supreme Court of New Jersey affirmed the decision of the trial court that did not allow the father of a disabled adult son to modify his child support obligation by creating a special needs trust for the child. The court said that the father did not demonstrate how the proposed special needs trust would benefit the disabled son and did not present a sufficiently detailed plan to the court. A special needs trust is intended to supplement, rather than replace, government benefits the disabled person receives. The assets of the special needs trust cannot be used for food, clothing, or shelter. The purpose of child support is to provide food, clothing, shelter, and the other basic needs of the person who is the subject of the child support order. If the trustee of the proposed special needs trust in this case had used the trust assets in place of child support, expenditures on food, clothing, or shelter would be considered as in-kind support and maintenance to the beneficiary of the trust. The amount of in-kind support and maintenance would count as income to the beneficiary, and would disqualify him for government assistance programs. In other words, replacing child support with a special needs trust and using the assets of that trust to pay for the disabled person's food, clothing, shelter, and other necessities would defeat the very purpose of a special needs trust.

Special needs trusts can, when used correctly, protect the child's eligibility for government assistance programs. Let's say that a grandparent wants to leave money to a disabled grandchild in the grandparent's will or living trust. If the grandparent leaves the money directly to the grandchild and receiving that money would take the child's total countable assets over the asset limit for Medicaid, the child would no longer qualify for Medicaid benefits. With the current limit of $2,000 in countable assets, even a modest inheritance could destroy a child's eligibility for Medicaid benefits.

A disabled person might receive free health care services and a monthly stipend of several hundred dollars in government assistance, and qualify for a subsidized housing and nutritional assistance if they qualify for Medicaid. A mere $5,000 inheritance could cost the person with special needs far more than $5,000, if the inheritance goes directly to the individual, rather than to his special needs trust.

Sometimes, a child or adult becomes disabled because of an accident or some other form of negligent conduct by another person. If a jury awards the disabled person money damages in the personal injury lawsuit or the individual receives settlement proceeds, those funds could make the person ineligible for public assistance. On the other hand, if the jury award or settlement proceeds goes straight into a special needs trust instead of getting paid directly to the individual, the special needs trust, if set up and used correctly, can preserve a person's eligibility for government programs.

While special needs trusts can provide valuable benefits for the family with special needs by making it possible for the disabled person to indirectly receive an inheritance, settlement proceeds, or jury award without losing eligibility for government assistance

2. J.B. v. W.B., 73 A.3d 405, 215 N.J. 305 (2013).

and services, those benefits come at a cost. People often assume that when the disabled person dies, the assets remaining in the special needs trust can then be distributed to surviving family members. Unfortunately, that is not the case.

A special needs trust allows a disabled person to continue receiving government assistance. Those benefits cost taxpayer dollars. The remaining assets in a special needs trust will go to the government first, to repay the benefits the person received during their lifetime. If there are any assets leftover after reimbursing the government, those assets can then be distributed under the terms of the special needs trust. Typically, there are no funds remaining after government reimbursement.

You will need to follow the strict legal requirements for setting up a special needs trust that works as intended. Those requirements change from time to time and vary from state to state. For that reason, we do not include a sample special needs trust in this text. You should follow the rules that apply in your jurisdiction.

II. GUARDIANSHIPS

There are several situations in which it might be appropriate to file for a guardianship of a person with special needs. A few examples of these circumstances include:

- The aging parents of a disabled minor or adult child might seek a guardianship naming older siblings of the disabled person as the legal guardians to provide a seamless transition of the care of the disabled individual when the parents die.
- Sometimes, only one parent provides the caregiving for the disabled person. The other parent might be deceased, unknown, or not involved in the life of the child with special needs. The parent might have concerns about what will happen to the child when the caregiver parent dies. It can be appropriate for the sole caregiver parent to name in their will or living trust a guardian who will be willing and appropriate to provide caregiving for the special needs child. If the uninvolved parent comes into the picture after the caregiver parent dies, the person nominated as guardian could request the surviving parent's consent for a legal guardianship. The parent who was not involved in the child's life often agrees to that arrangement.
- When a parent has special needs, particularly those that could reduce the parent's life expectancy, it can be prudent to make similar arrangements for someone to step in and serve as the caregiver for the surviving children if they have not yet become adults when the parent dies. This situation can apply to children who have special needs or to those who do not.

These are but a few examples of situations in which you might wish to discuss the topic of guardianships with your clients.

III. CONSERVATORSHIPS

A guardianship typically involves authority and responsibility for the needs of the person, like shelter, education, medical care, food, clothing, and appropriate activities. A conservatorship, on the other hand, involves managing the financial matters for the person who is the subject of the guardianship. Sometimes one person fulfills both roles, but it might be in the best interest of the child to have one person serve as the guardian and another person be the conservator. Regardless of how you resolve those relationships for your clients, you should always create safeguards to minimize the likelihood of the vulnerable person being the victim of financial abuse or mismanagement.

IV. ADDITIONAL ESTATE PLANNING OPTIONS FOR FAMILIES WITH SPECIAL NEEDS

Many people with special needs have the legal capacity to make their own decisions about medical care and handle their own finances. They have not been declared by a court to lack legal capacity and are not the subject of a legal guardianship.

When an individual in that situation needs emergency medical care and is 18 or older, the parent does not have legal authority to consent to that treatment. For this reason, it can be a prudent to have the disabled but legally competent adult child sign a medical power of attorney and a Health Insurance Portability and Accountability (HIPAA) medical records release authorization granting a parent or another responsible person the legal authority to serve as their medical attorney-in-fact. The power of attorney would only kick in if the disabled adult child is unable to make those decisions. The document would not allow the designated attorney-in-fact to control the child's medical care against the individual's wishes. The HIPAA release would allow the attorney-in-fact to review the special needs individual's medical records to make informed decisions.

For example, the parents of a minor with moderate to severe epilepsy get a divorce. When that child turns 18, the parents can no longer authorize medical care for the adult child. If the child were to have a medical emergency, the parents would have to obtain a court order to make medical decisions for the child until such time as he regains consciousness if they do not have a medical power of attorney signed by the adult child.

When a person with special needs turns 18, they should consider getting a durable power of attorney for financial management and to create a will or living trust. One should not automatically assume that because a person has special needs, they lack legal capacity or a need for these standard estate planning documents.

Also, when the person with special needs is one of the parents, they should think about getting these standard estate planning documents in place. The failure to do so can make things more difficult, stressful, and expensive for their family one day.

Most family lawyers are not also specialists in estate planning, but all attorneys handling family law matters like divorce, paternity, and modifications should talk to their clients about the need for revised or new estate planning documents when they wrap up the family law case.

CHAPTER 11

Forms and Samples

The following forms and samples have been developed or adapted for use in divorce cases involving children with special needs. They are organized in the order they would be used during a divorce. Use them as guidelines and suggestions, and modify as needed for the individual circumstances of each case.

The forms and samples developed or adapted for special needs include

1. Initial Intake Questionnaire
2. Petition for Dissolution
3. Statement of Income & Expenses
4. Answer to Petition for Dissolution
5. Counter-petition for Dissolution
6. Child Support Calculation
7. Motion for Appointment of Guardian ad Litem
8. Order Appointing Guardian ad Litem
9. Special Needs Parenting Plan
10. Settlement Agreement
11. Affidavit for Judgment
12. Judgment of Dissolution
13. Motion to Modify

1. INITIAL INTAKE QUESTIONNAIRE

Today's date: ________________ Referred by: ____________________________

Client:
Name: ______________________________ Maiden/former: ____________
Address:
____
____

How long at this address? __________
How long in ___________ county? _______________
How long in state? ______________

Jurisdiction: ________________________ Venue: _________________________

Address to send correspondence:
____
____

Want maiden/former name back? _________ SS# _____________________

DL# ____________________________ State ________

Date of marriage ____________ Place of marriage __________________

Place where marriage is registered _________________________

Date of separation _________________________

Home phone: ____________________ Cell phone _________________________

Work phone: ____________________ Other phone _________________________

Where may we leave messages? Home Cell Work Other
Where may we call? Home Cell Work Other

DOB __________ Place of birth—city, state, county ______________________

Years of education 1–12; 12+ _________ Race _________________________
[Required for Bureau of Vital Statistics form]
Employer ____

How long? _______ Title _______________________

Annual gross income ____________ Bonuses? ________________
Seeking maintenance? _________ How much? __________________

Prior marriages? YES/NO How many? ________
When ended? ______________ How? ____________
[Death, dissolution, annulment]
Where? __________________________ [City, county, state]
Active military? ______________________

Pregnant? YES/NO Of this marriage? YES/NO Due date: _____________

Opposing party:
Name: ___________________________ Maiden/former: ___________
Address: ____
____

How long at this address? __________
How long in ___________ county? _______________
How long in state? ______________

Jurisdiction: _______________________ Venue: ________________________

Address to send correspondence:
____
____

Want maiden/former name back? _________ SS# ____________________

DL# ___________________________ State ________

Date of marriage ____________ Place of marriage __________________

Place where marriage is registered ________________________

Date of separation ________________________

Home phone: ___________________ cell phone ________________________

Work phone: ___________________ other phone ________________________

Where may we leave messages? Home Cell Work Other
Where may we call? Home Cell Work Other

DOB __________ Place of birth—city, state, county ______________________

Years of education 1–12; 12+ _________ Race ____________________________
[Required for Bureau of Vital Statistics form]
Employer ____

How long? _______ Title _______________________
Annual gross income ____________ Bonuses? ________________
Seeking maintenance? _________ How much? __________________

Prior marriages? YES/NO How many? ________
When ended? ______________ How? ____________
[Death, dissolution, annulment]
Where? __________________________ [City, county, state]
Active military? _______________________

Pregnant? YES/NO Of this marriage? YES/NO Due date: _____________

* * * * * * * * * * *

Grounds for divorce ____

Prenuptial agreement? YES/NO Any pending lawsuits? YES/NO

Either receive government support? YES/NO Counseling? YES/NO

Restraining order? YES/NO Spouse already filed? YES/NO

Children of this marriage:

Name	DOB	SS#	Age	Special Needs

Current custody:
Physical custody ________________________
Legal custody___________________

Client's wishes as to custody:
Physical custody ________________________
Legal custody ___________________

Is child support being paid currently? YES/NO
$ __________ is being paid by MOTHER/FATHER
Calculated child support based on current estimates of financial situation:
$ _______________ to be paid by MOTHER/FATHER

Health insurance is currently carried by MOTHER/FATHER

Other children of either party ______________________________________

Is either paying or receiving child support or maintenance not related to these parties? YES/NO MOTHER/FATHER is PAYING/RECEIVING
$ __________ per WEEK/MONTH from ______________________
for CHILD SUPPORT/MAINTENANCE of ______________________

Special needs:
Do any of the children have **special needs**? YES/NO
If so, on separate pages write details, including the following

- Which child(ren)
- What type(s) of special needs
- Doctors, therapists
- Date of diagnosis
- Types of therapy
- Costs—direct and indirect
- Schedule; prognosis
- Short-term and long-term plans
- Regular caregiver(s)
- Respite care
- Educational situation including IEPs (Individual Educational Plan) and 504 Plans[1]
- Medications
- Effects on primary caregiver parent—job, stress, career, retirement savings program
- Specific needs of the child(ren)
- Sensory issues
- Transition and adjustment issues

Do any of the PARENTS have **special needs**? YES/NO
If so, on separate pages write details, including the following

- Which parent
- What type(s) of special needs

1. An IEP is a legal document, mandated by IDEA, that controls the procedural requirements. It is more involved than a 504 Plan. An IEP is required for students with disabilities who require specialized instruction. A 504 Plan is a written plan required for students with disabilities needing only reasonable accommodation. It is less involved than an IEP. An excellent explanation may be found in *A Parent's Guide to Special Education*, by L. Wilmhurst & A. W. Brue (Amacom, 2005). *See also* "IEPs vs. 504 Plans," and the entire Sevier County Special Education website. Retrieved July 17, 2022, from https://www.sevier.org/site/default.aspx?PageType=2&PageModuleInstanceID=486&ViewID=838b13a1-2ccb-4c74-83cb-0b9f098d6937&RenderLoc=0&FlexDataID=7938. Additional helpful materials include the Learning Disabilities OnLine website, http://www.LDonline.org (especially the materials on accommodations and modifications) and the Cleveland Heights Teachers Union website materials on 504 Plan Frequently Asked Questions, http://www.chtu.org. Both retrieved July 6, 2022.

- Doctors, therapists
- Date of diagnosis
- Prognosis—is the condition expected to be fatal? If so, what is the life expectancy? If so, how can the parenting plan support the relationship of the parent with the children in the time the parent has left?
- Prognosis—is the condition expected to worsen? If so, how can the parenting plan support the relationship of the parent with the children?
- Types of medical treatment and therapy
- Costs—direct and indirect
- Schedule
- Short-term and long-term plans
- Regular caregiver(s)
- Respite care
- Educational situation including IEPs (Individual Educational Plan) and 504 Plans[2]
- Medications
- Effects of the parent's special needs on each parent—job, stress, career, retirement savings program
- Effects of the parent's special needs on the parent's ability to parent
- Specific needs of the parent with special needs
- Sensory issues
- Transition and adjustment issues

FINANCIAL FORMS—TAKE HOME—COMPLETE—BRING BACK—OR WE EMAIL TO CLIENT WHO RETURNS BY EMAIL

What happens next: ____

Take case? __________ Fee deposit: ____________________

Contact person (emergency): ____

2. See footnote 1.

2. PETITION FOR DISSOLUTION

IN THE FAMILY COURT OF THE COUNTY OF ___________
STATE OF ____________

In Re the Marriage of:	)	For File Stamp Only
	)	
______________________,	)	
______________Street	)	
City, State ZIP	)	
_____________	)	
Petitioner,	)	
and	)	Case No. _____________
______________________,	)	
______________Street	)	
City, State ZIP	)	Division: _________
_____________	)	
Respondent.	)	

SERVE AT:
Office/Home
Street Address
City, State ZIP

PETITION FOR DISSOLUTION OF MARRIAGE

Comes now the Petitioner, _________________, and for her cause of action, states to the Court as follows:

1. Petitioner has been a resident of the State of _________ for _____ days/months immediately preceding the filing of this Petition for Dissolution, and has been a resident of _______ County, State, for _____ days/months immediately preceding the filing of this Petition for Dissolution.
2. Respondent has been a resident of the State of __________ for _____ days/months immediately preceding the filing of this Petition for Dissolution, and has been a resident of ____________ County, State, for _____ days/months immediately preceding the filing of this Petition for Dissolution.
3. Petitioner resides at ___________Street, City, County, State. Petitioner is currently employed at _____________.
4. Respondent is currently residing at _____________Street, City, County, State. Respondent is currently employed at ________________.
5. Petitioner states that the parties were married on Month, Day, Year, in the City of _______________, State, and that said marriage was registered in the County of _____________, State.

6. Petitioner and Respondent are residing in the same residence, but are no longer living together as husband and wife, and separated on or about Month, Day, Year.
7. Petitioner states that neither Petitioner nor Respondent are members of the armed forces of the United States of America on active duty and are not entitled to any benefits or immunities of the Servicemembers Civil Relief Act.
8. Petitioner states that there is no reasonable likelihood that the marriage can be preserved and, therefore, the marriage is irretrievably broken.
9. Petitioner and Respondent have acquired certain property and certain debts during the marriage and have not yet entered into a property settlement agreement which disposes of all matters between them, financial or otherwise.
10. Petitioner states that there was one unemancipated child born of the marriage, namely:
    Child's Name, DOB ________________
    AND THAT SUCH CHILD HAS SPECIAL NEEDS, NAMELY _______.
11. That Petitioner is not now pregnant.
12. For sixty days immediately preceding the filing of the Petition for Dissolution of Marriage, the minor child of the parties resided with Petitioner and Respondent at __________________ Dr., City, County, State.
13. The Petitioner requests that the Court award the parties joint care and custody of the minor child with the child's principal residence being with Petitioner.
14. There have been no arrangements made as to the custody and support of the parties' child.
15. The Petitioner has not participated in any capacity in any other litigation concerning the custody of the child in this or any other state; Petitioner has no information of any custody proceeding concerning the child pending in a court of this or any other state; and Petitioner knows of no person not a party to these proceedings who has physical custody of the child or claims to have custody or visitation rights with respect to the child.
16. That Respondent is hereby notified pursuant to Section _______________ that he may not terminate coverage for Petitioner or any minor child born of the marriage under any existing policy of health, dental, or vision insurance.
17. That the Court make provision for the maintenance of a health benefit plan for the minor child and for payment of non-covered medical, orthodontic, health, dental and optical expenses incurred with regard to the minor child all pursuant to the provisions of Section ________________.
18. That Petitioner requests that all child support payments be made through the Family Support Payment Center, P.O. Box ___________, City, State, ZIP.
19. That this Court order the Sheriff or other law enforcement office to enforce this Court's custody and/or visitation orders.
20. That this Court order terms of custody and visitation pursuant to the terms contained in Petitioner's Parenting Plan for Special Needs.
21. That this Court order Child Support pursuant to Petitioner's Child Support Chart for Special Needs.

WHEREFORE, Petitioner prays for a Judgment dissolving the marriage of the parties; that the Court set aside to Petitioner and Respondent their separate non-marital property; that the marital property and marital debts be divided in a fair and equitable manner; that the Court award custody of the minor child pursuant to Petitioner's Parenting Plan for Special Needs; that the Court order Respondent to pay to Petitioner child support pursuant to Petitioner's Child Support Chart for Special Needs retroactive to the date of filing; and for further and different relief as this Court deems just and proper in the premises.

STATE OF ______________

ss.

COUNTY OF ____________

Comes now ________________, Petitioner, being first duly sworn according to law, and states that she has read the foregoing Petition for Dissolution of Marriage and states that the facts contained therein are true and correct according to her best knowledge, information, and belief.

____
Petitioner

Subscribed and sworn to before me this _____ day of ___________, 20___

____
Notary Public

My commission expires:

Respectfully submitted,
[Attorney Signature Block]
ATTORNEY FOR PETITIONER

NOTICE TO PETITIONER AND RESPONDENT

Please take notice that pursuant to Section _________ of the ______________ Statutes, from the date of filing the petition for dissolution of marriage or legal separation, no party shall terminate coverage during the pendency of the proceeding for any other party or any minor child of the marriage under any existing policy of health, dental, or vision insurance.

3. SAMPLE STATEMENT OF INCOME AND EXPENSES

IN THE FAMILY COURT OF ____________ COUNTY
STATE OF ______________

In Re the Marriage of:	)	
	)	
____________________,	)	
_____________,	)	
Petitioner,	)	
	)	Case No. ____________________
____________________,	)	Division: ________
_____________,	)	
Respondent.	)	

STATEMENT OF INCOME AND EXPENSES OF PETITIONER—
SPECIAL NEEDS CASE

1. **Income**
   A. Name and Address of Employer: ____

Gross Wages or Salary and Commission Each Pay Period $_____________

PAID: __ Weekly Biweekly Semimonthly Monthly

Number of Dependents Claimed:

B. Payroll Deductions:
FICA (Social Security Tax $_____
Federal Withholding Tax $_____
State Withholding Tax $______
City Earnings Tax (If Applicable) $______
Union Dues $________
Others:
$____
$____
$____
Total Deductions Each Pay Period $_____
Net Take Home Pay Each Pay Period $______

Additional Income from Rentals, Dividends and Business Enterprises, Social Security, A.F.D.C. V.A. Benefits, Pensions, Annuities, Bonuses, "Commissions and All Other Sources" (give monthly average and list sources of income).

$ ______ Average Monthly Total ....

C. Total Average Net Monthly Income $

D. Your Share of the Gross Income Shown on Last Year's Federal Income Tax Return $ ___________

2. Expenses Required to Maintain Previous Standard of Living Stated on a MONTHLY Average

A. Rent or Mortgage Payments

B. Utilities

1. Gas
2. Water
3. Electricity
4. Telephone
5. Trash Service

C. Automobiles

1. Gas and Oil
2. Maintenance (Routine)
3. Taxes and License
4. Payment on the Auto Loan

D. Insurance

1. Life
2. Health & Accident
3. Disability
4. Homeowners (If Not Included in Mortgage Payment)
5. Automobile

E. Total Payment Installments Contracts

F. Child Support Paid to Others for Children Not in Your Custody (Excluding Children of This Marriage)

G. Maintenance or Alimony (Excluding Petitioner or Respondent Herein)

H. Church and Charitable Contributions

I. Other Living Expenses (Total of Items 1–7 Listed Below)

	YOURS	CHILDREN IN YOUR CUSTODY
1. Food		
2. Clothing		
3. Medical Care, Dental Care and Drugs		
4. Recreation		
5. Laundry and Cleaning		
6. Barber Shop or Beauty Shop		
7. School and Books		

J. Day Care Center or Babysitter

K. All Other Expenses Not Presently Identified (Give as Monthly Average)

L. Special Needs Expenses (Give as Monthly Average)

1. Medical Treatment
2. Doctors
3. Therapy
4. Other Medical Expenses

5. Equipment
6. Supplies
7. Training
8. Transportation
9. Caregiver
10. Companion
11. Professionals
12. Medication
13. Supplements
14. Dietary Modifications
15. Household Modifications
16. Daily/Personal Care Items
17. Respite Care
18. Activities
19. Meals
20. Sensory Items
21. Other Special Needs Items
22. Total Special Needs Items

M. Total Average Monthly Expenses

STATE OF ______________

SS

COUNTY OF ____________

COMES NOW_________, being of lawful age and after being duly sworn, states that Affiant has read the foregoing **STATEMENT OF INCOME AND EXPENSES**, and that the facts therein are true and correct according to the Affiant's best knowledge and belief.

____

Affiant

Subscribed and sworn to before me, the undersigned Notary Public, on this ___day of ______, 20___.

____

Notary Public

My commission expires:

4. SAMPLE ANSWER TO PETITION FOR DISSOLUTION

IN THE FAMILY COURT OF __________________ COUNTY
STATE OF __________________

In Re the Marriage of:	)	
	)	
__________________,	)	
____________,	)	
Petitioner,	)	
vs.	)	Case No. __________________
__________________,	)	Division: _______
____________,	)	
Respondent.	)	

ANSWER TO PETITION FOR DISSOLUTION

Comes now the Respondent, ______________________, by and through his attorney, ________________________, and in Answer to the Petition for Dissolution of Marriage, states to the Court as follows:

1. Respondent admits each and every allegation contained in paragraphs 1, 2, 3, 4, 5, 6, 7, 8, and 9 of the Petition, including every subpart thereof.
2. In further response to paragraph 4 of said Petition, Respondent states that the minor child, ___________________________, has **special needs**, namely_____________, therefore the use of the standard child support guidelines and standard parenting plan would be unjust and inappropriate.

WHEREFORE, Respondent having fully answered Petitioner's Petition for Dissolution of Marriage prays the Court find the marriage of the parties to be irretrievably broken and enter a Judgment dissolving the marriage; that the Court set aside to Petitioner and Respondent their separate non-marital property; that the marital property and marital debts be divided in a fair and equitable manner; that the Court award the parties joint care and custody of the minor child with the child's principal residence being with Petitioner; that the Court order child support pursuant to Respondent's Model Child Support Chart for Special Needs and visitation pursuant to Respondent's Model Parenting Plan for Special Needs; and for further and different relief as this Court deems just and proper in the premises.

STATE OF _____________

ss.

COUNTY OF ___________

Comes now ____________________, Respondent, being first duly sworn according to law, and states that the facts in the foregoing are true and correct to his best knowledge and belief.

____
Respondent

Subscribed and sworn to before me this _____ day of ___________, 20___

____
Notary Public

My commission expires:

Respectfully submitted,
[Attorney Signature Block]
ATTORNEY FOR PETITIONER

CERTIFICATE OF SERVICE

I hereby certify that a true and correct copy of the foregoing was deposited in the U.S. Mail, postage prepaid to:
Opposing Counsel's Name, Street Address, City, State ZIP
this ______ day of ________________, 20___.

____
Attorney for Respondent

5. SAMPLE COUNTER-PETITION FOR DISSOLUTION

IN THE FAMILY COURT OF ________________ COUNTY
STATE OF ________________

In Re the Marriage of:	)	
	)	
________________,	)	
___________,	)	
Petitioner,	)	
vs.	)	Case No. ________________
________________,	)	Division: _______
___________,	)	
Respondent.	)	

COUNTER-PETITION FOR DISSOLUTION OF MARRIAGE

Comes now the Respondent, ________________, and for his cause of action, states to the Court as follows:

1. Respondent has been a resident of the State of ___________ for _____ days/months immediately preceding the filing of this Petition for Dissolution, and has been a resident of ___________ County, _________, for _____ days/months immediately preceding the filing of this Petition for Dissolution.
2. Petitioner has been a resident of the State of _________ for _____ days/months immediately preceding the filing of this Petition for Dissolution, and has been a resident of __________ County, __________, for _____ days/months immediately preceding the filing of this Petition for Dissolution.
3. Respondent is currently residing at ________________Road, City, State. Respondent is currently employed by ________________.
4. Petitioner is currently residing at ______________ Dr., City, County, State. Petitioner is currently employed by ____________________.
5. Respondent states that the parties were married on Month, Day, Year, in City, County, State, and that said marriage was registered in County, State.
6. Petitioner and Respondent are residing in the same residence, but are no longer living together as husband and wife, and separated on Month, Day, Year.
7. Respondent states that neither Petitioner nor Respondent are members of the armed forces of the United States of America on active duty and are not entitled to any benefits or immunities of the Servicemembers Civil Relief Act.
8. Respondent states that there is no reasonable likelihood that the marriage can be preserved and, therefore, the marriage is irretrievably broken.
9. Petitioner and Respondent have acquired certain property and certain debts during the marriage but have not yet entered into a property settlement agreement.

10. Respondent states that there is one unemancipated child born of this marriage, to-wit:
    Child's Name, DOB ______________
    AND THAT SUCH CHILD HAS SPECIAL NEEDS, NAMELY __________.
11. That Petitioner is not now pregnant.
12. For sixty days immediately preceding the filing of the Petition for Dissolution of Marriage, the minor child of the parties resided with Respondent and Petitioner at __________________ Dr., City, County, State.
13. The Respondent requests that the Court award the parties joint care and custody of the minor child with the child's principal residence being with Respondent.
14. There have been no arrangements made as to the custody and support of the parties' child.
15. The Respondent has not participated in any capacity in any other litigation concerning the custody of the child in this or any other state; Respondent has no information of any custody proceeding concerning the child pending in a court of this or any other state; and Respondent knows of no person not a party to these proceedings who has physical custody of the child or claims to have custody or visitation rights with respect to the child.
16. That Petitioner is hereby notified pursuant to Section _______________ that she may not terminate coverage for Respondent or any minor child born of the marriage under any existing policy of health, dental, or vision insurance.
17. That the Court make provision for the maintenance of a health benefit plan for the minor child and for payment of non-covered medical, orthodontic, health, dental, and optical expenses incurred with regard to the minor child all pursuant to the provisions of Section _________________.
18. That Respondent requests that all child support payments be made through the Family Support Payment Center, P.O. Box ___________, City, State, ZIP.
19. That this Court order the Sheriff or other law enforcement office to enforce this Court's custody and/or visitation orders.
20. That this Court order terms of custody and visitation pursuant to the terms contained in Respondent's Parenting Plan for Special Needs.
21. That this Court order Child Support pursuant to Respondent's Child Support Chart for Special Needs.

WHEREFORE, Respondent prays for a Judgment dissolving the marriage of the parties; that the Court set aside to Petitioner and Respondent their separate non-marital property; that the marital property and marital debts be divided in a fair and equitable manner; that the Court award custody of the minor child pursuant to Respondent's Parenting Plan for Special Needs; that the Court order Petitioner to pay to Respondent child support pursuant to Respondent's Child Support Chart for Special Needs retroactive to the date of filing; and for further and different relief as this Court deems just and proper in the premises.

STATE OF ______________

ss.

COUNTY OF ____________

Comes now ______________________, Respondent, being first duly sworn according to law, and states that the facts in the foregoing are true and correct to his best knowledge and belief.

____
Respondent

Subscribed and sworn to before me this _____ day of ___________, 20___

____
Notary Public

My commission expires:

Respectfully submitted,
[Attorney Signature Block]
ATTORNEY FOR PETITIONER

CERTIFICATE OF SERVICE

I hereby certify that a true and correct copy of the foregoing was deposited in the U.S. Mail, postage prepaid to:

Opposing Counsel's Name, Street Address, City, State ZIP
this ______ day of ________________, 20___.

____
Attorney for Respondent

NOTICE TO PETITIONER AND RESPONDENT

Please take notice that pursuant to Section _________ of the _____________ Statutes, from the date of filing the petition for dissolution of marriage or legal separation, <u>no party</u> shall terminate coverage during the pendency of the proceeding for any other party or any minor child of the marriage under any existing policy of health, dental, or vision insurance.

6. SAMPLE CHILD SUPPORT CALCULATION

In re the Marriage of: ____

Form 14SN—CHILD SUPPORT AMOUNT CALCULATION WORKSHEET

CHILDREN	DATE OF BIRTH	CHILDREN	DATE OF BIRTH
Name		Name	

	Parent Receiving Support	Parent Paying Support	Combined
1. MONTHLY GROSS INCOME	$	$	
a. Court ordered maintenance being received	$	$	
2. ADJUSTMENTS (per month)	($)	($)	
a. Other court or administratively ordered child support being paid			
b. Court ordered maintenance being paid	($)	($)	
c. Support obligation for other children in parent's primary physical custody	($)	($)	
3. ADJUSTED MONTHLY GROSS INCOME (sum of lines 1 and 1a, minus lines 2a, 2b, and 2c).	$	$	$
4. PROPORTIONATE SHARE OF COMBINED ADJUSTED MONTHLY GROSS INCOME (each parent's line 3 income divided by combined line 3 income).	%	%	
5. BASIC CHILD SUPPORT AMOUNT (from support chart using combined line 3 income)			$
6. ADDITIONAL CHILD-REARING COSTS (per month)	$		
a. Reasonable work-related child care costs of the parent receiving support less any child care tax credit			
b. Reasonable work-related child care costs of the parent paying support		$	
c. Health insurance costs for the children who are subjects of this proceeding	$	$	

d. Uninsured extraordinary medical costs (agreed by parents or ordered by court)	$	$	
e. Other extraordinary child rearing costs (agreed by parents or ordered by court)	$	$	
f. Special needs expenses and costs: therapy equipment medications supplements dietary costs sensory items respite care other reasonable items			
7. TOTAL ADDITIONAL CHILD SUPPORT COSTS (sum of lines 6a, 6b, 6c, 6d, and 6e)	$	$	$
8. TOTAL COMBINED CHILD SUPPORT COSTS (sum of line 5 and combined line 7)			$
9. EACH PARENT'S SUPPORT OBLIGATION (multiply line 8 by each parent's line 4)	$	$	
10. CREDIT FOR ADDITIONAL CHILD-REARING COSTS (line 7 of parent paying support)		$	
11. ADJUSTMENTS FOR A PORTION OF THE AMOUNTS OF EXPENDED DURING PERIODS OF OVERNIGHT VISITATION OR CUSTODY (multiply line 5 by ___%)		$	
12. ADJUSTMENT FOR RESPITE CARE AND OTHER EXPENSES IF VISITATION IS NOT REGULARLY EXERCISED:			
13. PRESUMED CHILD SUPPORT AMOUNT (line 9 minus line 10 and 11 plus line 12).		**($)**	
PREPARED BY: Attorney for			
EXHIBIT # __________			

7. MOTION FOR APPOINTMENT OF GUARDIAN AD LITEM

IN THE FAMILY COURT OF ____________________ COUNTY
STATE OF ____________________

In Re the Marriage of:	)	
	)	
____________________,	)	
______________,	)	
Petitioner,	)	
vs.	)	Case No. ____________________
____________________,	)	Division: ________
______________,	)	
Respondent.	)	

MOTION FOR APPOINTMENT OF GUARDIAN AD LITEM

Comes now the Petitioner, ________________________, by and through his attorney, __________________________, and respectfully requests the Court appoint a Guardian Ad Litem for the minor children:

CHILD ONE
CHILD TWO
for the following reasons:

_____ credible allegations of child neglect
_____ credible allegations of child abuse
_____ special needs of the child(ren), specifically: ____________________
I AM/AM NOT AWARE OF ANY SPECIAL NEEDS OF THE CHILD(REN), SPECIFICALLY: ______________________________
____
_____ other

This Motion for Appointment of Guardian Ad Litem is supported by a sworn affidavit, a true and correct copy of which is attached hereto and marked as Exhibit 1.

Respectfully submitted,
[Attorney Signature Block]
ATTORNEY FOR PETITIONER

CERTIFICATE OF SERVICE

I hereby certify that a true and correct copy of the foregoing was deposited in the U.S. Mail, postage prepaid to:

Opposing Counsel's Name, Street Address, City, State ZIP
this ______ day of ________________, 20___.

____
Attorney for Respondent

8. ORDER APPOINTING GUARDIAN AD LITEM

IN THE FAMILY COURT OF ___________________ COUNTY
STATE OF ___________________

In Re the Marriage of:	)	
	)	
___________________,	)	
____________,	)	
Petitioner,	)	
vs.	)	Case No. ___________________
___________________,	)	Division: _______
____________,	)	
Respondent.	)	

ORDER APPOINTING GUARDIAN AD LITEM

IT IS HEREBY ORDERED that ___________________________ shall be appointed as Guardian Ad Litem for the minor children:

CHILD ONE
CHILD TWO
for the following reasons:

_____ credible allegations of child neglect
_____ credible allegations of child abuse
_____ special needs of the child(ren), specifically: _______________________
THE PARTIES STATE THAT THEY ARE/ARE NOT AWARE OF ANY SPECIAL NEEDS OF THE CHILD(REN), SPECIFICALLY:
____
____
_____ other

SO ORDERED:

____
The Honorable ______________________

9-A. SAMPLE SPECIAL NEEDS PARENTING PLAN—CHILD/CHILDREN WITH SPECIAL NEEDS

IN THE FAMILY COURT OF __________________ COUNTY
STATE OF __________________

In Re the Marriage of:	)	
	)	
__________________,	)	
____________,	)	
Petitioner,	)	
vs.	)	Case No. __________________
__________________,	)	Division: _______
____________,	)	
Respondent.	)	

CONSENT PARENTING PLAN FOR SPECIAL NEEDS

For purposes of this Parenting Plan, "Minor Children" refers to CHILD ONE, born Month, Day, Year, and CHILD TWO, born Month, Day, Year, either collectively or either child separately, as is appropriate.

Mother and Father shall have joint legal custody and Father shall have sole physical custody of said minor children.

Father's residence shall be designated as the primary residence of the minor children for mailing and educational purposes.

CUSTODY PARENTING TIME SCHEDULE

Due to the special needs of the children, the standard visitation schedule is not in the best interests of the children. The girls are 12-year-old twins. One of the children, CHILD ONE, has cerebral palsy. She receives intensive therapy for many hours every week, and by necessity, her life is extremely structured.

The two most important aspects of this Parenting Plan are:

- The best interests of the children, and
- Cooperation of the parents.

CUSTODY, VISITATION AND RESIDENTIAL TIME FOR EACH CHILD WITH EACH PARENT SHALL BE AT SUCH TIMES AS THE PARTIES SHALL AGREE. The parties are strongly encouraged to work together cooperatively and flexibly to reach by amicable agreement such custody, visitation, and residential times as shall be in the best interests of the children and keeping in mind their special needs. In the event the parties cannot agree, Mother shall have custody, visitation, or residential time as set forth below and Father shall have all other time as his custody, visitation, or residential time.

EACH PARENT IS STRONGLY ENCOURAGED TO PUT THE CHILDREN FIRST AND TO MAKE EVERY REASONABLE EFFORT TO MEET THE UNIQUE NEEDS OF THE SPECIAL NEEDS CHILD(REN). Each parent is strongly encouraged to take time every week to spend one-on-one time with the special needs child and to spend one-on-one time with the non-special needs child.

WEEKDAY VISITATION

Mother may come to Father's house to visit the children during the evenings whenever her schedule permits, as long as the parties shall so agree. In the event the parties cannot agree upon the night or nights of this visitation, Mother shall visit the children at Father's house or pick them up at Father's house on Wednesday evenings. Mother shall visit/pick up children at 6:00 pm and return them to Father's house by 7:15 pm, when she is welcome to participate in their bedtime routine, which usually lasts until 8:00 pm. Mother may extend this weekday visitation to overnight visitation. In the event the parties agree upon overnight visitation during the week, Mother shall either return the children to Father's house the next morning or take them to their morning activity, as agreed to by the parties.

WEEKENDS

The children are involved in many activities due to their special needs. These activities require great flexibility and cooperation by the parents regarding the weekend visitation. The general goal is that Mother shall have the children for approximately half of the weekends, although this will often not be every other weekend. The parties shall frequently consult each other regarding the scheduled activities and arrange the weekend visitation around the schedules and best interests of the children. If the parties cannot agree, Mother shall have visitation of the children every other weekend beginning at 6:00 pm on Friday through and ending at 6:00 pm on Sunday, beginning the weekend following the date of the judgment. If either parent's holiday weekend, as set forth below, conflicts with this, then the parent losing their regular weekend shall receive the other parent's next regular weekend to thereafter be followed by the original schedule so that each would have two consecutive weekends.

SUMMER

The children attend summer school for six weeks every year. This usually runs from June through August. There is a week or two between the regular school year letting out and the start of summer school, and there is a week or two between the end of summer school and the beginning of the next school year. During these weeks, the girls usually attend a special needs summer day camp. It is important for the girls to attend summer school. If they are registered for summer school but do not attend consistently, they will not be eligible to attend in subsequent years.

Mother may exercise periods of summer visitation during the summer regardless of whether it is during the weeks of summer school, as long as she shall take the children to summer school if her time periods fall during those weeks.

Since these arrangements must be made well in advance, Mother shall notify Father of her choice of option in writing by March 1st every year.

Mother may have liberal summer visitation as the parties shall agree. In the event the parties cannot agree, subject to the above provisions, Mother shall have three weeks each summer (to be divided into three seven-consecutive-day periods) to coincide with the children's school summer vacation. Mother may select the first week of this summer vacation by notifying Father of same (each notification herein to be in writing) by February 1st of each year, one week may then be excluded by Father by February 15th and then the next week may be selected by Mother by March lst, one more week may then be excluded by Father by March 15th, the final week may be selected by Mother by April lst. Father's excluded weeks shall prevail over Mother's weekend and weekday periods set forth above.

HOLIDAYS AND SPECIAL DAYS

1. Holiday and special day custody shall prevail over weekend, weekday and summer vacation set forth above. Birthday periods shall not prevail when in conflict with other Holidays and Special Days.
2. Mother shall have the minor children on her birthday and on Mother's Day of each year from 9:00 am to 9:00 pm; plus "Holiday Group A" in even-numbered years and "Holiday Group B" in odd-numbered years.
3. Father shall have the minor children on his birthday and on Father's Dayof each year from 9:00 am to 9:00 pm; plus "Holiday Group A" in odd-numbered years and "Holiday Group B" in even-numbered years.
4. Mother and Father are encouraged to communicate to attempt to arrange a combined event/activity for the children's birthday. In the event they cannot agree, the following provisions regarding the children's birthday shall apply.
5. Due to the serious special needs of the children, the conditions stated in the above paragraphs concerning WEEKDAY, WEEKEND, and SUMMER visitation shall apply to HOLIDAY GROUPS A & B.

HOLIDAY GROUP A

1. PRESIDENT'S DAY/WASHINGTON'S BIRTHDAY (OBSERVED) weekend from 5:00 pm the Friday prior to 8:00 am the following Tuesday.
2. A period of 7 (seven) days during the children's school spring break, the exact days to be selected and notice given in writing to the other parent by February lst.
3. INDEPENDENCE DAY — If July 4th falls on a: (a) Tuesday, Wednesday or Thursday from 5:00 pm on July 3rd until 9:00 am on July 5th (b) Friday or Saturday from 5:00 pm on the Thursday before until 9:00 am on the following Monday, (c) Sunday or Monday from 5:00 pm on the Friday before until 9:00 am on the following Tuesday.
4. HALLOWEEN (October 31st) night from 4:00 pm until 9:00 am the following day.
5. CHRISTMAS VACATION from December 25th beginning at 10:00 am through 9:00 am on December 31st.
6. Each child's birthday from 9:00 am until 9:00 am the following day.

HOLIDAY GROUP B

1. MARTIN LUTHER KING weekend from 5:00 pm the Friday prior through 8:00 am the following Tuesday.
2. MEMORIAL DAY weekend from 5:00 pm the Friday prior through 8:00 am the following Tuesday.
3. LABOR DAY weekend from 5:00 pm the Friday prior through 8:00 am the following Tuesday.
4. THANKSGIVING weekend from 5:00 pm the Wednesday prior through 8:00 am the following Monday.
5. CHRISTMAS VACATION from 5:00 pm the day the children's school Christmas vacation begins through 10:00 am on December 25th and December 31st beginning at 9:00 am through 8:00 am the day the children's school Christmas vacation ends.
6. The day prior to each child's birthday beginning at 9:00 am through 9:00 am the day of the birthday.

The serious special needs of the children requires that Mother and Father be far more cooperative and flexible than the parents of children without special needs.

EXCHANGES

[X] When school is in session:

Exchanges of all children from Mother to Father shall occur at:
[ ] Residence of Mother [X] Residence of Father [ ] School
[ ] Other Location-Parents currently reside at same location, exchanges not applicable.

Exchanges of all children from Father to Mother shall occur at:
[ ] Residence of Mother [X] Residence of Father [ ] School
[ ] Other Location

[ ] When school is not in session or if all children are not school age:
Exchange of all children from Mother to Father shall occur at:
[ ] Residence of Mother [X] Residence of Father
[ ] Other Location

Exchange of all children from Father to Mother shall occur at:
[ ] Residence of Mother [X] Residence of Father
[ ] Other Location

[ ] If an exchange occurs at a location other than a parent's residence, the parent scheduled to have time with the children shall pick up and return the children to the specified location and the other parent shall be responsible for assuring the children are at the specified location for pick up, unless other arrangements are described.

TRANSPORTATION

Transportation arrangements for all children for all scheduled parenting time(s) including weekdays, weekends, holidays, and vacation times shall be as follows:

[X] Mother shall be responsible for transportation of the children at the beginning of the visit. Mother shall be responsible for transportation of the children at the end of the visit.

Mother and Father shall share responsibility for all transportation of the children, including cost, as follows:

[ ] Extraordinary transportation costs (bus, taxi, train, airfare) shall be the responsibility of [ ] Mother [ ] Father [ ] Shared % Mother % Father

CHANGES

The parents' schedules and commitments may require occasional changes in the parenting time schedule. Parents shall attempt to agree on any changes, but the parent receiving a request for a change shall have the final decision on whether the change shall occur.

The parent making the request may make such request
[X] in person [X] by phone [X] in writing to the other parent [X] other—email

The request for change shall be made no later than:
[ ] 24 hours [X] one week [ ] two weeks [ ] other
prior to the date of the requested change.

The parent receiving the request shall respond no later than:
[ ] 24 hours [ ] one week [ ] two weeks [X] other - 72 hours after receiving the requested change.

The response to the request may be made
[X] in person [X] by phone [X] in writing to the other parent [X] other—email
Any parent requesting a change of schedule shall be responsible for any additional child care or transportation costs resulting from the change.

Mother and Father shall cooperate to allow the children to meet their therapeutic, school, and social commitments.

TELEPHONE CONTACTS

Each parent shall have reasonable access to all children by telephone during any period in which the children are with the other parent, unless otherwise specified.

RELOCATION

Absent exigent circumstances as determined by a court with jurisdiction, you, as a party to this action, are ordered to notify, in writing by certified mail, return receipt requested, and at least 60 days prior to the proposed relocation, each party to this action of any proposed relocation of the principal residence of the children, including the following information: (1) the intended new residence, including the specific address and mailing address, if known, and if not known, the city; (2) the home telephone number of the new residence, if known; (3) the date of the intended move or proposed relocation; (4) a brief statement of the specific reasons for the proposed relocation of the children; and (5) a proposal for a revised schedule of custody or visitation with the children. Your obligation to provide this information to each party continues as long as you or any other party by virtue of this order is entitled to custody of a child covered by this order. Your failure to obey the order of this court regarding the proposed relocation may result in further litigation to enforce such order, including contempt of court. In addition, your failure to notify a party of a relocation of the child may be considered in a proceeding to modify custody or visitation with the children. Reasonable costs and attorney fees shall be assessed against you if you fail to give the required notice.

LEGAL CUSTODY

Legal Custody: The parties shall agree before making any final decisions on issues affecting the growth and development of the children; including, but not limited to, choice of religious upbringing, choice of child care provider, choice of school, course of study, special tutoring, extracurricular activities including, but not limited to, music, art, dance, and other cultural lessons or activities and gymnastics or other athletic activities, choice of camp or other comparable summer activity, nonemergency medical and dental treatment, psychological, psychiatric, or like treatment or counseling, the choice of particular health care providers, the extent of any travel away from home, part or full-time employment, purchase or operation of a motor vehicle, contraception and sex education, and decisions relating to actual or potential litigation on behalf of the children. However, each parent may make decisions regarding the day-to-day care and control of the children and in emergencies affecting the health and safety of the children while the children are residing with him or her. The parents shall endeavor, whenever reasonable, to be consistent in such day-to-day decisions.

Communication: Each parent shall ensure that the other parent is provided with copies of all communications or information received from a child's school, and if a second copy of the communication is not provided by the school shall make a copy for with him the other parent. Each parent shall notify the other of any activity such as school conferences, programs, sporting, and other special events etc., where parents are invited to attend and each shall encourage and welcome the presence of the other.

Children Not Involved in Court or Financial Communications: The parties shall not talk about adult issues, parenting matters, financial issues, and other court-related topics, when the children are present. Such discussions shall not be had during custody exchanges of the children or during telephone visits. The children shall not be used to carry such messages, written communication or child support payments between the parents.

Medical Care Information: Each parent shall have the authority to seek any emergency medical treatment for the children when in his or her custody. Each shall advise the other of any medical emergency or serious illness or injury suffered by the minor children as soon as possible after learning of the same, and shall give the other parent details of the emergency, injury or illness and the name and telephone numbers of all treating doctors. Each parent shall inform the other before any routine medical care, treatment or examination by a health care provider including said provider's name and telephone number. Each party shall direct all doctors involved in the care and treatment of the minor children to give the other parent all information regarding any injury or illness and the medical treatment or examination, if requested. For purposes of this paragraph, a serious injury or illness is one which requires a child (1) to be confined to home for more than 48 hours; or (2) to be admitted to, or treated at, a hospital or surgical facility; or (3) to receive any type of general anesthesia or invasive surgical procedure or test.

Child Care Provider: If both parents will need to use a child care provider during periods of custody or visitation they shall use the same child care provider, unless the distances between their residences or places of employment make the use of the same child care provider unreasonable.

Access to Records: Each parent shall be entitled to immediate access from the other or from a third party to records and information pertaining to the children including, but not limited to, medical, dental, health, child care, school or educational records; and each shall take whatever steps are necessary to ensure that the other parent has such access.

Activities Not to Conflict with Custody or Visitation: The parties shall enroll the children in activities, particularly outside of school, that, to the extent possible, are scheduled at times and places that avoid interruption and disruption of the custody or visitation time of the other party unless consented to by that parent. The special needs of the children require far greater cooperation and flexibility by the parents than is required of the parents of children without special needs.

Resolution of Disputes: If the parties fail to agree on the interpretation of the Parenting Plan, or are unable to agree upon a final decision on issues affecting the growth and development or health and safety of the children, they shall submit the dispute to a mutually agreed-upon Special Needs Coordinator who shall hear and arbitrate the issue. In the event they are not able to agree on a Special Needs Coordinator they shall each select a Special Needs Coordinator from the list of approved Special Needs Coordinators maintained by the ___________ County Family Court and the two Special Needs Coordinators shall determine who shall arbitrate the case. The Special Needs Coordinator shall be a quick and informal tribunal to arbitrate issues which may arise in the future including, but not limited to, increasing or decreasing child support; changes in therapy, treatment, education, custody, and/or visitation; and issues relating to expenses.

CHILD SUPPORT AND OTHER EXPENSES

Due to the special needs of the children, the application of Standard Child Support Guidelines would be inappropriate and/or unjust. The initial amount of child support shall be $_________ per month, payable by Mother to Father. This amount shall be modifiable. This is the base amount, which DOES include the current amount for nutritional supplements/regimens, and DOES NOT include additional support for therapy, activities, camps, or other expenses necessitated by their special needs. Parents shall pay for these additional items based upon their proportional share of income. Parents acknowledge that future nutritional supplements/regimens may involve an increased cost, and parents agree to pay such increased cost based upon their proportional income.

Child support shall terminate for CHILD TWO in accordance with § _______ [Statutes of state of _______________]

The Parties recognize that due to the special needs of CHILD ONE, child support may not terminate at age 18 or at any particular age and may continue if the child is physically or mentally incapacitated from supporting herself and insolvent and unmarried as per § _______ [Statutes of state of _______________].

In addition, each party will continue to contribute to child support as long as they are able to provide child support.

The child support shall be paid 50% on the 1st and 50% on the 15th day of each month.

HEALTH CARE COSTS

The children are currently covered by _______________ medical insurance through Father's employer. Both parents shall cooperate to keep the children covered under this insurance or under another plan. In the event it becomes appropriate to obtain other health insurance for the children, the parents shall pay the expense of such coverage based upon their proportionate share of income. Both parents shall cooperate to provide insurance ID cards to the other parent as applicable, and to complete all forms required by the coverage.

Unless both parties have agreed to use a health care provider that is not covered by the health benefit plan, if a parent incurs an expense to a health care provider that is not covered by the health benefit plan that would have been covered, or covered at a more favorable rate, if a provider included in the plan had been used, then that parent shall pay seventy-five percent (75%) and the other parent twenty-five percent (25%) of the uncovered expenses.

"Health expenses" shall be defined in accordance with Internal Revenue Code (1987) § 213 "Medical, Dental, etc., Expenses" or any other section enacted in replacement, in addition or in substitution thereof, and/or any Internal Revenue Regulation including, but not limited to, § 1.213-1 or any relevant Regulation enacted in replacement, in addition or in substitution thereof, or any relevant Treasury Decision, Regulation or any Revenue Ruling defining those types or kinds of medical costs that are deductible under the Internal Revenue Code, and shall also include orthodontia and optical care (including, but not limited to, prescription eyeglasses or contact lenses and eye examinations conducted by an optician, optometrist, or ophthalmologist), treatment, and appliances. Psychological and counseling expenses shall be paid as the parties agree, or absent agreement to the extent they are included as "Health Expenses" defined above or are determined by the child's case manager to be in the best interests of the child.

All health expenses incurred on behalf of the children and not paid by the health benefit plan shall be paid based upon each parent's proportionate share of income. The health expenses covered by this paragraph are not limited to just the usual medical, dental, orthodontic, optical, and psychological expenses of children without special needs. Due to the special needs of the children, they have and are expected to continue to have extraordinary medical, therapeutic and other expenses, which shall be paid by the parents based upon proportionate share of income, in addition to the base amount of child support.

The Parties recognize that due to the special needs of CHILD ONE, payment of health care costs may not terminate at age 18 or at any particular age and may continue if the child is physically or mentally incapacitated from supporting herself and insolvent and unmarried as per § _______ [Statutes of state of _______________].

In addition, each party will continue to contribute to health care as long as they are able to provide health care.

FOR EACH CHILD WITH SPECIAL NEEDS, ATTACH AN EXHIBIT CONTAINING A SUMMARY OF:

[ ] Diagnosis
[ ] Doctors, therapists, and other professionals
[ ] Child's current daily schedule and routine
[ ] Child's current therapy plan
[ ] Summary of how special needs affect the child's daily life
[ ] Itemization and explanation of the costs involved in or caused by the special needs
[ ] Who is the primary caregiver of the child
[ ] Primary caregiver's daily schedule
[ ] Statement as to the impact of transitions and schedule changes on the child
[ ] List of equipment and special items needed by the child and the location of such items
[ ] Suggested physical custody arrangement
[ ] Suggested legal custody arrangement
[ ] Suggested visitation—daily, weekly, weekends, holidays, summers, and special days

EDUCATION AND EXTRAORDINARY EXPENSES

Due to the special needs of the children, they currently incur and are expected to continue to incur extraordinary educational and other expenses. These shall be paid by the parties based upon their proportionate share of income. If the parties cannot agree on the extraordinary expenses for education, therapy, activities, equipment, supplements, and/or other items, the parties agree to pay (based upon their proportionate share of income) for the items determined by the child's/children's Special Needs Coordinator to be in the best interest of the child/children.

_______________________   _______________________
Petitioner   Respondent

_______________________   _______________________
Attorney for Petitioner   Attorney for Respondent

[Adapted from Special Needs Parenting Plan coauthored with Kieran Coyne, attorney in St. Louis, Missouri.]

9-A. SAMPLE SPECIAL NEEDS PARENTING PLAN—PARENT WITH SPECIAL NEEDS

IN THE FAMILY COURT OF ________________ COUNTY
STATE OF ________________

In Re the Marriage of:	)	
	)	
________________,	)	
____________,	)	
Petitioner,	)	
vs.	)	Case No. ________________
________________,	)	Division: _______
____________,	)	
Respondent.	)	

CONSENT PARENTING PLAN—PARENT WITH SPECIAL NEEDS

Mother and Father shall have joint legal custody and Mother shall have sole physical custody of said minor child. Mother's residence shall be designated as the primary residence of the minor child for mailing and educational purposes.

CUSTODY PARENTING TIME SCHEDULE

Due to the special needs of the Father, the standard visitation schedule is not in the best interests of the child. The Father has severe epilepsy, currently not controlled by medication. He experiences frequent seizures without warning. He cannot legally operate a motor vehicle. He relies on public transportation, ride-share services, and taxicabs for transportation. At the time of this court action, the child is a nine-year-old boy.

The two most important aspects of this Parenting Plan are:

- The best interests of the child, and
- Cooperation of the parents.

CUSTODY, VISITATION AND RESIDENTIAL TIME OF THE CHILD WITH EACH PARENT SHALL BE AT SUCH TIMES AS THE PARTIES SHALL AGREE. The parties are strongly encouraged to work together cooperatively and flexibly to reach by amicable agreement such custody, visitation and residential times as shall be in the best interests of the child and keeping in mind the Father's special needs. In the event the parties cannot agree, Father shall have custody, visitation, or residential time as set forth below, and Mother shall have all other time as his custody, visitation, or residential time.

EACH PARENT IS STRONGLY ENCOURAGED TO PUT THE CHILD FIRST AND TO MAKE EVERY REASONABLE EFFORT TO MEET THE UNIQUE NEEDS OF THE FATHER DUE TO HIS SPECIAL NEEDS.

FATHER CURRENTLY HAS AN ELECTRONIC DEVICE HE WEARS ON HIS WRIST OR ON A LANYARD AROUND HIS NECK TO SUMMON EMERGENCY MEDICAL ASSISTANCE WHEN HE HAS A SEIZURE. FATHER SHALL WEAR SUCH A DEVICE AT ALL TIMES WHEN WITH THE CHILD. THE CHILD KNOWS WHEN AND HOW TO ACTIVATE THE DEVICE.

WEEKDAY VISITATION

Mother may bring the child to Father's house for visits during the evenings whenever her schedule permits, as long as the parties shall so agree. In the event the parties cannot agree upon the night or nights of this visitation, Mother shall bring the child to Father's house on Wednesday evenings at 6:00 pm and pick the child up from Father's house at 8:00 pm. The parties may extend this weekday visitation to overnight visitation. In the event the parties agree upon overnight visitation during the week, Father shall either return the child to Mother's house the next morning or take him to his morning activity, as agreed to by the parties.

WEEKENDS

Father's medical condition requires great flexibility and cooperation by the parents regarding the weekend visitation. The general goal is that Father shall have the child for approximately half of the weekends, although this will often not be every other weekend. The parties shall frequently consult each other regarding the Father's medical status and arrange the weekend visitation around the health of the Father and best interests of the child. If the parties cannot agree, Father shall have visitation of the child every other weekend beginning at 6:00 pm on Friday through and ending at 6:00 pm on Sunday, beginning the weekend following the date of the judgment. If either parent's holiday weekend, as set forth below, conflicts with this, then the parent losing their regular weekend shall receive the other parent's next regular weekend to thereafter be followed by the original schedule so that each would have two consecutive weekends.

SUMMER

The child attends various activities during the summer. By February 1 of each year, the parents will divide the child's summer school break into two-week blocks. Each parent will have approximately half of the summer break with the child. The parents agree to cooperate on dividing any remaining days left over from the two-week blocks, for example, if the summer break has an odd number of weeks. If the school summer break is less than 12 weeks, the parties shall each designate half of the remaining break time as their third choice instead of two-week blocks.

In even-numbered years, Father will designate his first two-week block in writing to Mother by February 15; Mother will designate her first two-week block in writing to Father by February 22; Father will designate his second two-week block in writing to Mother by March 1; Mother will designate her second two-week block in writing to Father by March 8; Father will designate his third two-week block in writing to Mother by March 15; Mother will designate her first two-week block in writing to Father by March 22; the parties agree to divide any remaining summer school break days by March 30.

In odd-numbered years, Mother will designate her first two-week block in writing to Father by February 15; Father will designate his first two-week block in writing to Mother by February 22; Mother will designate her second two-week block in writing to Father by March 1; Father will designate his second two-week block in writing to Mother by March 8; Mother will designate her third two-week block in writing to Father by March 15; Father will designate his first two-week block in writing to Mother by March 22; the parties agree to divide any remaining summer school break days by March 30.

Each parent shall be responsible for getting the child to his activities during the parent's summer break time unless the parents agree otherwise. No parent shall schedule the child for activities that take place during the other parent's summer break time without the other parent's written consent.

HOLIDAYS AND SPECIAL DAYS

1. Holiday and special day custody shall prevail over weekend, weekday and summer vacation set forth above. Birthday periods shall not prevail when in conflict with other Holidays and Special Days.
2. Mother shall have the minor child on her birthday and on Mother's Day of each year from 9:00 am to 9:00 pm; plus "Holiday Group A" in even-numbered years and "Holiday Group B" in odd-numbered years.
3. Father shall have the minor child on his birthday and on Father's Day of each year from 9:00 am to 9:00 pm; plus "Holiday Group A" in odd-numbered years and "Holiday Group B" in even-numbered years.
4. Mother and Father are encouraged to communicate to attempt to arrange a combined event/activity for the child's birthday. In the event they cannot agree, the following provisions regarding the child's birthday shall apply.

HOLIDAY GROUP A

1. PRESIDENT'S DAY/WASHINGTON'S BIRTHDAY (OBSERVED) weekend from 5:00 pm the Friday prior to 8:00 am the following Tuesday.
2. A period of 7 (seven) days during the child's school spring break, the exact days to be selected and notice given in writing to the other parent by February lst.
3. INDEPENDENCE DAY—If July 4th falls on: (a) Tuesday, Wednesday or Thursday from 5:00 pm on July 3rd until 9:00 am on July 5th, (b) Friday or Saturday from 5:00 pm on the Thursday before until 9:00 am on the following Monday, (c) Sunday or Monday from 5:00 pm on the Friday before until 9:00 am on the following Tuesday.
4. HALLOWEEN (October 31st) night from 4:00 pm until 9:00 am the following day.
5. CHRISTMAS VACATION from December 25th beginning at 10:00 am through 9:00 am on December 31st.
6. The child's birthday from 9:00 am until 9:00 am the following day.

HOLIDAY GROUP B

1. MARTIN LUTHER KING weekend from 5:00 pm the Friday prior through 8:00 am the following Tuesday.
2. MEMORIAL DAY weekend from 5:00 pm the Friday prior through 8:00 am the following Tuesday.
3. LABOR DAY weekend from 5:00 pm the Friday prior through 8:00 am the following Tuesday.
4. THANKSGIVING weekend from 5:00 pm the Wednesday prior through 8:00 am the following Monday.
5. CHRISTMAS VACATION from 5:00 pm the day the child's school Christmas vacation begins through 10:00 am on December 25th and December 31st beginning at 9:00 am through 8:00 am the day the child's school Christmas vacation ends.
6. The day prior to the child's birthday beginning at 9:00 am through 9:00 am the day of the birthday.

EXCHANGES

[ ] When school is in session:

Exchanges of the child from Mother to Father shall occur at:
[ ] Residence of Mother [ ] Residence of Father [ ] School
[ ] Other Location-Parents currently reside at same location, exchanges not applicable.

Exchanges of the child from Father to Mother shall occur at:
[ ] Residence of Mother [ ] Residence of Father [ ] School
[ ] Other Location
[ ] When school is not in session:

Exchange of the child from Mother to Father shall occur at:
[ ] Residence of Mother [ ] Residence of Father
[ ] Other Location

Exchange of the child from Father to Mother shall occur at:
[ ] Residence of Mother [ ] Residence of Father
[ ] Other Location

[ ] If an exchange occurs at a location other than a parent's residence, the parent scheduled to have time with the child shall pick up and return the child to the specified location and the other parent shall be responsible for assuring the child is at the specified location for pick up, unless other arrangements are described.

TRANSPORTATION

Transportation arrangements for the child for all scheduled parenting time(s) including weekdays, weekends, holidays, and vacation times shall be as follows:

[ ] Mother shall be responsible for transportation of the child at the beginning of the visit. Mother shall be responsible for transportation of the child at the end of the visit.

Mother and Father shall share responsibility for all transportation of the child, including cost, as follows:

[ ] Extraordinary transportation costs (bus, taxi, train, airfare) shall be the responsibility of [ ] Mother [ ] Father [ ] Shared % Mother % Father

CHANGES

The parents' schedules and commitments may require occasional changes in the parenting time schedule. Parents shall attempt to agree on any changes, but the parent receiving a request for a change shall have the final decision on whether the change shall occur.

The parent making the request may make such request
[X] in person [X] by phone [X] in writing to the other parent [X] other—email

The request for change shall be made no later than:
[ ] 24 hours [X] one week [ ] two weeks [ ] other—prior to the date of the requested change.

The parent receiving the request shall respond no later than:
[ ] 24 hours [ ] one week [ ] two weeks [X] other—72 hours after receiving the requested change.

The response to the request may be made
[X] in person [X] by phone [X] in writing to the other parent [X] other—email
Any parent requesting a change of schedule shall be responsible for any additional child care or transportation costs resulting from the change.

Mother and Father shall cooperate to allow the child to meet his school and social commitments.

TELEPHONE CONTACTS

Each parent shall have reasonable access to the child by telephone during any period in which the child is with the other parent, unless otherwise specified.

RELOCATION

Absent exigent circumstances as determined by a court with jurisdiction, you, as a party to this action, are ordered to notify, in writing by certified mail, return receipt requested, and at least 60 days prior to the proposed relocation, each party to this action of any proposed relocation of the principal residence of the child, including the following information: (1) the intended new residence, including the specific address and mailing address, if known, and if not known, the city; (2) the home telephone number of the new residence, if known; (3) the date of the intended move or proposed relocation;

(4) a brief statement of the specific reasons for the proposed relocation of the child; and (5) a proposal for a revised schedule of custody or visitation with the child. Your obligation to provide this information to each party continues as long as you or any other party by virtue of this order is entitled to custody of a child covered by this order. Your failure to obey the order of this court regarding the proposed relocation may result in further litigation to enforce such order, including contempt of court. In addition, your failure to notify a party of a relocation of the child may be considered in a proceeding to modify custody or visitation with the child. Reasonable costs and attorney fees shall be assessed against you if you fail to give the required notice.

LEGAL CUSTODY

Legal Custody: The parties shall agree before making any final decisions on issues affecting the growth and development of the child including, but not limited to, choice of religious upbringing, choice of child care provider, choice of school; course of study; special tutoring; extracurricular activities, including but not limited to, music, art, dance, and other cultural lessons or activities and gymnastics or other athletic activities, choice of camp or other comparable summer activity, nonemergency medical and dental treatment, psychological, psychiatric, or like treatment or counseling; the choice of particular health care providers; the extent of any travel away from home; part or full-time employment; purchase or operation of a motor vehicle, contraception and sex education, and decisions relating to actual or potential litigation on behalf of the child. However, each parent may make decisions regarding the day-to-day care and control of the child and in emergencies affecting the health and safety of the child while the child is residing with him or her. The parents shall endeavor, whenever reasonable, to be consistent in such day-to-day decisions.

Communication: Each parent shall ensure that the other parent is provided with copies of all communications or information received from the child's school, and if a second copy of the communication is not provided by the school shall make a copy for the other parent. Each parent shall notify the other of any activity such as school conferences, programs, sporting and other special events etc., where parents are invited to attend and each shall encourage and welcome the presence of the other.

Child Not Involved in Court or Financial Communications: The parties shall not talk about adult issues, parenting matters, financial issues, and other court-related topics when the child is present. Such discussions shall not be had during custody exchanges of the child or during telephone visits. The child shall not be used to carry such messages, written communication, or child support payments between the parents.

Medical Care Information: Each parent shall have the authority to seek any emergency medical treatment for the child when in his or her custody. Each shall advise the other of any medical emergency or serious illness or injury suffered by the minor child as soon as possible after learning of the same, and shall give the other parent details of the emergency, injury, or illness and the name and telephone numbers of all treating doctors. Each parent shall inform the other before any routine medical care, treatment, or examination by a health care provider including said provider's name and telephone number. Each party shall direct all doctors involved in the care and treatment of the minor child to give the other parent all information regarding any injury or illness and the medical treatment or examination, if requested. For purposes of this paragraph, a serious injury or illness is one that requires a child (1) to be confined to home for more than 48 hours; or (2) to be admitted to, or treated at, a hospital or surgical facility; or (3) to receive any type of general anesthesia or invasive surgical procedure or test.

Child Care Provider: If both parents will need to use a child care provider during periods of custody or visitation, they shall use the same child care provider, unless the distances between their residences or places of employment make the use of the same child care provider unreasonable.

Access to Records: Each parent shall be entitled to immediate access from the other or from a third party to records and information pertaining to the child including, but not limited to, medical, dental, health, child care, school or educational records; and each shall take whatever steps are necessary to ensure that the other parent has such access.

Activities Not to Conflict with Custody or Visitation: The parties shall enroll the child in activities, particularly outside of school, which, to the extent possible, are scheduled at times and places that avoid interruption and disruption of the custody or visitation time of the other party unless consented to by that parent. The special needs of the FATHER require far greater cooperation and flexibility by the parents than is required of parents without special needs.

Resolution of Disputes: If the parties fail to agree on the interpretation of the Parenting Plan, or are unable to agree upon a final decision on issues affecting the growth and development or health and safety of the child, they shall submit the dispute to a mutually agreed-upon Special Needs Coordinator who shall hear and arbitrate the issue. In the event they are not able to agree on a Special Needs Coordinator they shall each select a Special Needs Coordinator from the list of approved Special Needs Coordinators maintained by the ___________ County Family Court and the two Special Needs Coordinators shall determine who shall arbitrate the case. The Special Needs Coordinator shall be a quick and informal tribunal to arbitrate issues which may arise in the future including, but not limited to, increasing or decreasing child support; changes in therapy, treatment, education, custody and/or visitation; and issues relating to expenses.

CHILD SUPPORT AND OTHER EXPENSES

[Standard language]

HEALTH CARE COSTS

[Standard language]

______________________	______________________
Petitioner	Respondent
______________________	______________________
Attorney for Petitioner	Attorney for Respondent

10. SAMPLE SETTLEMENT AGREEMENT

____

IN THE FAMILY COURT OF ____________________ COUNTY
STATE OF ____________________

In Re the Marriage of:	)	
	)	
____________________,	)	
______________,	)	
Petitioner,	)	
vs.	)	Case No. ____________________
____________________,	)	Division: ________
______________,	)	
Respondent.	)	

MARITAL SETTLEMENT AGREEMENT

This MARITAL SETTLEMENT AGREEMENT (hereinafter the "AGREEMENT") is made on the ________ day of ______________, 20__, between ____________, (hereinafter the "WIFE"), and ______________, (hereinafter the "HUSBAND"), and collectively referred to as the "PARTIES".

WITNESSETH that:

WHEREAS, the PARTIES to this AGREEMENT were married on the ____ day of ____________, ______, and because of irreconcilable differences which have arisen between them, which render it impossible for them to live together as husband and wife, and

WHEREAS, the PARTIES believe there is no reasonable likelihood that the marriage of the PARTIES can be preserved, and that the marriage is irretrievably broken, and

WHEREAS, there are two Children born of the marriage to wit: Child One, born Month, Day, Year, and Child Two, born Month, Day, Year, (hereinafter the "Minor Children"), and

WHEREAS, there is now pending an action in the Family Court of the County of ______________, State of ______________ praying that the marriage of the PARTIES be dissolved, and

WHEREAS, the PARTIES hereby desire to fully and finally settle all property rights, and claims between them and make provisions regarding the disposition of their property, maintenance, child support, child custody, attorneys' fees and the costs of these proceedings;

NOW, THEREFORE, for valuable consideration, each received by the other and for mutual promises herein contained, it is agreed as follows:

I. AGREEMENT CONTINGENT UPON COURT REVIEW
All of the stipulations, conditions, and agreements hereinafter contained are contingent upon the Family Court of the County of __________, State of _______, entering an order and judgment dissolving the marriage of the PARTIES and are contingent upon the Court's determination that this AGREEMENT is not unconscionable.

II. CHILD CUSTODY AND SUPPORT MATTERS
The PARTIES agree that the provisions of the PARENTING PLAN (hereinafter the "PLAN") attached as Exhibit "A" shall govern the terms of the Minor Children's custody, visitation, and support arrangements. The PARTIES agree that they will abide by the terms of the PLAN. (Mother shall Pay Father the sum of $_________ per month in child support).

III. DIVISION OF PROPERTY

A. NON-MARITAL PROPERTY

The PARTIES agree that there is non-marital property to be set apart by the Court, which property is divided as indicated on Exhibit B attached.

B. MARITAL PROPERTY

1. PERSONAL PROPERTY

a. Division of Personal Property

The PARTIES make specific reference to the division of personal property identified on Exhibit B attached, with the property being awarded to the PARTY indicated. Any household goods and personal effects not identified on said exhibit or awarded by this Agreement is awarded to the party who has possession or control of such unidentified goods or personal effects. Each PARTY is to be responsible for the payment of personal property taxes, if any, that are due for the personal property they are awarded by this agreement.

<u>1998 Dodge Caravan</u>
The PARTIES agree that HUSBAND is awarded the 1998 Dodge Caravan as his sole and separate property. Further, HUSBAND shall pay and be responsible for any loan or obligation secured by said vehicle, any personal property tax obligations for said vehicle, any leases for said vehicle, and the cost of insuring and operating said vehicle and shall indemnify and hold harmless WIFE for such debts.

<u>2002 Toyota Camry</u>
The PARTIES agree that WIFE is awarded the 2002 Toyota Camry as her sole and separate property. Further, WIFE shall pay and be responsible for any loan or obligation secured by said vehicle, any personal property tax obligations for said vehicle, any leases for said vehicle, and the cost of insuring and operating said vehicle and shall indemnify and hold harmless HUSBAND for such debts.

Bank A (Savings)
The PARTIES agree that the parties will close this account and share the proceeds from this account equally.

Bank B (Sav) and (Chk)
The PARTIES agree that HUSBAND is awarded the checking and savings accounts at Bank B as his sole and separate property.

Bank C (Sav)(W) (in Wife's name)
The PARTIES agree that WIFE is awarded the account at Bank C (Sav)(W) as her sole and separate property.

Bank D (Chk) (in Wife's name)
The PARTIES agree that WIFE is awarded the account at Bank D (Chk) as her sole and separate property.

Bank E (Sav)(H) (in Husband's name)
The PARTIES agree that HUSBAND is awarded the account at Bank E (Sav)(H) as his sole and separate property.

Bank F (Chk)(H) (in Husband's name)
The PARTIES agree that HUSBAND is awarded the account at Bank F (Chk)(H) as his sole and separate property.

Pensions and IRAs
The PARTIES acknowledge that each Party is currently receiving retirement and/or disability benefits as a result of their respective military services and the PARTIES agree that each Party shall be awarded their own retirement/pension/disability benefits as their respective property. Neither Party will make any claims for any portion of the retirement/pension/disability benefits in the name of the other Party and both Parties do hereby waive and release any interest they have in the retirement/pension/disability benefits in the name of the other Party. HUSBAND is awarded the IRA in his name as his property. Even though Father is the primary caregiver for Child One, the child with Special Needs, and thus is unable to work to his otherwise full ability, thereby decreasing the amount he is able to contribute to a retirement plan for his future benefit, the parties agree that this is a fair and equitable distribution of the Pensions and IRAs, for the reason that both parties have full military pensions.

Life Insurance
The PARTIES are each awarded the life insurance policies in their respective names (on their respective lives) as their property. The PARTIES agree that they will continue to maintain their children as the sole beneficiaries on the existing life insurance policies until their children are emancipated by law. Further, Each Party shall provide the other Party documentation regarding the terms of the POLICY and its current status, upon the other Party's request. Further, The PARTIES consent to the insurance company issuing, and/or managing, such POLICY providing to the OTHER PARTY such information about the POLICY that is reasonably necessary to determine the existence, terms, beneficiaries, and status of the POLICY.

Additionally, the PARTIES agree that there are GERBER life insurance policies insuring each of their children, and the PARTIES agree to maintain such insurance POLICIES and to each pay one-half of the insurance premiums for said POLICIES until the insured minor child is emancipated. The PARTIES further agree that they will each be designated as equal co-beneficiaries on such POLICIES, and in the event of the death of an insured minor child, the insurance proceeds will be used to satisfy the burial costs of the child, the child's outstanding uninsured medical bills, if any, the child's outstanding educational expenses, and thereafter such remaining proceeds shall be shared equally between the PARTIES.

b. Titles and Papers

Each PARTY shall promptly deliver to the other all property or documents evidencing ownership of property which by the terms of this AGREEMENT is to remain or become the property of the other. Each PARTY shall execute and deliver to the other PARTY such Affidavits of Gift and Limited Powers of Attorney that are reasonably required to transfer each PARTY'S interest in the cars, automobiles, and vehicles awarded the other PARTY and to permit the other PARTY to act as attorney in fact for the sole purpose of transferring title of the car, automobile or vehicle awarded by this AGREEMENT.

Further, each party agrees to keep all property, and documents evidencing ownership of property, which by the terms of this AGREEMENT is to remain or become the property of the other in good condition, normal wear and tear excepted, until such time as delivery of such property and documentation to the other PARTY has occurred. The PARTIES agree that neither PARTY shall be obligated to store or keep the property or documentation of ownership of such property, which by the terms of this AGREEMENT, is to remain or become the property of the other, for more than 30 days after written notice of a request to pick up such property and documentation has been mailed by certified mail, return receipt requested, to the PARTY to whom such property and documentation is awarded by this AGREEMENT. (Such notice to pick up property shall be addressed to the last known mailing address of the recipient PARTY and shall specify a date, time and place, where the property and documentation in question is to be picked up, which date and time shall be reasonable, and not sooner than five days from the date of mailing of such notice.)

2. REAL PROPERTY

a. Identification of Real Property

The PARTIES acknowledge that they now own or have a marital interest in the following real property:

i. 1234 AnyStreet, City, State located in the County of ________, State of __________, with the legal description contained on Exhibit ___ attached (hereinafter the "MARITAL RESIDENCE") Which real property is security for an obligation, evidenced by a Deed of Trust, in favor of XYZ Bank (hereinafter the "MORTGAGEE FOR MARITAL RESIDENCE").

b. Division of Real Property

The PARTIES agree that the real property in which they have a marital interest shall be disposed of as follows:

i. MARITAL RESIDENCE

The PARTIES agree that the *MARITAL RESIDENCE* is awarded to HUSBAND as his sole and exclusive property.

HUSBAND shall assume and pay the unpaid balance of approximately $_______, owing on the *MARITAL RESIDENCE,* to XYZ Credit Union (hereinafter the "MORTGAGEE FOR MARITAL RESIDENCE"). HUSBAND shall also assume and pay the unpaid balance of any other obligation or line of credit that is secured by the *MARITAL RESIDENCE* and shall indemnify and hold WIFE harmless for such other obligations, if any.

HUSBAND shall indemnify and hold WIFE harmless should the MORTGAGEE FOR MARITAL RESIDENCE, or its assigns or successors, proceed against WIFE upon HUSBAND'S failure to assume or pay the obligation owed to the MORTGAGEE FOR MARITAL RESIDENCE, or upon HUSBAND'S default under any provision of the loan instruments, promissory notes, or Deed of Trust evidencing or securing the obligation to the MORTGAGEE FOR MARITAL RESIDENCE.

HUSBAND shall also be responsible for any obligation for taxes, subdivision dues, insurance costs, repair costs and utility costs, and any other costs, associated with the ownership, possession or use of the *MARITAL RESIDENCE.* HUSBAND shall indemnify and hold WIFE harmless on such costs.

HUSBAND agrees to take such reasonable action as is necessary to remove WIFE'S name from the obligation to the MORTGAGEE FOR MARITAL RESIDENCE, including but not limited to, refinancing the obligation. WIFE'S name shall be removed from the obligation within four weeks of the date of a Judgment of Dissolution of Marriage between the parties.

WIFE shall deliver a Quitclaim Deed, transferring her interest in the MARITAL RESIDENCE to HUSBAND concurrently with the removal of her name from the mortgage obligation.

WIFE shall pay all unpaid mortgage payments due on the MARITAL RESIDENCE for any period prior to the delivery of a Quitclaim Deed to HUSBAND.

WIFE does herewith assign, transfer and set over to the HUSBAND all of her interest in the Escrow fund, if any, held on MARITAL RESIDENCE and further the WIFE assigns, transfers and sets over to the HUSBAND all of WIFE'S interest in all existing insurance on the MARITAL RESIDENCE.

WIFE waives any interest in any deposit previously paid to any utility service providers, whether for phone, water, trash, electric, gas, and sewer service, for service to the MARITAL RESIDENCE. WIFE agrees to cooperate with HUSBAND and to do all things reasonably necessary to have the water, phone, electric, gas, sewer, and trash utilities for the MARITAL RESIDENCE put in the name of the HUSBAND.

c. Other Real Property

The PARTIES each acknowledge and represent to the other that neither party has any interest in any real property in the State of __________ or elsewhere, whether in their names alone or with others, except as identified above.

3. NATURE OF PROPERTY DIVIDED

The PARTIES agree that all of the property divided by Section B above is marital property (except for property listed on Petitioner's Statement of Property filed with the

Court as being separate/non-marital property). The transfers represent fair and equitable divisions of property after consideration of the other financial provisions of this AGREEMENT

4. TRANSFERS OF PROPERTY INTEREST

The PARTIES stipulate and agree that the transfers of property interests, which take place in order to satisfy the terms of this Agreement, shall be transfers pursuant to Section 1041 of the Internal Revenue Code, and the PARTIES agree to execute any forms or other documents as might be necessary to establish this intent.

IV. **MAINTENANCE**

The PARTIES agree, after examining all relevant factors, including the factors specified under Section __________ (statutes of state of _________), that WIFE shall pay to HUSBAND the sum of $_______ per month as and for maintenance, such payments are due on the first day of each month, beginning on first of _____, 20___. The PARTIES agree that this provision as to maintenance shall be modifiable. Maintenance shall automatically terminate upon the first of the following to occur: HUSBAND'S death, WIFE'S death, HUSBAND'S remarriage. The PARTIES agree that no wage withholding orders are required at this time, although the PARTIES understand that in the event maintenance or child support is not paid in a timely fashion, then a wage withholding order may be applied for by HUSBAND.

V. **DEBTS**

A. **Assumption of Debts and Liabilities:** From and after the date the petition in this cause was filed, each PARTY will be solely liable for the debts acquired by him or her.

B. **Terms of Payments:** The PARTIES' debts and liabilities will be assumed and paid as provide on the exhibits attached hereto (i.e., Exhibit "B") and incorporated herein by reference. Each PARTY is responsible for any debt or obligation that is incurred in connection with the ownership, possession or use of an asset of property, whether real or personal, unless specifically indicated otherwise in this Agreement.

C. **Indemnification:** The PARTIES agree to indemnify and hold harmless each other and defend the other from and against all claims and liabilities and will reimburse the other for any and all expenses made or incurred by the other, either directly or indirectly, including a reasonable attorney's fee, as a result of his or her failure to pay or otherwise satisfy the debts and liabilities assumed by each in this AGREEMENT.

D. **No Undisclosed Debts:** The PARTIES warrant to each other that, he or she has not incurred any debt or obligation which is either (1) an obligation on or for which the other PARTY is or may become personally liable, or (2) an obligation that could be enforced at any time against an asset held or to be received under this AGREEMENT by the other PARTY, except as disclosed on attached Exhibit B. Each PARTY covenants not to incur any such obligations or debts on or after the execution of this AGREEMENT.

VI. **INCORPORATION IN DECREE**

It is the intent of the PARTIES that the terms of this AGREEMENT be incorporated and fully set forth in any Decree of Dissolution of Marriage entered by the Court, and the Parties shall be ordered to perform the terms thereof.

VII. **SEVERABILITY OF PROVISIONS**

In the event that any provision of the AGREEMENT is unenforceable when incorporated as part of the Court's judgment, it shall be considered severable and enforceable by an action based on contractual obligation, and it shall not invalidate the remainder of this AGREEMENT as incorporated in any Decree.

VIII. **PROVISIONS FOR FAILURE TO PERFORM WITH NOTICE REQUIRED**

In the event that either PARTY brings an action for failure to perform any of the obligations imposed by the AGREEMENT due him or her, or for enforcement or clarification of the AGREEMENT, the prevailing PARTY in such action shall have the right to recover his or her reasonable attorney's fees and litigation costs reasonably expended in prosecuting or defending the action. However, no attorney fees shall be so recovered by a PARTY filing an action unless the PARTY seeking to recover said attorney fees and costs shall have mailed to the other PARTY written notice of the alleged failure to perform and said alleged failure was not cured within ten (10) days after the date of mailing of said notice by certified mail to the alleged breaching PARTY'S residential address. Provided further, that no such notice shall be necessary as to any periodic child support obligation which Petitioner has failed to perform in a timely fashion in accordance with this Agreement on more than two occasions. Provided further, that no such notice shall be necessary as to any periodic maintenance obligation which Wife has failed to perform in a timely fashion in accordance with this AGREEMENT on more than two occasions.

No fees or costs authorized by this paragraph shall be recovered except as determined and awarded by the Court in an action brought for enforcement, breach, or clarification of the AGREEMENT.

IX. **MODIFICATION AND APPROVAL**

The terms of this AGREEMENT shall be subject to modification or change only by a mutual agreement of the PARTIES in writing. It is understood that this provision is not applicable to the terms of the AGREEMENT dealing with child custody, visitation, and child support. The PARTIES recognize that the provisions relating to custody, visitation, and child support are subject to the approval of the Court, and may be modified by the Court regardless of this paragraph.

X. **MUTUAL RELEASE**

Subject to the provisions of the AGREEMENT, each PARTY has remised, released and forever discharged and, by these presents, does himself or herself and his or her heirs, legal representatives, executors, administrators and assigns remise, release and forever discharge the other PARTY, and the other PARTY'S family, employees, agents and attorneys, of and from all cause or causes of action, claims, rights or demands whatsoever in law or equity, which either PARTY hereto ever had or now has against the other, except any and all cause or causes of action for dissolution of marriage or rights arising from this AGREEMENT or subsequent Court Order.

XI. **MUTUAL WAIVER OF RIGHTS IN ESTATES**
Except as otherwise provided in this AGREEMENT, each PARTY shall have the right to dispose of his or her property of whatsoever nature, real or personal, and each PARTY, for himself or herself, respectively, and for their respective heirs, legal representatives, executors, administrators, personal representatives and assigns, hereby waives any right of election which he or she may have or hereafter acquire regarding the estate of the other or to take against any Last Will and Testament of the other or any codicil thereto, whether heretofore or hereafter executed, as provided for in any law now or hereinafter effective of this state or any other state or territory of the United States or any foreign country and renounces and releases all interest, right or claim of distributive share or interstate succession or dower or courtesy, or community property or statutory exemption or allowance or otherwise, that he or she now has or might otherwise have against the other or the estate of the other, or the property of whatsoever nature, real or personal, of the other PARTY under or by virtue of the laws of any state or country. Nothing contained in this particular paragraph, however, shall affect any obligation undertaken in the other paragraphs of the AGREEMENT by either PARTY.

XII. **DISPOSAL OF PROPERTY**
Except as set forth in this agreement, each of the PARTIES shall, from the date of the execution of this AGREEMENT, have the right to dispose of his or her property by *intervivos* conveyance, gift, Last Will or otherwise, as though a single person.

XIII. **EXECUTION OF PAPERS**
The PARTIES agree that they shall take any and all steps to execute, acknowledge and deliver to the other any and all instruments, assurances and affidavits that the other PARTY may reasonably require or find convenient, expedient or businesslike for the purpose of giving full force and effect to the provisions of this AGREEMENT.

XIV. **PERFORMANCE OF ACTS REQUIRED IN AGREEMENT**
Where acts and things are required to be performed under the terms of this Agreement and no time is specified for their performance, they shall be done as soon as practical after a judgment of dissolution of marriage is entered between the PARTIES, or within 15 days of the date of judgment of dissolution of marriage is entered between the PARTIES, whichever is sooner.

XV. **VOLUNTARY AGREEMENT AND INVESTIGATION AND DISCLOSURE**
Each of the PARTIES hereby affirms that they each are entering into this AGREEMENT freely and voluntarily; that they have ascertained and weighed all the facts and circumstances likely to influence his or her judgment herein; that they have given due

consideration to such provisions in question; that they have sought independent advice of counsel in regard to all details and particulars of the AGREEMENT (or, they had an opportunity to seek independent advice of counsel) and the underlying facts; and that they clearly understand and assent to all the provisions hereof.

Each PARTY further warrants that they have each disclosed to the other the full extent of their respective properties and income, either on the Statements of Property and/or Statements of Income and Expenses filed with the Court, or on the attachments to this AGREEMENT. Each PARTY further warrants that they have not secreted, hidden, transferred, or disposed of any assets that either PARTY may have an interest in. Each PARTY warrants that neither PARTY has since the ___ day of ________, 20___ withdrawn, consumed or borrowed, except for ordinary, regular and normal living expenses, funds from the bank accounts, stock holdings, retirement plans, 401k plans, pension plans, and Thrift Savings Plans, in their respective names or control. Each PARTY warrants that the equity values or balances of the bank accounts, stock holdings, retirement plans, 401k plans, pension plans, and Thrift Savings Plans, except as values fluctuate with the market or accounts are subject to third party charges, are as disclosed on each PARTY'S Statements of Property filed with the Court, or as disclosed on the account statements or documentation provided the other PARTY in response to Requests for the Production of Documents, whichever documentation contains the most current information.

Each PARTY agrees that in the event property, assets or interests are discovered that have not been disclosed on their Statements of Property or on attachments to this AGREEMENT, and which property, assets or interests were acquired in whole or in part during the marriage and not by way of inheritance or gift or in exchange for non-marital property, that such property, assets or interests shall be divided equally between the PARTIES promptly after the discovery of the same.

XVI. **WAIVER OF DISCOVERY**

Each party acknowledges that he or she has had the opportunity to complete the discovery each as Interrogatories, Request for Production of Documents, appraisals, real estate and other property, and depositions, and has chosen not to do same. Each party acknowledges the risks of proceeding without completion of such discovery. Each party has, nevertheless directed his or her attorneys to proceed without completion of such discovery. Each party acknowledges that without such completed discovery, his or her counsel has not conducted any investigation or analysis that would permit his or her counsel to determine the full extent and value of the parties' marital property, debts, income and expenses, and whether there is any marital component in any non-marital property. The settlement has been based on the personal knowledge of each party, and the review of limited documents exchanged between the parties and Statement of Income and Expenses and Statement of Property filed by each party herein.

XVII. **RIGHTS TO TRIAL**

Both Parties understand they have a right to trial. The Parties agree and stipulate, having been fully advised by their respective attorneys of the consequences and considerations that could result if fully litigated and that trying the case could be more favorable or could be less favorable than the terms of this Property Settlement and Separation Agreement. Nevertheless, the Parties have agreed it is in their respective best interests to waive any trial of this matter and settle the case.

XVIII. **LIVING APART**

The PARTIES shall continue to live separate and apart and from the date of the execution of this AGREEMENT, free from any interference by the other, as if fully unmarried, and further, neither will molest, malign, annoy or trouble the other in any manner.

XIX. **JOINT INCOME TAX RETURNS**

The PARTIES agree to file joint income tax returns for the tax year ending December 31, 20 ___, and each shall be entitled to one-half (1/2) of any refund on any joint returns filed for said tax year and will likewise be responsible for one-half (1/2) of any taxes, interest and penalties on returns which are jointly filed.

The PARTIES agree that in the event any jointly filed income tax return is audited by the appropriate taxing authorities, they will cooperate with each other and their respective attorneys, and accountants, to investigate, respond to or comply with such audit. Any non-cooperating PARTY shall indemnify and hold harmless the other PARTY for failure to perform any reasonable request to assist the attorney/accountants in investigating, responding to or complying with said audit.

The PARTIES agree that in the event either PARTY receives any notice or documentation from the Internal Revenue Service, or any state taxing authority, that references or involves an income tax return that was filed by either PARTY, or the PARTIES jointly, during the course of the marriage, they shall promptly forward a copy of such notice or documentation to the other PARTY at their last known mailing address. In the event a PARTY fails to promptly forward a copy of such notice or documentation to the other PARTY and additional taxes, interest or penalties are assessed against the other PARTY after the date of receipt of such notice or documentation by the non-forwarding PARTY, then the non-forwarding PARTY shall indemnify and hold harmless the other PARTY for such additional taxes, interest, and penalties.

XX. **PAYMENT OF ATTORNEY'S FEES**

The PARTIES agree that they shall each pay their own respective attorney fees incurred in this cause.

XXI. **PAYMENT OF COURT COSTS**

The PARTIES agree that the court costs, excluding deposition costs, of this proceeding shall be equally shared between the PARTIES. Any deposition costs shall be borne solely by the PARTY taking the deposition. In the event the Court orders court costs paid from any deposits already on hand with the Court, then the Respondent shall indemnify, hold harmless, and reimburse Petitioner for Respondent's share of court costs as agreed to in this paragraph

XXII. **BINDING EFFECT**
This AGREEMENT shall be binding on the heirs, representatives and assigns of the PARTIES hereto except as to the specific paragraphs which contain provisions for termination of obligations on the death of one or both of the PARTIES.

XXIII. **EXECUTION**
Each PARTY hereto acknowledges that each of them is making this AGREEMENT of his or her own free will and volition and acknowledges that no coercion, force, pressure, or undue influence has been used against either PARTY in the making of this AGREEMENT or by any other person or persons.

XXIV. **STATUTORY COMPLIANCE**
The validity and construction of this AGREEMENT shall be determined in accordance with the laws of the State of Missouri.

XXV. **SIGNATURES**
IN WITNESS WHEREOF, the PARTIES set their signatures to this document hereafter.

STATE OF _______________)
)ss.
COUNTY OF _____________)

_____________, of lawful age, being first duly sworn on her oath, states that she is the Petitioner (and Wife) named herein and that she has read the above and foregoing Agreement; she further states that the facts and matters contained therein are true and correct to the best of her knowledge, information and belief and she has executed this document voluntarily and of her free will.

____
Petitioner

On this ____ day of ________________, 20___ before me a Notary Public in and for said State personally appeared ______________ to me known to be the person described in and who executed the foregoing instrument, and acknowledged and stated under oath and/or affirmed that she executed the same as her free act and deed, and that the facts and matters contained therein are true and correct to the best of her knowledge, information and belief.

IN TESTIMONY WHEREOF, I have hereunto set my hand and affixed my official seal in the County and State aforesaid, the day and year first above written

____
Notary Public

My Commission expires:

____

STATE OF ______________)
)ss.
COUNTY OF ____________)

____________, of lawful age, being first duly sworn on his oath, states that he is the Respondent (and Husband) named herein and that he has read the above and foregoing Agreement; he further states that the facts and matters contained therein are true and correct to the best of his knowledge, information and belief, and he has executed this document voluntarily and of his free will.

____
Respondent

On this ____ day of ________________, 20___ before me a Notary Public in and for said State personally appeared _____________ to me known to be the person described in and who executed the foregoing instrument, and acknowledged and stated under oath and/or affirmed that he executed the same as his free act and deed, and that the facts and matters contained therein are true and correct to the best of his knowledge, information and belief.

IN TESTIMONY WHEREOF, I have hereunto set my hand and affixed my official seal in the County and State aforesaid, the day and year first above written

____
Notary Public

My Commission expires:

____

EXHIBIT "A"
PARENTING PLAN

EXHIBIT "B"
DIVISION OF PROPERTY

EXHIBIT "C"
Legal Description for MARITAL RESIDENCE

[Adapted from Settlement Agreement coauthored with Kieran Coyne, an attorney in St. Louis, Missouri.]

11. AFFIDAVIT FOR JUDGMENT

IN THE FAMILY COURT OF ________________ COUNTY
STATE OF ________________

In Re the Marriage of:	)	For File Stamp Only
	)	
________________,	)	
___________,	)	
Petitioner,	)	
vs.	)	Case No. ________________
________________,	)	Division: _______
___________,	)	
Respondent.	)	

AFFIDAVIT OF PETITIONER REQUESTING DISSOLUTION OF MARRIAGE—SPECIAL NEEDS CASE

Petitioner, upon her oath submits the following affidavit pursuant to local rules, to form a basis for the court's entering a judgment in this case upon affidavit and without the necessity of a formal hearing.

1. The Petition in this case was filed on _____________, 20___.
2. Respondent was served with summons in this case on ________ (date) and filed a responsive pleading on ________ (date).
3. Respondent is and has been a resident of the State of _________ for more than _______ days/months immediately preceding the filing of the petition in this case.
4. Both parties are over eighteen years of age.
5. At the time of filing, Petitioner resided at ___________ (street address, city, county, state, zip code).
6. At the time of filing, Respondent resided at ___________ (street address, city, county, state, zip code).
7. Petitioner's social security number is XXX-XX-XXXX (if applicable).
8. Respondent's social security number is XXX-XX-XXXX (if applicable).
9. Petitioner is represented by ____________ (attorney name and address).
10. Respondent is represented by ____________ (attorney name and address).
11. Petitioner is employed as a _________ (occupation) at _______ (employer name) located at ___________________ (employer address).
12. Respondent is employed as a _________ (occupation) at _______ (employer name) located at ___________________ (employer address).

13. Petitioner and Respondent were married on __________(date) at __________ (city, county, state). The marriage was recorded in the County of ________, State of ______.
14. Petitioner and Respondent separated on or about ________, 20___.
15. Petitioner believes that there is no reasonable likelihood that the marriage of Petitioner and Respondent can be preserved and, therefore, believes that the marriage is irretrievably broken.
16. Petitioner is not on active duty with the Armed Forces of the United States of America or its allies.
17. Respondent is not on active duty with the Armed Forces of the United States of America or its allies.
18. Petitioner is not pregnant.
19. The parties have entered into a written agreement for the division of their property which includes all assets and debts and identifies and divides the marital property and debts and sets apart to each party his or her nonmarital property. This agreement is attached to this affidavit and incorporated herein by reference.
20. Petitioner and Respondent have agreed to spousal maintenance payable by Respondent to Petitioner in the amount of $ _____ per month as and for Petitioner's maintenance until further order of the Court. Said maintenance obligation shall be modifiable. The parties ask that the court incorporate this agreed upon spousal maintenance in the Judgment of Dissolution.
21. Petitioner is unaware of any genuine issue as to any material fact in this proceeding.
22. There are two minor, unemancipated children of the marriage, to wit:
    CHILD ONE DOB: ______
    CHILD TWO DOB: ______
23. CHILD ONE (Child's name) HAS A SPECIAL NEEDS, NAMELY CEREBRAL PALSY, WHICH SPECIAL NEEDS HAVE BEEN COMPLETELY ADDRESSED IN THE SETTLEMENT AGREEMENT, PARENTING PLAN, AND PROPOSED JUDGMENT. THESE DOCUMENTS HAVE BEEN APPROVED BY THE SPECIAL NEEDS COORDINATOR ASSIGNED TO THIS CASE.
24. The children lived with Petitioner and Respondent at ____ (street address, city, county, state) for six months immediately preceding the filing of this petition.
25. That Petitioner has not participated in any capacity in any other litigation concerning the custody of the children in this or any other state. Petitioner has no information of any custody proceeding concerning the children pending in a court of this or any other state; and knows of no person not a party to these proceedings who has physical custody of the children or claims to have custody or visitation rights with respect to the children.
26. Petitioner and Respondent have entered into a custody agreement, which is attached and incorporated herein by reference. Petitioner and Respondent request that the Court incorporate the terms of the custody agreement in the Judgment of Dissolution.

27. Attached hereto is a special needs child support worksheet (Form 14SN) which has been agreed to by both parties. Petitioner attests to the truth of the contents of the child support worksheet.
28. The parties agree that the amount of support calculated by the Child Support Guidelines as modified for Special Needs is not rebutted as being unjust or inappropriate and agree that Respondent shall pay $____ per month child support.
29. The child support rights have not been assigned to the State of ________.
30. Costs paid by Petitioner and Respondent equally.

____
Petitioner

STATE OF ______________)
)ss.
COUNTY OF ____________)

________________ personally appeared before me on ___________________, who upon being duly sworn stated that the foregoing statements were true and accurate to their best knowledge and belief.

____
Notary Public

CERTIFICATE OF MAILING

I hereby certify that a copy of the foregoing was mailed on the ___ day of _____, 20__ by U.S. Mail, postage prepaid to: _________ (opposing counsel's name, street address, city, state and zip code)

____

[Adapted from portions of Affidavit form, Missouri Attorney Assistant, Legal Easy, Inc.]

12. JUDGMENT OF DISSOLUTION

IN THE FAMILY COURT OF __________________ COUNTY
STATE OF __________________

In Re the Marriage of:	)	
	)	
__________________,	)	
____________,	)	
Petitioner,	)	
vs.	)	Case No. __________________
__________________,	)	Division: _______
____________,	)	
Respondent.	)	

JUDGMENT OF DISSOLUTION

Now on this ____ day of (month), (year), this cause comes on for hearing; Petitioner, (name), appearing in person and with her attorney, (name). Respondent, (name), appearing in person and with his attorney, (name).

Whereupon, all matters contained in the petition are submitted to the Court for trial. All parties announce ready for hearing. After hearing all the evidence, reviewing the Property Settlement Agreement and being fully advised in the premises, the Court finds that Petitioner has been a resident of the State of ___________ for more than ____ days next preceding the commencement of this proceeding and that more than ___ days have elapsed since the filing of the Petition. The Court finds that the Petitioner, ___________ is not now pregnant. The Court finds that there remains no reasonable likelihood that the marriage can be preserved and that the marriage is irretrievably broken.

IT IS THEREFORE ORDERED, ADJUDGED AND DECREED by the Court that the parties hereto be and they are hereby granted the dissolution of their marriage and restored to all rights and privileges of single and unmarried persons.

The Court finds that the Property Settlement Agreement is presented to the Court and after being duly examined is found not to be unconscionable, and is to be made a part of the Judgment. The Court finds that said agreement disposes of all marital and non-marital property and debt.

The Court finds that there were two children born of the marriage, namely;
CHILD ONE (name) born _________
CHILD TWO (name) born _________

THE COURT FINDS THAT CHILD ONE (Child's name) HAS A SPECIAL NEEDS, NAMELY CEREBRAL PALSY, WHICH SPECIAL NEEDS HAVE BEEN COMPLETELY ADDRESSED IN THE SETTLEMENT AGREEMENT, PARENTING PLAN,

AND PROPOSED JUDGMENT. THESE DOCUMENTS HAVE BEEN APPROVED BY THE SPECIAL NEEDS COORDINATOR ASSIGNED TO THIS CASE.

The Court finds that it is in the best interests of the children for the parents to the awarded joint physical and joint legal custody of both children.

In determining the custody of the children, the Court has considered the wishes of the children's parents as to custody and the proposed parenting plan submitted by both parties; the needs of the children for a frequent, continuing and meaningful relationship with both parents and the ability and willingness of parents to actively perform their function as mother and father for the needs of the children; the interaction and interrelationship of the children with parents, siblings, and any other person who may significantly affect the children's best interests; which parent is more likely to allow the children frequent, continuing and meaningful contact with the other parent; the children's adjustment to the children's home, school, community; the mental and physical health of all individuals involved, including any history of abuse of any individuals involved; the intention of either parent to relocate the principal residence of the children; and the wishes of a children as to the children's custodian.

In the event either party relocates their principal residence, then you are advised pursuant to Section ____ of the Statutes of the State of __________ as follows: Absent exigent circumstances as determined by a Court with jurisdiction, you, as a party to this action, are ordered to notify, in writing by certified mail, return receipt requested, and at least 60 days prior to the proposed relocation, each party to this action shall notify the other of any proposed relocation of the principal residence of the children, including the following information:

a. The intended new residence, including the specific address and mailing address, if known, and if not known, the city;
b. The home telephone number of the new residence, if known;
c. The date of the intended move or proposed relocation;
d. A brief statement of the specific reasons for the proposed relocation of the children; and
e. A proposal for a revised schedule of custody or visitation with the children.

Your obligation to provide this information to each party continues as long as you or any other party by virtue of this order is entitled to custody of a child covered by this order. Your failure to obey this order of this court regarding the proposed relocation may result in further litigation to enforce such order including contempt of court. In addition, your failure to notify a party of a relocation of the children may be considered in a proceeding to modify custody or visitation with the children. Reasonable costs and attorney fees may be assessed against you if you fail to give the required notice.

The Court orders that each party pay their respective pro rata share of the 20__ personal property taxes based upon the assessed value of the vehicles awarded to each party. Each party shall pay their share prior to December 31, 20__.

The Court orders the Sheriff or other Law Enforcement Officer to enforce visitation or custody rights.

The Court orders Petitioner to pay to Respondent the sum of $______ per month as and for Respondent's maintenance until further order of the Court. Said maintenance obligation shall be modifiable.

It is contemplated by and the intention and agreement of the parties that the amounts of maintenance payable by Petitioner to Respondent under this Section shall be deductible on Petitioner's Federal and (state) income tax returns and shall constitute income to Respondent for Federal and (state) income tax purposes.

The Court orders each party to pay their own attorney fees.

The Court orders Petitioner and Respondent to equally pay all court costs incurred herein.

The Court finds that this Judgment has disposed of all marital and non-marital property and debts.

IT IS FURTHER ORDERED, ADJUDGED AND DECREED by the Court that the parties shall sign any and all documents necessary to effectuate the terms of this Judgment Entry.

IT IS SO ORDERED.
Dated this _______ day of ___________________, 20____.

____
The Honorable ________________
Case No. ____________

APPROVED AS TO FORM:

ATTORNEY SIGNATURE BLOCK
ATTORNEY FOR PETITIONER

ATTORNEY SIGNATURE BLOCK
ATTORNEY FOR RESPONDENT

[Adapted from portions of Judgment form, Missouri Attorney Assistant, Legal Easy, Inc.]

13. MOTION TO MODIFY

IN THE FAMILY COURT OF __________________ COUNTY
STATE OF __________________

In Re the Marriage of:	)	For File Stamp Only
	)	
________________,	)	
____________,	)	
Petitioner,	)	
vs.	)	Case No. __________________
________________,	)	Division: _______
____________,	)	
Respondent.	)	

MOTION TO MODIFY—SPECIAL NEEDS

Comes now the Petitioner, ____________, by and through her counsel,_________ , and for his cause of action, alleges and states:

1. On _____________ this Court entered a Decree of Dissolution in this matter. There were two children born of the marriage, namely;
   CHILD ONE (name) born _________
   CHILD TWO (name) born _________
   THE COURT FOUND THAT CHILD ONE (Child's name) HAS A SPECIAL NEEDS, NAMELY CEREBRAL PALSY, AND FOUND THAT THE SPECIAL NEEDS HAD BEEN COMPLETELY ADDRESSED IN THE SETTLEMENT AGREEMENT, PARENTING PLAN AND PROPOSED JUDGMENT. THESE DOCUMENTS WERE APPROVED BY THE SPECIAL NEEDS COORDINATOR ASSIGNED TO THIS CASE.
2. The Decree of Dissolution further awarded Petitioner and Respondent the joint physical and legal custody of the minor children.
3. The Decree of Dissolution awarded Respondent as support for said children the sum of $_____ per month.
4. The Decree of Dissolution further ordered Petitioner to pay maintenance to Respondent.
5. The Decree of Dissolution has not been modified.
6. Since the date of the original Decree of Dissolution was entered, there have been changed circumstances so substantial and continuing as to make the terms of said Decree of Dissolution unreasonable in regard to the children. As a result of such changed circumstances, a modification of the Decree of Dissolution is necessary to serve the best interests of the parties.

7. The changed circumstances, include but are not limited to the following:

   ____
8. Petitioner requests the court award sole physical and legal custody of the minor child to her due to the change of circumstances listed above.
9. Petitioner requests the visitation schedule originally ordered be modified as follows:

   ____
10. Petitioner is unable to provide the ordered child support originally ordered due to the change of circumstances listed above.
11. Petitioner is unable to provide maintenance to Respondent.
12. Petitioner is presently employed by _____________.
13. Respondent is presently employed by ____________.
14. As a result of the above, all of which involve a substantial and continuing change of conditions and circumstances, the Petitioner prays that a new Order be entered by this Court.

WHEREFORE, Petitioner prays that the Court enter an Order modifying the decree of dissolution The to award visitation as stated above to serve the best interests of the minor children; to decrease the child support paid by Petitioner, retroactive to the date of the service of this Motion, to a sum which is reasonable in light of the above-described changes in conditions and circumstances; awarding custody of the minor children to Petitioner; to decrease the award of maintenance paid by Petitioner; and further Ordering that in all other respects, the Court's Order entered __________, 20___, shall remain in full force and effect; and for such further Orders as to this Court shall seem just and proper.

____

ATTORNEY SIGNATURE BLOCK
ATTORNEY FOR PETITIONER

STATE OF ______________)
)ss.
COUNTY OF ____________)

Comes now _________, Petitioner, being first duly sworn according to law, and states that she has read the foregoing Motion to Modify and states that the facts contained therein are true and correct according to her best knowledge, information and belief.

____

Subscribed and sworn to before me this _____ day of ________, 20___.

____

Notary Public

My commission expires:

CHAPTER 12

Resources

This chapter contains information about resources where judges, attorneys, parents, educators, and other persons working with children with special needs can get additional information on these subjects. A wealth of information is available, and more is being discovered every day. Because this field is growing and changing so quickly, the best ways to supplement the following information and stay up to date are to check the following websites for new material and do thorough internet searches.

This information is organized into three categories:

I. Center for Parent Information and Resources
II. State Councils on Developmental Disabilities
III. State Departments of Education

I. CENTER FOR PARENT INFORMATION AND RESOURCES

The Center for Parent Information and Resources (CPIR) has replaced the National Dissemination Center for Children with Disabilities as a central source of information on disabilities from birth and throughout childhood, on the IDEA (special education law), on "No Child Left Behind," and on educational practices. This entity has a website at http://www.parentcenterhub.org. CPIR can connect you to Parent Centers with private workspaces for people to exchange information on resources and solve common challenges. This organization is also a useful resource for attorneys and judges to educate themselves on specific disabilities and special needs they encounter in cases.

The CPIR provides educational materials on many different disabilities, including:

- Attention deficit/hyperactivity disorder (ADHD)
- Autism spectrum disorder
- Deafness/blindness
- Developmental delays and disabilities
- Down syndrome
- Emotional disturbance
- Intellectual disabilities
- Learning disabilities
- Pervasive developmental disorders (PDD)
- Reading and learning disabilities
- Speech–language impairments
- Traumatic brain injury
- Visual impairments

(Source: https://www.parentcenterhub.org/resourcelibrary/index/d/d1/d12/)

CPIR also has numerous webinars created by the Office of Special Education Programs (OSEP).

The preceding paragraphs are but a thumbnail sketch of the vast amount of information you will find at this organization's extremely valuable website. Do not overlook their publications, which are extensive.

II. STATE COUNCILS ON DEVELOPMENTAL DISABILITIES

The National Association of Councils on Developmental Disabilities (NACDD) provides information on all 50 state councils on developmental disabilities. These councils can be valuable resources for people working with children with disabilities. The Developmental Disabilities Councils receive federal funding for programs that promote inclusion, integration, and self-determination for people with developmental disabilities throughout the United States (https://www.nacdd.org/).

A summary of the NACDD listing of state councils on developmental disabilities follows. Each state agency's website contains additional information, such as names of specific contact people. This information was not included in this book, both because this information will change over time and because it was too detailed for this book. Please refer to specific websites for more information.

State Councils on Developmental Disabilities

ALABAMA

Phone: (334) 242-3973
www.acdd.org/

ALASKA

Phone: (907) 269-8990
www.dhss.alaska.gov

AMERICAN SAMOA

Phone: (684) 633-2696

ARIZONA

Phone: (602) 542-8977
www.azdes.gov/addpc

ARKANSAS

Phone: (501) 682-2897
www.ddcouncil.org

CALIFORNIA

Phone: (916) 322-8481
https://scdd.ca.gov

COLORADO

Phone: (720) 941-0176
www.coddc.org

COMMONWEALTH OF THE NORTHERN MARIANA ISLANDS

Phone: (670) 664-7000/1
https://cnmicdd.gov.mp/about-us/

CONNECTICUT

Phone: (860) 418-6160
www.ct.gov/ctcdd

DELAWARE

Phone: (302) 739-3333
www.ddc.delaware.gov

DISTRICT OF COLUMBIA

Phone: (202) 724-8612
http://ddc.dc.gov

FLORIDA

Phone: (850) 488-4180
www.fddc.org

GEORGIA

Phone: (888) 275-4233
www.gcdd.org

GUAM

Phone: (671) 735-9127
www.gddc.guam.gov

HAWAII

Phone: (808) 586-8100
www.hiddcouncil.org

IDAHO

Phone: (208) 334-2178
www.icdd.idaho.gov

ILLINOIS

Phone: (217) 782-9696
Fax: (312) 814-2080
www2.illinois.gov/sites/icdd

INDIANA

Phone: (317) 232-7770
www.in.gov/gpcpd

IOWA

Phone: (515) 281-9083
Toll Free: (800) 452-1936
http://iddcouncil.idaction.org

KANSAS

Phone: (785) 296-2608
www.kcdd.org

KENTUCKY

Phone: (502) 564-7841
www.ccdd.ky.gov

LOUISIANA

Phone: (225) 342-6804
www.laddc.org

MAINE

Phone: (207) 287-4213
www.MaineDDC.org

MARYLAND

Phone: (410) 767-3670
www.md-council.org

MASSACHUSETTS

Phone: (617) 770-7676
www.mass.gov/mddc

MICHIGAN

Phone: (517) 335-3158
https://www.michigan.gov/disabilityresources

MINNESOTA

Phone: (651) 296-4018
www.mnddc.org

MISSISSIPPI

Phone: (601) 359-6238
www.mscdd.org

MISSOURI

Phone: (573) 751-8611
www.moddcouncil.org

MONTANA

Phone: (406) 443-4332
www.mtcdd.org

NEBRASKA

Phone: (402) 471-2330
http://dhhs.ne.gov/Pages/dd-planning-council.aspx

NEVADA

Phone: (775) 684-8619
www.nevadaddcouncil.org

NEW HAMPSHIRE

Phone: (603) 271-3236
www.nhddc.org

NEW JERSEY

Phone: (609) 292-3745
www.njddc.org

NEW MEXICO

Phone: (505) 841-4519
www.nmddpc.com

NEW YORK

Phone: (518) 486-7505
www.ddpc.ny.gov

NORTH CAROLINA

Phone: (919) 850-2901
https://www.ncdhhs.gov/assistance/disability-services

NORTH DAKOTA

Phone: (701) 328-4847
www.nd.gov/scdd

OHIO

Phone: (614) 466-5205
www.ddc.ohio.gov

OKLAHOMA

Phone: (405) 521-4984
www.okddc.ok.gov

OREGON

Phone: (503) 945-9941
www.ocdd.org

PENNSYLVANIA

Phone: (717) 787-6057
www.paddc.org

PUERTO RICO

Phone: (787) 722-0590
http://portals.jp.pr.gov/SiteDirectory/CED_EN/Pages/Home2.aspx

RHODE ISLAND

Phone: (401) 737-1238
www.riddc.org

SOUTH CAROLINA

Phone: (803) 734-0465
www.scddc.state.sc.us

SOUTH DAKOTA

Phone: (605) 773-6369
https://dhs.sd.gov/developmentaldisabilities/

TENNESSEE

Phone: (615) 532-6615
www.tn.gov/cdd

TEXAS

Phone: (512) 437-5432
www.tcdd.texas.gov

UTAH

Phone: (801) 245-7350
www.utahddcouncil.org

VERMONT

Phone: (802)828-1310
www.ddc.vermont.gov

VIRGIN ISLANDS

Phone: (340) 773-2323 Ext. 2137
http://www.dhs.gov.vi/disabilities/dd_counsel.html

VIRGINIA

Phone: (804) 786-0016
www.vaboard.org

WASHINGTON

Phone: (360) 586-3560
www.ddc.wa.gov

WEST VIRGINIA

Phone: (304) 558-0416
www.ddc.wv.gov

WISCONSIN

Phone: (608) 266-7826
www.wi-bpdd.org

WYOMING

Phone: (307) 777-7230
https://health.wyo.gov/healthcarefin/hcbs/dd-advisory-council/

III. STATE DEPARTMENTS OF EDUCATION

State departments of education can be great resources for people who work with children with disabilities. Much of the legislation and case law concerning children with special needs has arisen in the educational arena. Contact information for the state departments of education follows. Information for the U.S. Department of Education can be found at ihttps://www2.ed.gov/about/contacts/state/ar.html.

Alabama State Department of Education

Phone: (334) 694-4900
www.alsde.edu/Pages/home.aspx

Alaska Department of Education

Phone: (907) 465-2800
http://education.alaska.gov

American Samoa Department of Education (Utulei)

Phone: (684) 633-5237
www.doe.as

Arizona Department of Education

Phone: (602) 542-5393
www.ade.az.gov

Arkansas Department of Education

Phone: (501) 682-4475
http://ade.arkansas.gov/

California Department of Education

Phone: (916) 319-0800
www.cde.ca.gov/

Colorado Department of Education

Phone: (303) 866-6600
www.cde.state.co.us/

Connecticut State Department of Education

Phone: (860) 713-6743
www.sde.ct.gov/

Delaware Department of Education

Phone: (302) 735-4000
www.doe.k12.de.us/

District of Columbia Public Schools

Phone: (202) 727-6436
http://osse.dc.gov/

Federated States of Micronesia Department of Education

Phone: (691) 320-2609
http://national.doe.fm

Florida Department of Education

Phone: (850) 245-0505
www.fldoe.org/

Georgia Department of Education

Phone: (404) 656-2800
www.gadoe.org

Guam Department of Education

Phone: (671) 300-1536
www.gdoe.net/

Hawaii Department of Education

Phone: (808) 784-6200
www.hawaiipublicschools.org/Pages/home.aspx

Idaho Department of Education

Phone: (208) 332-6800
http://sde.idaho.gov/index.html

Illinois State Board of Education

Phone: (217) 782-4321
www.isbe.net/

Indiana Department of Education

Phone: (317) 232-6610
www.doe.in.gov

Iowa Department of Education

Phone: (515) 281-5294
http://educateiowa.gov

Kansas State Department of Education

Phone: (785) 296-3201
www.ksde.org/

Kentucky Department of Education

Phone: (502) 564-3141
www.education.ky.gov

Louisiana Department of Education

Phone: (225) 342-4253
www.lousianabelieves.com/

Maine Department of Education

Phone: (207) 624-6600
www.maine.gov/doe/

Maryland Department of Education

Phone: (410) 767-0100
www.marylandpublicschools.org

Massachusetts Department of Education

Phone: (781) 338-3000
www.doe.mass.edu/

Michigan Department of Education

Phone: (833) 633-5788
www.michigan.gov/mde/

Minnesota Department of Children, Families, and Learning

Phone: (651) 582-8200
http://education.state.mn.us/mde/index.html

Mississippi Department of Education

Phone: (601) 359-3513
www.mdek12.org/

Missouri Department of Education

Phone: (573) 751-4212
http://dese.mo.gov/

Montana Office of Public Instruction

Phone: (406) 444-3680
www.opi.mt.gov/

Nebraska Department of Education

Phone: (402) 471-2295
www.education.ne.gov

Nevada Department of Education

Phone: (775) 687-9115
www.doe.nv.gov/

New Hampshire Department of Education

Phone: (603) 271-3494
www.education.nh.gov/

New Jersey Department of Education

Phone: (609) 376-3500
www.state.nj.us/education/

New Mexico State Department of Education

Phone: (505) 827-5800
https://webnew.ped.state.nm.us/

New York State Education Department

Phone: (518) 474-3852
www.nysed.gov/

North Carolina Department of Public Instruction

Phone: (984) 236-2100
www.ncpublicschools.org/

North Dakota Department of Public Instruction

Phone: (701) 328-2260
www.dpi.state.nd.us

Northern Mariana Islands Department of Education

Phone: (670) 237-3027
https://www2.ed.gov/about/contacts/state/mp.html

Ohio Department of Education

Phone: (877) 644-6338
www.ode.state.oh.us/

Oklahoma Department of Education

Phone: (405) 521-3301
www.ok.gov/sde/

Oregon Department of Education

Phone: (503) 947-5600
www.oregon.gov/ode/Pages/default.aspx

Pennsylvania Department of Education

Phone: (717) 783-6788
www.education.pa.gov

Puerto Rico Department of Education

Phone: (787) 759-2000
https://de.pr.gov

Republic of Palau Department of Education

Phone: (680) 488-6425
https://www.palaugov.pw/executive-branch/ministries/education/

Republic of the Marshall Islands Department of Education

Phone: (692) 625-5261
https://pss.edu.mh/

Rhode Island Department of Education

Phone: (401) 222-4600
www.ride.ri.gov/

South Carolina Department of Education

Phone: (803) 734-8500
http://ed.sc.gov/

South Dakota Department of Education

Phone: (605) 773-3455
http://doe.sd.gov/

Tennessee Department of Education

Phone: (615) 741-5158
www.tn.gov/education

Texas Education Agency

Phone: (512) 463-9734
www.tea.state.tx.us/

Utah State Office of Education

Phone: (801) 538-7500
www.schools.utah.gov

Vermont Department of Education

Phone: (802) 828-1130
www.education.vermont.gov/

Virgin Islands Department of Education

Phone: (340) 773-1095 St. Croix
Phone: (340) 774-0100 St. Thomas
www.vide.vi/

Virginia Department of Education

Phone: (804) 292-3820
www.doe.virginia.gov/

Washington Department of Education

Phone: (360) 725-6000
www.k12.wa.us/

West Virginia Department of Education

Phone: (304) 558-2681
http://wvde.state.wv.us/

Wisconsin Department of Public Instruction

Phone: (608) 266-3390
http://dpi.wi.gov/

Wyoming Department of Education

Phone: (307) 777-7675
http://edu.wyoming.gov/

CHAPTER 13

Bibliography

There are thousands of books on the various types of special needs. Attorneys and judges need to properly educate themselves when handling special needs cases, but may not have time to read thousands of books. The following is a list of suggested books by subject. This is not an endorsement of any of these books or of the ideas expressed in them. You must evaluate each book and its contents for yourself. This list suggests books on many, but not all, of the topics in this book. No slight was intended by not including every subject. Many more books can easily be found at the bookstore, in a library, or online.

ADD/ADHD

100 Questions and answers about your child's attention deficit hyperactivity disorder, by Ruth D. Nass & Fern Leventhal (Jones and Bartlett Publishers, 2005).

Attention deficits and hyperactivity in children and adults: Diagnosis, treatment, and management (2nd ed.), Pasquale Accardo, Ed. (Informa Healthcare, 1999).

Driven to distraction: Recognizing and coping with attention deficit disorder from childhood through adulthood (Reprint Ed.), by Edward M. Hallowell & John J. Ratey (Touchstone, 1995).

Taking charge of ADHD: The complete, authoritative guide for parents (Rev. Ed.), by Russell A. Barkley (Guilford Press, 2000).

Teaching teens with ADD and ADHD: A quick reference guide for teachers and parents, by Chris A. Zeigler Dendy (Woodbine House, 2000).

The ADHD book of lists: A practical guide for helping children and teens with attention deficit disorders, by Sandra F. Rief (Jossey-Bass, 2003).

ALLERGIES AND ASTHMA

American Academy of Pediatrics guide to your children's allergies and asthma: Breathing easy and bringing up healthy, active children, by Michael J. Welch (Villard, 2000).

Asthma: The complete guide to integrative therapies, by Jonathan Brostoff & Linda Gamlin (Healing Arts Press, 2000).

Breathe easy! A teen's guide to allergies and asthma, by Jean Ford (Mason Crest Publishers, 2005).

Understanding and managing your child's food allergies (A Johns Hopkins Press Health Book), by Scott H. Sicherer (Johns Hopkins University Press, 2006).

AUTISM/ASPERGER'S SYNDROME

Asperger's syndrome: A guide for parents and professionals, by Tony Attwood (Jessica Kingsley Publishers, 1998).

Raising a child with autism: A guide to applied behavior analysis for parents, by Shira Richman (Jessica Kingsley Publishers, 2001).

Emergence: Labeled autistic, by Temple Grandin & Margaret M. Scariano (Arena Press, Warner Books, 1986).

Overcoming autism, by Lynn Kern & Claire Lazebnik (Penguin, 2004).

BIPOLAR

New hope for children and teens with bipolar disorder: Your friendly, authoritative guide to the latest in traditional and complementary solutions, by Boris Birmaher (Three Rivers Press, 2004).

Parenting a bipolar child: What to do and why, by Gianni L. Faedda & Nancy B. Austin (New Harbinger Publications, 2006).

The bipolar child: The definitive and reassuring guide to childhood's most misunderstood disorder (3rd ed.), by Demitri Papolos, & Janice Papolos (Broadway, 2007).

The bipolar disorder survival guide: What you and your family need to know, by David J. Miklowitz (Guilford Press, 2002).

The bipolar teen: What you can do to help your child and your family, by David J. Miklowitz, & Elizabeth L. George (Guilford Press, 2007).

BLINDNESS AND VISUAL IMPAIRMENT

Blindness and early childhood development, by David H. Warren (American Foundation for the Blind, 1977).

Children with visual impairments: A guide for parents (2nd ed.), by M. Cay Holbrook, Ed. (Woodbine House, 2006).

Cognitive development in blind children, by Sara Begum (Discovery Publishing House, 2003).

How to thrive, not just survive: A guide to developing independent life skills for blind and visually impaired children and youths, by Rose-Marie Swallow; Kathleen Mary Huebner, Ed. (American Foundation for the Blind, 1987).

CANCER

Childhood cancer: A handbook from St. Jude Children's Research Hospital, by Joseph Mirro, & R. Grant Steen (Da Capo Press, 2000).

Childhood cancer—A medical dictionary, bibliography, and annotated research guide to internet references (ICON Health Publications, 2004).

Childhood cancer: A parent's guide to solid tumor cancers (2nd ed.), by Honna James-Hodder & Nancy Keene (Patient Centered Guidance, 2002).

Childhood cancer: Information for the patient and family (2nd ed.), by Ronald D. Barr, Mary Crockett, Susan Dawson, Marilyn Eves, Anthony Whitton, & John Wiernikowski (BC Decker Inc., 2001).

Childhood cancer: Understanding and coping, by Henry Ekert (Informa Healthcare, 1989).

Communication disorders in childhood cancer, by Bruce E. Murdoch, Ed. (Whurr Publishers, 1999).

Living with childhood cancer: A practical guide to help families cope, by Leigh A. Woznick & Carol D. Goodheart (American Psychological Association, 2001).

Pediatric oncology (M. D. Anderson Cancer Care Series), by Ka Wah Chan, Jr., & R. Beverly Raney, Eds. (Springer Publishing, 2005).

CELIAC DISEASE

Celiac disease: A guide to living with gluten intolerance, by Sylvia Llewellyn Bower; Mary Kay Sharrett & Steve Plogsted, contributors (Demos Medical Publishing, 2006).

Celiac disease: A hidden epidemic, by Peter H. R. Green & Rory Jones (Collins Living, 2006).

Kids with celiac disease: A family guide to raising happy, healthy, gluten-free children, by Danna Korn (Woodbine House, and 2001).

The GF kid: A celiac disease survival guide, by Melissa London (Woodbine House, 2005).

CEREBRAL PALSY

Cerebral palsy: A complete guide for caregiving (A Johns Hopkins Press Health Book) (2nd ed.), by Freeman Miller & Steven J. Bachrach (Johns Hopkins University Press, 2006).

Children with cerebral palsy: A manual for therapists, parents and community workers (2nd ed.), by Archie Hinchcliffe (Sage Publications, 2007).

Children with cerebral palsy: A parents' guide (2nd ed.), by Elaine Geralis, Ed. (Woodbine House, 1998).

Handling the young child with cerebral palsy at home (3rd ed.), by Nancie R. Finnie (Butterworth-Heinemann, 1997).

CHILD ABUSE

A parent's and teacher's handbook on identifying and preventing child abuse, by James A. Monteleone (G.W. Medical Publishing, 1998).

A sourcebook on child sexual abuse, by David Finkelhor (Sage Publications, 1986).

Child abuse and culture: Working with diverse families, by Lisa Aronson Fontes (Guilford Press, 2008).

Child abuse and neglect: Guidelines for identification, assessment and case management, by Marilyn S. Peterson, Michael Durfee, & Kevin Coulter, Eds. (Volcano Press, 2003).

Child Abuse, Gender and Society (Routledge Research in Gender and Society), by Jacqueli Turton (Routledge, 2007).

Child sexual abuse curriculum for the developmentally disabled, by Sol R. Rappaport, Sandra A. Burkhardt, & Anthony F. Rotatori (C.C. Thomas Publishing, 1997).

Child sexual abuse: Disclosure, delay, and denial, by Margaret-Ellen Pipe, Michael E. Lamb, Yael Orbach, & Ann-Christin Cederborg, Eds. (Erlbaum Publishing, 2007).

Understanding child abuse and neglect (7th ed.), by Cynthia Crosson-Tower (Allyn & Bacon, 2007).

CHRONIC ILLNESS

Chronic illness in children: An evidence-based approach, by Laura L. Hayman, Margaret M. Mahon, & J. Rick Turner, Eds. (Springer Publishing, 2002).

Chronic illness in children and adolescents, by Ronald T. Brown, Brian P. Daly, & Annette U. Rickel (Hogrefe & Huber Publishers, 2007).

Cognitive aspects of chronic illness in children, by Ronald T. Brown, Ed. (Guilford Press, 1999).

Coping with your child's chronic illness, by Alesia T. Singer (Robert D. Reed Publishers, 1999).

In sickness and in play: Children coping with chronic illness, by Cindy Dell Clark (Rutgers University Press, 2003).

CROHN'S DISEASE

Learning sickness: A year with Crohn's disease, by Jim Lang (Capital Books, 2004).

Managing your child's Crohn's disease and ulcerative colitis, by Keith J. Benkov & Harland S. Winter (Mastermedia Publishing, 1996).

The angry gut: Coping with colitis and Crohn's disease, by W. Grant Thompson (Da Capo Press, 1993).

The first year—Crohn's disease and ulcerative colitis: An essential guide for the newly diagnosed, by Jill Sklar, & Manuel Sklar (Marlowe & Co., 2002).

CYSTIC FIBROSIS

Cystic fibrosis: A guide for patient and family (3rd ed.), David M. Orenstein, Ed. (Lippincott Williams & Wilkins, 2003).

Cystic fibrosis: Everything you need to know, by Wayne Kepron (Firefly Books, 2004).

Cystic fibrosis: The ultimate teen guide, by Melanie Ann Apel (Scarecrow Press, 2006).

Understanding cystic fibrosis, by Karen Hopkin (University Press of Mississippi, 1998).

DEAFNESS AND HEARING IMPAIRMENT

Deafness in childhood, by Freeman McConnell (University of Illinois Press, 1967).

IDEA Advocacy for children who are deaf or hard of hearing: A question and answer book for parents and professionals, by Bonnie P. Tucker (Singular, 1997).

Keys to raising a deaf child, by Virginia Frazier-Malwald & Lenore M. Williams (Barron's Educational Series, 1999).

Raising and educating a deaf child: A comprehensive guide to the choices, controversies, and decisions faced by parents and educators (2nd ed.), by Marc Marschark (Oxford University Press, USA, 2007).

The young deaf or hard of hearing child: A family-centered approach to early education, by Barbara Bodner-Johnson, & Marilyn Sass-Lehrer, Eds. (Brookes Publishing, 2003).

Understanding childhood deafness, by Wilhma Rae Quinn (Thorsons Publishers, 1996).

DEPRESSION

Growing up sad: Childhood depression and its treatment, by Leon Cytryn, & Donald H. McKnew (W.W. Norton, 1998).

Handbook of depression in children and adolescents, by John R.Z. Abela & Benjamin L. Hankin, Eds. (Guilford Press, 2007).

Stress and depression in children and teenagers, by Vicki Maud (Sheldon Press, 2003).

Raising a moody child: How to cope with depression and bipolar disorder, by Mary A. Fristad & Jill S. Goldberg Arnold (Guilford Press, 2003).

Understanding teenage depression: A guide to diagnosis, treatment and management, by Maureen Empfield & Nicholas Bakalar (Owl Books, 2001).

DEVELOPMENTAL DISORDERS

A parent's to guide to developmental delays: Recognizing and coping with missed milestones in speech, movement, learning, and other areas, by Laurie Fivozinsky LeComer (Perigee Trade, 2006).

Cognition in children (developmental psychology), by Usha Goswami (Psychology Press, 1998).

Development and disabilities: Intellectual, sensory and motor impairments, by Robert M. Hodapp (Cambridge University Press, 1998).

Developmentally delayed children (child psychology) (3rd ed.), by Wain K. Brown (William Gladden Press, 2008).

Manual of developmental and behavioral problems in children (pediatric habilitation), by Vidya Gupta (Informa Healthcare, 1999).

Pervasive developmental disorders: Diagnosis, options, and answers, by Mitzi Waltz (Future Horizons, 2003).

DIABETES

Growing up with diabetes: What children want their parents to know, by Alicia McAuliffe (Wiley, 1998).

Parenting a child with diabetes: A practical, empathetic guide to help you and your child live with diabetes (2nd ed.), by Gloria Loring (McGraw-Hill, 1999).

Practical endocrinology and diabetes in children (2nd ed.), by Joseph E. Raine, Malcolm D.C. Donaldson, John W. Gregory, Martin O. Savage, & Raymond L. Hintz (Wiley-Blackwell, 2006).

The everything parent's guide to children with juvenile diabetes: Reassuring advice for managing symptoms and raising a happy, healthy child, by Moira McCarthy; Jake Kushner, contributor (Adams Media, 2007).

Type 1 diabetes in children, adolescents, and young adults: How to become an expert on your own diabetes (3rd ed.), by Dr. Ragnar Hanas (Da Capo Press, 2005).

Understanding insulin-dependent diabetes, by H. Peter Chase (Childrens' Diabetes Foundation, 2000).

DOWN SYNDROME

Understanding Down syndrome: An introduction for parents, by Cliff Cunningham (Brookline Books, 1996).

Communication skills in children with Down syndrome: A guide for parents, by Libby Kumin (Woodbine House, 1994).

Fine motor skills in children with Down syndrome: A guide for parents and professionals, by Maryanne Bruni (Woodbine House, 1998).

Gross motor skills in children with Down syndrome: A guide for parents and professionals, by Patricia C. Winders (Woodbine House, 1997).

DRUG AND ALCOHOL ABUSE AND ADDICTION

Children of addiction: Research, health, and public policy issues, by H. Fitzgerald (Garland Science Publishing, 2002).

Drug addiction and families, by Marina Barnard & Fergal Keane (Jessica Kingsley Publishers, 2006).

Etiology of substance use disorder in children and adolescents: Emerging findings from the center for education and drug abuse research, Center for Education and Drug Abuse Research; by Ralph E. Tarter & Michael M. Vanyukov, Eds. (Routledge Publishing, 2002).

Impact of substance abuse on children and families: Research and practice implications (Haworth Social Work Practice), by Shulamith Lala Ashenberg Straussner & Christine Huff Fewell, Eds. (Routledge Publishing, 2006).

On the rocks: Teens and alcohol, by David Aretha (Franklin Watts Publishing, 2007).

Our children are alcoholics: Coping with children who have addictions, by Sally B. & David B. (Islewest Publishing, 1997).

DYSLEXIA

How to reach and teach children and teens with dyslexia: A parent and teacher guide to helping students of all ages academically, socially, and emotionally, by Cynthia M. Stowe (Jossey-Bass Publishing, 2000).

Supporting children with dyslexia (Learning Service, David Fulton Publishing, 2004).

The everything parent's guide to children with dyslexia: All you need to ensure your child's success (Everything: Parenting and Family), by Abigail Marshall (Adams Media, 2004).

The secret life of the dyslexic child: How she thinks. How he feels. How they can succeed, by Robert Frank & Kathryn E. Livingston (Rodale Books, 2004).

EATING DISORDERS AND OBESITY

A parent's guide to eating disorders and obesity (The Children's Hospital of Philadelphia Series), by Martha Moraghan Jablow & C. Everett Koop (Dell Publishing, 1991).

Children and adolescent obesity: Causes and consequences, prevention and management, by Walter Burniat, Tim J. Cole, Inge Lissau, & Elizabeth M.E. Poskitt, Eds. (Cambridge University Press, 2006).

Eating disorders: A guide for families and children (Guide for Families), by Valerie Eisbree; foreword by Sarah Mountbatten-Windsor (Merit Publishing International, 2007).

Eating disorders in children and adolescents (Cambridge Child and Adolescent Psychiatry), by Brett McDermott; Tony Jaffa, Ed. (Cambridge University Press, 2006).

Handbook of childhood and adolescent obesity (Issues in Clinical Child Psychology), by Elissa Jeialian & Ric G. Steele, Eds. (Springer Publishing, 2008).

EPILEPSY AND SEIZURES

Children with seizures: A guide for parents, teachers, and other professionals, by Martin L. Kutscher; foreword by Gregory L. Holmes (Jessica Kingsley Publishers, 2006).

Epilepsy in childhood and adolescence (2nd ed.), by R. E. Appleton & John Gibbs (Taylor & Francis, 1998).

Growing up with epilepsy: A practical guide for parents, by Lynn Bennett Blackburn (Demos Medical Publishing, 2003).

Pediatric epilepsy: Diagnosis and therapy (3rd ed.) by John M. Pellock, Blaise F. D. Bourgeois, W. Edwin Dodson, Douglas R. Nordill, Jr., & Raman Sankar, Eds. (Demos Medical Publishing, 2007).

Seizures and epilepsy in childhood: A guide (3rd ed.), by John H. Freeman, Eileen P. G. Vining, & Diana J. Pillas (Johns Hopkins University Press, 2002).

FETAL ALCOHOL SYNDROME

Alcohol, pregnancy and the developing child: Fetal alcohol syndrome, by Hans-Ludwig Spohr & Hans-Christoph Steinhausen, Eds. (Cambridge University Press, 1996).

Finding perspective . . . raising successful children affected by fetal alcohol spectrum disorders, by Liz Lawryk (OBD Triage Institute, 2005).

Reaching out to children with FAS/FAE: A handbook for teachers, counselors, and parents who live and work with children affected by fetal alcohol syndrome, by Diane Davis (Center for Applied Research in Education, 1994).

Recognizing and managing children with fetal alcohol syndrome/fetal alcohol effects: A guidebook, by Brenda McCreight (Child Welfare League of America Press, 1997).

FRAGILE X SYNDROME

Children with fragile X syndrome: A parents' guide, by Jayne Dixon Weder, Ed. (Woodbine House, 2000).

Educating children with fragile X syndrome: A multi-professional view, by D. Dew-Hughes (RoutledgeFalmer, 2003).

Fragile X syndrome: Diagnosis, treatment, and research (Johns Hopkins Series in Contemporary Medicine and Public Health) (3rd ed.), by Randi Jenssen Hagerman, & Paul J. Hagerman, Eds. (Johns Hopkins University Press, 2002).

Supporting children with fragile X syndrome (Learning Service, David Fulton Publishing, 2004).

HEADACHES AND MIGRAINES

Frequently asked questions about migraines and headaches (FAQ: Teen Life Set 6), by Allan B. Cobb (Rosen Publishing Group, 2008).

Headache and your child: The complete guide to understanding and treating migraine and other headaches in children and adolescents, by Seymour Diamond & Amy Diamond (Fireside, 2001).

Headaches and migraine (your child), by Maggie Jones (Robson Books, 2002).

Headaches and migraines in childhood, by Charles F. Barlow (Cambridge University Press, 1991).

HEART DISORDERS AND DISEASE

Encyclopedia of heart diseases, by M. Gabriel Kahn (Academic Press, 2005).

Heart defects in children: What every parent should know, by Cheryl J. Wild, (Wiley, 1998).

The heart of a child: What families need to know about heart disorders in children (Johns Hopkins Press Health Book) (2nd ed.), by Catherine A. Neill, Edward B. Clark, & Carleen Clark (Johns Hopkins University Press, 2001).

The parent's guide to children's congenital heart defects: What they are, how to treat them, how to cope with them, by Gerri Freid Kramer & Shari Maurer; foreword by Sylvester Stallone (Three Rivers Press, 2001).

HIV/AIDS

Children and HIV/AIDS, by Gary Anderson, & Constance Ryan, Eds. (Transaction Publishers, 1999).

Children and the HIV/AIDS crisis: Youth who are infected and affected, by Carrie McVicker (Youth Advocate Program International, 1999).

Children, families, and HIV/AIDS: Psychosocial and therapeutic issues, by Nancy Boyd-Franklin, Gloria L. Steiner, & Mary G. Boland, Eds. (Guilford Press, 1995).

School children with HIV/AIDS: Quality of life experiences in public schools, by Jillian Roberts; Kathleen Cairns, contributor (Detselig Enterprises, 1999).

HODGKIN'S DISEASE

Hodgkin's and non-Hodgkin's lymphoma, by John P. Leonard & Morton Coleman (Springer, 2006).

Hodgkin's disease (Diseases and Disorders), by Sheila Wyborny (Lucent Books, 2008).

Hodgkin lymphoma (2nd ed.), by Richard T. Hoppe, Peter M. Mauch, James O. Armitage, Volker Diehl, & Lawrence M. Weiss, Eds. (Lippincott Williams & Wilkins, 2007).

The official parent's sourcebook on childhood Hodgkin's disease: A revised and updated directory for the internet age (ICON Health Publications, 2002).

IEPS

IEP and inclusion tips for parents and teachers handout version, by Anne I. Eason & Kathleen Whitbread (IEP Resources, 2006).

Nolo's IEP guide: Learning disabilities (3rd ed.), by Lawrence M. Siegel (NOLO, 2007).

The complete IEP guide: How to advocate for your special ed. child (5th ed.), by Lawrence M. Siegel (NOLO, 2007).

Understanding, developing, and writing effective IEPs: A step-by-step guide for educators, by Roger Pierangelo & George A. Guiliani (Corwin Press, 2007).

KIDNEY AND LIVER DISEASE

ABC of kidney disease (ABC Series), by David Goldsmith, Satish Jayawardene, & Penny Ackland, Eds. (BMJ Books, 2007).

A parent's guide to kidney disorders (University of Minnesota Guides to Birth and Childhood Disorders), by Glenn H. Bock, Edward J. Ruley, & Michael P. Moore (University of Minnesota Press, 1993).

Kidney disorders in children and adolescents: A practical handbook, by Ronald J. Hogg, Ed. (Informa Healthcare, 2006).

Liver disease in children (3rd ed.), by Frederick J. Suchy, Ronald J. Sokol, & William F. Balistreri, Eds. (Cambridge University Press, 2007).

Pediatric nephrology, by Ellis D. Avner, William E. Harmon, & Patrick Niaudet, Eds. (Lippincott Williams & Wilkins, 2003).

LEARNING DISABILITIES

College and career success for students with learning disabilities, by Roslyn Dobler (McGraw-Hill, 1996).

Learning disabilities: A to Z: A parent's complete guide to learning disabilities from preschool to adulthood, by Corinne Smith & Lisa Strick (Free Press, 1999).

Learning disabilities: From identification to intervention, by Jack M. Fletcher, G. Reid Lyon, Lynn S. Fuchs, & Marcia A. Barnes (Guilford Press, 2006).

Learning disabilities information for teens, by Sandra Augustyn Lawton (Omnigraphics, 2005).

Parenting children with learning disabilities, by Jane Utley Adelizzi & Diane B. Goss (Bergin & Garvey Trade, 2001).

Surviving learning disabilities successfully: 16 rules for managing a child's learning disabilities, by Nancy E. Graves & Danielle E. Graves (iUniverse, 2007).

The misunderstood child: Understanding and coping with your child's learning disabilities, by Larry B. Silver (Three Rivers Press, 1998).

LEUKEMIAS, LYMPHOMAS, AND MYELOMAS

100 Q & A about leukemia (2nd ed.), by Edward D. Ball (Jones and Bartlett Publishers, 2007).

Childhood leukemia: A guide for families, friends and caregivers (3rd ed.), by Nancy Keene (Patient Centered Guides, 2002).

Childhood leukemias (2nd ed.), by Ching-Hon Pui, Ed. (Cambridge University Press, 2006).

Pediatric lymphomas (Pediatric oncology), by Howard J. Weinstein, Melissa M. Hudson, & Michael P. Link, Eds. (Springer, 2007).

Understanding leukemias, lymphomas and myelomas, by Tarig Mughal, John M. Goldman, & Sabena Mughal (Informa Healthcare, 2005).

MENTAL RETARDATION

Educating mentally retarded children, by R. K. Shah (Aavishkar Publishers, 2004).

Mental retardation and developmental delay: Genetic and epigenetic factors (Oxford Monographs on Medical Genetics), by Moyra Smith (Oxford University Press, USA, 2005).

Teacher of children with retarded mental development, by Jack Rudman (National Learning Corp., 1997).

The mentally retarded child, by Abraham Levinson (Greenwood Press, [Reprint] 1978).

MULTIPLE DISABILITIES

Including children with severe and multiple disabilities in typical classrooms: Practical strategies for teachers (2nd ed.), by June Downing, Joanne Eichinger, & Maryann Demchak (Paul H. Brookes Publishing, 2001).

Supporting the children with multiple disabilities (2nd ed.), by Michael Mednick (Continuum International Publishing Group, 2007).

Teaching individuals with physical or multiple disabilities (5th ed.), by Sherwood J. Best, Kathryn W. Heller, & June L. Bigge (Prentice Hall, 2004).

Understanding physical, health, and multiple disabilities (2nd ed.), by Kathryn Wolff Heller, Paula E. Forney, Paul A. Alberto, Sherwood J. Best, & Morton N. Schwartzman (Prentice Hall, 2008).

MULTIPLE SCLEROSIS

Multiple sclerosis: A guide for families (2nd ed.), by Rosalind C. Kalb (Demos Medical Publishing, 1998).

Multiple sclerosis: Diagnosis, medical management, and rehabilitation, by Jack S. Burks, & Kenneth P. Johnson (Demos Medical Publishing, 2000).

Multiple sclerosis Q&A: Researching answers to frequently asked questions, by Beth Ann Hill (Avery, 2003).

The first year—Multiple sclerosis: An essential guide for the newly diagnosed, by Margaret Blackstone; foreword by Sadiq A. Saud (Marlowe & Company, 2002).

MUSCULAR/NEUROMUSCULAR DISORDERS

Muscular dystrophy in children: A guide for families, by Irwin M. Siegel (Demos Medical Publishing, 1999).

Neuromuscular diseases of infancy, childhood, and adolescence (a clinician's approach), by H. Royden Jones, Darryl De Vivo, & Basil T. Darras (Butterworth-Heinemann, 2002).

Occupational therapy and Duchenne muscular dystrophy, by Kate Stone, Claire Tester, Joy Blakeney, Alex Howarth, Heather McAndrew, Nicola Traynor, Mary McCutcheon, & Ruth Johnston (Wiley, 2007).

Raising a child with a neuromuscular disorder: A guide for parents, grandparents, friends and professionals, by Charlotte Thompson (Oxford University Press, 1999).

PREGNANCY

Books, babies, and school-age parents: How to teach pregnant and parenting teens to succeed, by Jeannie Warren Lindsay & Sharon Githens Enright (Morning Glory Press, 1997).

Preteen and teenage pregnancy: A twenty-first century reality, by June L. Leishman (M&K Publishing, 2007).

The unplanned pregnancy book for teens and college students, by Dorrie Williams-Wheeler (Sparkledoll Productions, 2004).

Your pregnancy & newborn journey: A guide for pregnant teens (2nd ed.), by Jeannie Warren Lindsay & Jean Brunelli (Morning Glory Press, 2004).

PSYCHIATRIC/PSYCHOLOGICAL DISORDERS

Childhood schizophrenia, by Sheila Cantor (Guilford Press, 1988).

Helping your troubled teen: Learn to recognize, understand, and address the destructive behavior of today's teens and preteens, by Cynthia Kaplan, Blaise Aguirre, & Michael Rater (Fair Winds Press, 2007).

Should I medicate my child? Sane solutions for troubled kids with—and without—psychiatric drugs, by Lawrence H. Diller (Basic Books, 2003).

The American Psychiatric Publishing textbook of child and adolescent psychiatry (3rd ed.), by Jerry M. Wiener & Mina K. Dulcan (American Psychiatric Publishing, 2003).

The handbook of psychiatric drug therapy for children and adolescents, by Karen A. Theesen (Haworth Press, 1997).

SENSORY DISORDERS

Raising a sensory smart child: The definitive handbook for helping your child with sensory integration issues, by Lindsey Biel & Nancy Peske (Penguin, 2005).

Sensory integration and the child: 25th anniversary edition, by A. Jean Ayres (Western Psychological Services, 2005).

The out-of-sync child: Recognizing and coping with sensory integration dysfunction (Rev. Ed.), by Carol Stock Kranowitz; foreword by Larry B. Silver (Perigree, Penguin Group, 2005).

Too loud, too bright, too fast, too tight: What to do if you are sensory defensive in an overstimulating world, by Sharon Heller (Harper, 2003).

SEXUAL ASSAULT

21st century complete medical guide to sexual assault, rape, teen sexual violence, Progressive Management Medical Health News (Progressive Management, 2004).

Overcoming childhood sexual trauma: A guide to breaking through the wall of fear for practitioners and survivors, by Sheri Oz & Sarah-Jane Ogiers (Routledge, 2006).

Sexual assault of children and adolescents, by Ann Wolbert Burgess (Lexington Books, 1978).

The trauma of sexual assault: Treatment, prevention and practice, by Jenny Petrak & Barbara Hedge (Wiley, 2002).

SEXUALLY TRANSMITTED DISEASES

Color atlas and synopsis of sexually transmitted diseases (2nd ed.), by H. Hunter Handsfield (McGraw-Hill Professional, 2000).

Sexual health information for teens: Health tips about sexual development, human reproduction, and sexually transmitted diseases, by Deborah A. Stanley, Ed. (Omnigraphics, 2003).

Staying safe: A teen's guide to sexually transmitted diseases, by Miranda Hunter & William Hunter (Mason Crest Publishers, 2004).

The real truth about teens and sex: From hooking up to friends with benefits—what teens are thinking, and doing, and talking about, and how to help them make smart choices, by Sabrina Weill (Perigree Trade, 2005).

What every parent should know about teen sex: The secret STD epidemic, by Becky Ettinger (Xulon Press, 2007).

SICKLE-CELL ANEMIA

Comprehensive handbook of childhood cancer in sickle cell disease: A biopsychosocial approach, by Ronald T. Brown (Oxford University Press, USA, 2006).

Sickle cell anemia: What does it mean to have? (3rd ed.), Heinemann, Ed. (Heinemann Library, 2005).

Sickle cell anemia, by Lizabeth Peak (Lucent Books, 2007).

Understanding sickle cell disease, by Miriam Bloom (University Press of Mississippi, 1995).

SPECIAL NEEDS—GENERAL

A difference in the family: Living with a disabled child (Reprint Ed.), by Helen Featherstone (Penguin, 1981).

A matter of dignity: Changing the world of the disabled, by Andrew Potok (Bantam, 2002).

Adopting the hurt child: Hope for families with special-needs kids: A guide for parents and professionals (Revised & Updated), by Gregory C. Keck & Regina M. Kupecky (Navpress Publishing Group, 1998).

Children with special needs in early childhood settings, by Carol L. Paasche, Lola Gorrill, & Bev Strom (Thomson Delmar Learning, 2003).

Parenting through crisis: Helping kids in time of loss, grief and change, by Barbara Coloroso (Collins, 2001).

Quirky kids; understanding and helping your child who doesn't fit in—when to worry and when not to worry, by Perri Klass & Eileen Costello (Ballantine Books, 2004).

Disability is natural, by Kathie Snow (Braveheart Press, 2001).

The child with special needs: Encouraging intellectual and emotional growth, by Stanley I. Greenspan, Serena Weider, & Robin Simons (Perseus Books, 1998).

The early intervention dictionary: A multidisciplinary guide to terminology, by Jeanine G. Coleman (Woodbine House, 1993).

Uncommon voyage: Parenting a special needs child (2nd ed.), by Laura Shapiro Kramer; foreword by Seth Kramer (North Atlantic Books, 2001).

Views from our shoes: Growing up with a brother or sister with special needs, by Donald J. Meyer (Woodbine House, 1997).

SPECIAL NEEDS TRUSTS

Special needs trust administration manual: A guide for trustees, by Barbara D. Jackins, Richard S. Blank, Peter M. Macy, Ken W. Shulman, & Harriet H. Onello (People with Disabilities Press Series, 2005).

Tax, estate, and lifetime planning for minors, by Carmina Y. D'Aversa (American Bar Association, 2006).

The basics of special needs planning: Protecting your clients who need the most protection (Audio CD Package), by Harry S. Margolis & Vincent J. Russo (American Bar Association, 2007).

Third-party and self-created trusts: Planning for the elderly and disabled client (3rd ed.), by Clifton B. Kruse, Jr. (American Bar Association, 2002).

SPEECH AND LANGUAGE IMPAIRMENTS

Childhood speech, language and listening problems: What every parent should know (2nd ed.), by Patricia McAleer Hamaguchi (Wiley, 2001).

Children with specific language impairment, by Laurence B. Leonard (MIT Press, 2000).

Preschool language disorders resource guide: Specific language impairment, by Amy L. Weiss (Singular, 2001).

Speech and language impairments in children: Causes, characteristics, intervention and outcome, by Dorothy Bishop (Psychology Press, 2001).

SPINA BIFIDA

Caring for the child with spina bifida: Shriners Hospitals for children, by John F. Sarwak (American Academy of Orthopaedic Surgeons, 2002).

Children with spina bifida: A parent's guide, by Marlene Lutkenhoff (Woodbine House, 1999).

Living with spina bifida: A guide for families and professionals, by Adrian Sandler (University of North Carolina Press, 2003).

Spinabilities: A young person's guide to spina bifida, by Marlene Lutkenhoff & Sonya G. Oppenheimer (Woodbine House, 1997).

SUICIDE

Aftershock: Help, hope, and healing in the wake of suicide, by Arrington Cox & David Candy (B&H Publishing Group, 2003).

Let's talk facts about teens suicide: Healthy minds, healthy lives, by the American Psychiatric Association (American Psychiatric Publishing, 2005).

Teen Suicide, by Judith Peacock (LifeMatters, 2000).

The power to prevent suicide: A guide for teens helping teens, by Richard E. Nelson (Free Spirit Publishing, 1994).

When nothing matters anymore: A survival guide for depressed teens, by Bev Cobain; foreword by Peter S. Jensen (Free Spirit Publishing, 2007).

TERMINALLY ILL CHILDREN

Loss and grief recovery: Help caring for children with disabilities, chronic or terminal illness, by Joyce Ashton & Dennis Ashton (Baywood Publishing, 1996).

Supporting the child and the family in pediatric palliative care, by Erica Brown & Brian Warr; foreword by Sheila Shribman (Jessica Kingsley Publishers, 2007).

The private worlds of dying children, by Myra Bluebond-Langner (Princeton University Press, 1980).

When children die: Improving palliative and end-of-life care for children and their families (Committee on Palliative and End of Life Care for Children and Their Families), by Marilyn J. Field, & Richard E. Behrman, Eds. (National Academies Press, 2003).

TRAUMA

An adult's guide to childhood trauma, by Sharon Lewis (David Phillips Publishers, 2000).

Childhood trauma: Your questions answered, by Ursula Markham (Element Books, 1998).

Effects of interventions for childhood trauma from infancy through adolescence: Pain unspeakable, by Sandra B. Hutchison (Routledge, 2004).

Handbook for treatment of attachment-trauma problems in children, by Beverly James (Free Press, 1994).

The trauma spectrum: Hidden wounds and human resiliency, by Robert C. Scaer (W.W. Norton, 2005).

Too scared to cry: Psychic trauma in childhood (Reprint Ed.), by Lenore Terr (Basic Books, 1992).

Trauma and sexuality: The effects of childhood sexual, physical, and emotional abuse on sexual identity and behavior, by James A. Chu; & Elizabeth S. Bowman, Eds. (Informa Healthcare, 2003).

Treating trauma and traumatic grief in children and adolescents, by Judith A. Cohen, Anthony P. Mannarino, & Esther Deblinger (Guilford Press, 2006).

TRAUMATIC BRAIN INJURY

Children with traumatic brain injury: A parent's guide, by Lisa Schoenbrodt, Ed. (Woodbine House, 2001).

Traumatic brain injury in children and adolescents: A sourcebook for teachers and other school personnel (2nd ed.), by Janet Tyler & Mary Mira (Pro-Ed, 1999).

Traumatic brain injury in children and adolescents: Assessment and intervention, by Margaret Semrud-Clikeman (Guilford Press, 2001).

Traumatic brain injury rehabilitation: Children and adolescents (2nd ed.), by Mark Ylvisaker (Butterworth-Heinemann, 1998).

CHAPTER 14

Checklists

This chapter presents the following checklists. These checklists are for guidance only; they are not intended to be exhaustive.

1. *Initial Interview*—what to ask the client
2. *Client File Contents*—items the lawyer should have in her client file when handling a special needs divorce case
3. *Drafting the Petition*—special subject areas for the Petition
4. *Statement of Income and Expenses*—what should be included in the Statement of Income and Expenses
5. *Answer and Cross-Petition*—how to prepare the Answer and Cross-Petition
6. *Discovery*—subjects to explore through the discovery process
7. *Temporary Orders*—do you need to file a PDL Motion? (Interim Order)
8. *Child Support*—special considerations regarding child support
9. *Custody*—special considerations regarding custody
10. *Visitation*—special considerations regarding visitation
11. *Support Systems for the Special Needs Child*—help for the special needs child during and after divorce
12. *Property Distribution*—special considerations regarding property distribution, including retirement accounts
13. *Counseling*—special issues for counseling

1. INITIAL INTERVIEW—WHAT TO ASK THE CLIENT

1. Do any of the children have **special needs**? These can include any physical, mental, or emotional disability; learning disability; behavior or mood disorder; or any other issue that might require special consideration in the divorce, for purposes of medication, medical treatment, therapy, custody, visitation, or child support.
2. Do any of the children receive special **assistance at school**?
3. Do any of the children have an **Individualized Education Plan (IEP)** or **504 Plan**[1] at school?

1. An IEP is a legal document mandated by IDEA, that controls the procedural requirements. It is more involved than a 504 Plan. An IEP is required for students with disabilities who require specialized instruction. A 504 Plan is a written plan that is required for students with disabilities needing only reasonable accommodation. It is less involved than an IEP. An excellent explanation may be found in L. Wilmhurst & A. W. Brue, *A Parent's Guide to Special Education* (2005, Amacom). *See also* "IEPs vs. 504 Plans," and the entire Sevier County Special Education website. Retrieved July 18, 2022, from https://www.sevier.org/site/default.aspx?PageType=2&PageModuleInstanceID=486&ViewID=838b13a1-2ccb-4c74-83cb-0b9f098d693

4. Are any of the children on **medication**?
5. Are any of the children in **counseling,** physical **therapy**, behavior therapy, or psychological counseling?
6. What is the official **diagnosis**?
7. **Who** made the diagnosis?
8. **When** was the diagnosis made?
9. When had the **first symptoms** appeared?
10. What **testing** was done to evaluate the child's condition?
11. **Why** was the child seen by the person who made the diagnosis? (What made the parents believe the child **needed to be evaluated**?)
12. Has any other professional **confirmed** the diagnosis?
13. What is the child's **current condition**?
14. What is the child's **prognosis**? (expected outcome)
15. Is the condition **curable**?
16. Is the condition **treatable**?
17. Is the condition **terminal**?
18. Is the child expected to ever be able to get a high school **diploma**, get a college degree, live on her own, hold a regular job, **live** completely **independently**, marry, have children?
19. What is the child's **life expectancy**?
20. How does this condition **affect** the child's life **now**?
21. How is it expected to **affect** the child's life in the **future**?
22. How does this condition **affect siblings'** lives **now**?
23. How is it expected to **affect siblings'** lives in the **future**?
24. How does this condition **affect** the **parents'** lives **now**?
25. How is it expected to **affect** the **parents'** lives in the **future**?
26. Who is the **primary caregiver**?
27. How has the condition **affected** the **careers** of the **parents**?
28. How will the condition affect the **parents' career advancement** and **retirement plan contributions**?
29. What are the names, addresses, telephone numbers, and credentials of all **persons the child currently sees** for this condition?
30. List all **medications** the child currently takes, the frequency and dosage, the reason for the medication, and the expected result from the medication.
31. List all **therapies** the child currently receives, including therapies received at home and at school. *For each therapy, identify:*
    a. The **person** or **organization** who provides the therapy
    b. Who **referred** the child to that person or organization
    c. **Where** the therapy is received
    d. The **type** of therapy and **methodology** used (for example: behavior therapy using ABA-applied behavior analysis method)
    e. The **frequency** and **duration** of therapy (for example: three times per week, one hour each time)
    f. The **length of time** therapy is **expected to continue** (for example: for the entire school year, for six weeks after the cast is removed, indefinitely, for six months)

7&RenderLoc=0&FlexDataID=7938. Additional helpful materials include the Learning Disabilities OnLine website, http://www.LDonline.org (especially the materials on accommodations and modifications) and the Cleveland Heights Teachers Union website materials on 504 Plan Frequently Asked Questions, http://www.chtu.org. (Both websites retrieved on July 6, 2022).

   g. **Cost** of the therapy
   h. **How** this cost is **paid** (private pay, insurance, funding program)
   i. Amount of **uncovered cost** of this therapy
   j. **Incidental costs** of this therapy—transportation, caregiver, supplies, meals, equipment
   k. **Who takes** the child to the therapy
32. What are the expectations regarding future therapies and medications?
33. Is the child on a waiting list for any therapy, program, school, or funding?
34. Itemize all **direct and indirect costs** resulting from the child's special needs, including therapy, doctors, other practitioners, medications, supplements, equipment, supplies, caregiver training, special nutritional requirements, special clothing and personal care item requirements, home modifications, vehicle modifications, modifications at school, nonparental caregiver costs, transportation, and any other costs.
35. Do either of the PARENTS have **special needs**? These can include any physical, mental, or emotional disability; learning disability; behavior or mood disorder; or any other issue that might require special consideration in the divorce, for purposes of medication, medical treatment, therapy, custody, visitation, or child support.
36. Do either of the PARENTS receive **accommodations for a disability at work**?
37. Are either of the PARENTS on **medication**?
38. Are any of the PARENTS in **counseling**, physical **therapy**, behavior therapy, or psychological counseling?
39. What is the official **diagnosis**?
40. **Who** made the diagnosis?
41. **When** was the diagnosis made?
42. When did the **first symptoms** appeared?
43. What **testing** was done to evaluate the PARENT'S condition?
44. **Why** was the PARENT seen by the person who made the diagnosis? (Was there a medical or psychiatric crisis?)
45. Has any other professional **confirmed** the diagnosis?
46. What is the PARENT'S **current condition**?
47. What is the PARENT'S **prognosis**? (expected outcome)
48. Is the condition **curable**?
49. Is the condition **treatable**?
50. Is the condition **terminal**?
51. Is the PARENT expected to **live** entirely **independently**, or will the parent need in-home assistance, a group home setting, or long-term care?
52. What is the PARENT'S **life expectancy**?
53. How does this condition **affect** the PARENT'S life **now**?
54. How is it expected to **affect** the PARENT'S life in the **future**?
55. How does this condition **affect the children's** lives **now**?
56. How is it expected to **affect the children's** lives in the **future**?
57. How does this condition **affect** the **other parent's** life **now**?
58. How is it expected to **affect** the **other parent's** life in the **future**?
59. How has the condition **affected** the **careers** of the **parents**?
60. How will the condition affect the **parents' career advancement** and **retirement plan contributions**?
61. What are the names, addresses, telephone numbers, and credentials of all **persons the PARENT currently sees** for this condition?
62. List all **medications** the PARENT currently takes, the frequency and dosage, the reason for the medication, and the expected result from the medication.

63. List all **therapies and ongoing medical treatments** the PARENT currently receives. *For each therapy and medical treatment, identify:*
    a. The **person** or **organization** who provides the therapy or medical treatment
    b. Who **referred** the PARENT to that person or organization
    c. **Where** the therapy or medical treatment is received
    d. The **type** of therapy or medical treatment and **methodology** used (for example: behavior therapy using ABA-applied behavior analysis method)
    e. The **frequency** and **duration** of therapy or medical treatment (for example: three times per week, one hour each time)
    f. The **length of time** therapy or medical treatment is **expected to continue** (for example: for another six months from today's date, for six weeks after the cast is removed, indefinitely
    g. **Cost** of the therapy or medical treatment
    h. **How** this cost is **paid** (private pay, insurance, funding program)
    i. Amount of **uncovered cost** of this therapy or medical treatment
    j. **Incidental costs** of this therapy or medical treatment—transportation, caregiver, supplies, meals, equipment
64. What are the expectations regarding future therapies, medications, and medical treatment?
65. Itemize all **direct and indirect costs** resulting from the PARENT'S special needs, including therapy, medical treatments, doctors, other practitioners, medications, supplements, equipment, supplies, special nutritional requirements, special clothing and personal care item requirements, home modifications, vehicle modifications, modifications at work, nonparental caregiver costs, transportation, and any other costs.

2. CLIENT FILE CONTENTS—ITEMS THE LAWYER SHOULD HAVE IN HER CLIENT FILE WHEN HANDLING A SPECIAL NEEDS DIVORCE CASE

In addition to the usual items contained in a divorce client file, a lawyer handling a divorce case involving special needs of a child or parent should have the following items:

1. **Medical** reports, test results, diagnoses
2. **Evaluations**
3. **Treatment** plans
4. **Therapy** plans
5. **Medication** plans
6. Child's or parent's **safety plans** for home, school, work, and away
7. Medical **bills**
8. Documentation of all **costs**—see checklist 1
9. **IEPs** (Individual Education Plans) and **504 Plans** current and previous (IEPs and 504 Plans are explained in footnote 1.)
10. **Information** on every treating **professional**—see checklist 1
11. Copies of **articles** or **book excerpts** providing basic information on child's or parent's particular **condition**
12. Detailed therapy and treatment **schedule**
13. Detailed daily schedule
14. **Documentation** for all other items contained in checklist 1

3. DRAFTING THE PETITION—SPECIAL SUBJECT AREAS FOR THE PETITION

After you gather the information contained in checklists 1 and 2, *make sure you understand it.* If necessary, consult an expert in the field so you feel comfortable discussing the issues inherent in the child's or parent's condition and arguing the merits of the case to the judge.

In addition to the usual items contained in a standard Petition, assess the following topics and include in the Petition if relevant:

1. A recital of the child's or parent's **special needs**
2. A recital of the **need** to use a **different child support or spousal support amount**
3. A recital of the **need** to use a **different parenting plan**
4. A statement of the type of **physical custody** appropriate
5. A statement of the type of **legal custody** appropriate
6. A statement of the type of **visitation** appropriate
7. A statement of the need for **maintenance**
8. A statement of the need for different property distribution

4. STATEMENT OF INCOME AND EXPENSES—WHAT SHOULD BE INCLUDED IN THE STATEMENT OF INCOME AND EXPENSES

In addition to the standard items disclosed in the Statement of Expenses, the Statement of Income and Expenses should also disclose all *direct and indirect costs* resulting from the child's or parent's *special needs*, including

1. Therapy
2. Doctors
3. Other practitioners
4. Medications
5. Supplements
6. Equipment
7. Supplies
8. Caregiver training
9. Special nutritional requirements
10. Special clothing and personal care item requirements
11. Home modifications
12. Vehicle modifications
13. Modifications at school or work
14. Nonparental caregiver costs
15. Transportation
16. Any other costs

5. ANSWER AND CROSS-PETITION—HOW TO PREPARE THE ANSWER AND CROSS-PETITION

1. If the child's or parent's **special needs** have not been recited in the Petition, they should be alleged in the Answer and Cross-Petition.
2. If the child's or parent's special needs have been recited in the Petition **accurately**, this should be acknowledged in the Answer and Cross-Petition.

3. If the child's or parent's special needs have been **inaccurately alleged** in the Petition, this should be alleged in the Answer and Cross-Petition, with the **Respondent's view** of the child's condition.
4. If the need to use a **different child support or spousal support amount** is appropriate but not alleged in the Petition, this should be alleged in the Answer and Cross-Petition.
5. If the need to use a different child support or spousal support amount is **not appropriate** but is alleged in the Petition, this should be alleged in the Answer and Cross-Petition.
6. If the need to use a **different parenting plan** is appropriate but not alleged in the Petition, this should be alleged in the Answer and Cross-Petition.
7. If the need to use a different parenting plan is **not appropriate** but is alleged in the Petition, this should be alleged in the Answer and Cross-Petition.
8. Appropriate **physical custody** should be addressed in the Answer and Cross-Petition.
9. Appropriate **legal custody** should be addressed in the Answer and Cross-Petition.
10. Appropriate **visitation** should be addressed in the Answer and Cross-Petition.
11. The need for **maintenance** should be addressed in the Answer and Cross-Petition.

6. DISCOVERY—SUBJECTS TO EXPLORE THROUGH THE DISCOVERY PROCESS

Often, the documentation the clients provide to the lawyers is incomplete. In addition to the usual items that may be explored during a standard divorce, special needs cases demand exploring special subjects through the discovery process.

These special subjects can include the following information:

1. Whether any of the children or parents have **special needs**. Determine with regard to *all* of the children and parents whether they have any physical, mental, or emotional disability; learning disability; or behavior or mood disorder. Often there will be more than one special need within a family. Ask about this subject through interrogatories and/or depositions. Follow up with Request for Production of Documents. Obtain signed and notarized releases so you can obtain medical records of all medical and therapeutic professionals and record keepers.
2. Whether any of the children receive special **assistance at school or parents receive any disability accommodations at work**. Ask about this subject through interrogatories and/or depositions. Follow up with Request for Production of Documents. Obtain signed and notarized releases of school records.
3. Do any of the children have an **Individualized Education Plan (IEP)** or **504 Plan** at school? (IEPs and 504 Plans are explained in footnote 1.) Ask about this subject through interrogatories and/or depositions. Follow up with Request for Production of Documents. Obtain signed and notarized release of school records. In some educational settings, you may need to obtain two releases, one for the general education program and one for the entity that provides the special education/therapy in the school setting.
4. Are any of the children or parents on **medication**? Ask about this subject through interrogatories and/or depositions. Follow up with Request for Production of Documents. Obtain signed and notarized releases of medical records.
5. Are any of the children or parents in **counseling**, physical **therapy**, behavior therapy, or psychological counseling? Ask about this subject through interrogatories and/or depositions. Follow up with Request for Production of Documents. Obtain signed and notarized releases so you may obtain the records of all counselors and therapists.
6. What is the official **diagnosis**? Ask about this subject through interrogatories and/or depositions. Follow up with Request for Production of Documents. Obtain signed and

notarized release so you may obtain the records of the diagnostician. Sometimes this might be a doctor or therapist. Other times, it might be a diagnostic clinic or other entity.

7. **Who** made the diagnosis? Ask about this subject through interrogatories and/or depositions. Follow up with Request for Production of Documents. Obtain signed and notarized release so you may obtain the records of the diagnostician. Sometimes this may be a doctor or therapist. Other times, it might be a diagnostic clinic or other entity.
8. **When** was the diagnosis made? Ask about this subject through interrogatories and/or depositions. Follow up with Request for Production of Documents. Obtain signed and notarized releases so you may obtain the records of the diagnostician. Sometimes this might be a doctor or therapist. Other times, it might be a diagnostic clinic or other entity.
9. When did the **first symptoms** appear? Ask about this subject through interrogatories and/or depositions. Follow up with Request for Production of Documents. Be prepared to follow up with discovery on all persons or entities involved in the first appearance of symptoms. These may be preschools and their personnel, babysitters, pediatricians, emergency room personnel, law enforcement personnel, relatives of the child, Parents As Teachers, or other early childhood programs. Obtain all appropriate releases.
10. What **testing** was done to evaluate the child's or parent's condition? Ask about this subject through interrogatories and/or depositions. Follow up with Request for Production of Documents. Obtain all appropriate releases.
11. **Why** was the child or parent seen by the person who made the diagnosis? (What made the parents believe the child **needed to be evaluated**? Why did the parent seek treatment?) Ask about this subject through interrogatories and/or depositions. Follow up with Request for Production of Documents. Obtain all appropriate releases.
12. Has any other professional **confirmed** the diagnosis? Ask about this subject through interrogatories and/or depositions. Follow up with Request for Production of Documents. Obtain all appropriate releases.
13. What is the child's or parent's **current condition**? Ask about this subject through interrogatories and/or depositions. Follow up with Request for Production of Documents. Obtain all appropriate releases. Do research on the child's or parent's actual condition. Obtain authoritative and scholarly materials to educate yourself and the court on the child's or parent's particular condition. Research your state and local court evidentiary rules regarding admissibility of this evidence.
14. What is the child's or parent's **prognosis** (expected outcome)? Ask about this subject through interrogatories and/or depositions. Follow up with Request for Production of Documents. Obtain all appropriate releases. Obtain authoritative and scholarly materials to educate yourself and the court on the child's or parent's particular prognosis. Research your state and local court evidentiary rules regarding admissibility of this evidence.
15. Is the condition **curable** (can they make it "go away")? Ask about this subject through interrogatories and/or depositions. Follow up with Request for Production of Documents. Obtain all appropriate releases. Obtain authoritative and scholarly materials to educate yourself and the court on the curability of the child's or parent's particular condition. Research your state and local court evidentiary rules regarding admissibility of this evidence.
16. Is the condition **treatable** (they can't make it go away but they can make things better or perhaps make things not get worse for the patient)? Ask about this subject through interrogatories and/or depositions. Follow up with Request for Production of Documents. Obtain authoritative and scholarly materials to educate yourself and the court

on the treatment of the child's or parent's particular condition. Research your state and local court evidentiary rules regarding admissibility of this evidence.

17. Is the condition **terminal** (fatal)? Ask about this subject through interrogatories and/or depositions. Follow up with Request for Production of Documents. Obtain authoritative and scholarly materials to educate yourself and the court on whether the child's or parent's particular condition is terminal. Research your state and local court evidentiary rules regarding admissibility of this evidence.
18. Is the child expected to ever be able to get a high school **diploma**, get a college degree, live on her own, hold a regular job, **live** completely **independently**, marry, have children? Is the parent expected to live independently or need in-home assistance, a group home setting, or long-term care? Ask about this subject through interrogatories and/or depositions. Follow up with Request for Production of Documents. Obtain authoritative and scholarly materials to educate yourself and the court on the lifetime implications of the child's or parent's particular condition. Research your state and local court evidentiary rules regarding admissibility of this evidence.
19. What is the child's or parent's **life expectancy**? Ask about this subject through interrogatories and/or depositions. Follow up with Request for Production of Documents. Obtain authoritative and scholarly materials to educate yourself and the court on the life expectancy of the child's or parent's particular condition. Research your state and local court evidentiary rules regarding admissibility of this evidence.
20. How does this condition **affect** the child's or parent's life **now**? Ask about this subject through interrogatories and/or depositions. Follow up with Request for Production of Documents. Obtain authoritative and scholarly materials to educate yourself and the court on the current impact of the child's or parent's particular condition. Research your state and local court evidentiary rules regarding admissibility of this evidence.
21. How is it expected to **affect** the child's or parent's life in the **future**? Ask about this subject through interrogatories and/or depositions. Follow up with Request for Production of Documents. Obtain authoritative and scholarly materials to educate yourself and the court on the future impact of the child's or parent's particular condition. Research your state and local court evidentiary rules regarding admissibility of this evidence.
22. How does this condition **affect siblings'** lives **now**? Ask about this subject through interrogatories and/or depositions. Follow up with Request for Production of Documents. Obtain authoritative and scholarly materials to educate yourself and the court on the impact of the child's particular condition on siblings. Research your state and local court evidentiary rules regarding admissibility of this evidence.
23. How is it expected to **affect siblings'** lives in the **future**? Ask about this subject through interrogatories and/or depositions. Follow up with Request for Production of Documents. Obtain authoritative and scholarly materials to educate yourself and the court on the future impact of the child's particular condition on siblings. Research your state and local court evidentiary rules regarding admissibility of this evidence.
24. How does this condition **affect** the **parents'** lives **now**? Ask about this subject through interrogatories and/or depositions. Follow up with Request for Production of Documents. Obtain authoritative and scholarly materials to educate yourself and the court on the current impact of the child's particular condition on parents. Research your state and local court evidentiary rules regarding admissibility of this evidence.
25. How is it expected to **affect** the **parents'** lives in the **future**? Ask about this subject through interrogatories and/or depositions. Follow up with Request for Production of Documents. Obtain authoritative and scholarly materials to educate yourself and the court on the future impact of the child's particular condition on parents. Research your state and local court evidentiary rules regarding admissibility of this evidence.

26. Who is the **primary caregiver**? Ask about this subject through interrogatories and/or depositions. Follow up with Request for Production of Documents. Obtain all appropriate releases.
27. How has the condition **affected** the **careers** of the **parents**? Ask about this subject through interrogatories and/or depositions. Follow up with Request for Production of Documents. Obtain authoritative and scholarly materials to educate yourself and the court on the impact of the child's particular condition on careers of the parents. Research your state and local court evidentiary rules regarding admissibility of this evidence. Obtain employer and retirement account records from three time periods: one, prior to the child's special need; two, at the time the child's special need occurred; and three, at the current time.
28. How will the condition affect the **parents' career advancement** and **retirement plan contributions**? Ask about this subject through interrogatories and/or depositions. Follow up with Request for Production of Documents. Obtain authoritative and scholarly materials to educate yourself and the court on the impact of the child's particular condition on career advancement and retirement plan contributions of the parents. Research your state and local court evidentiary rules regarding admissibility of this evidence. Obtain employer and retirement account records from three time periods: one, prior to the child's special need; two, at the time the child's special need occurred; and three, at the current time.
29. What are the names, addresses, telephone numbers, and credentials of all **persons the child or parent currently sees** for this condition? Ask about this subject through interrogatories and/or depositions. Follow up with Request for Production of Documents. Obtain all appropriate releases.
30. List all **medications** the child or parent currently takes, the frequency and dosage, the reason for the medication, and the expected result from the medication. Ask about this subject through interrogatories and/or depositions. Follow up with Request for Production of Documents. Obtain all appropriate releases.
31. List all **therapies and medical treatments** the child or parent currently receives, including therapies received at home and school. Ask about this subject through interrogatories and/or depositions. Follow up with Request for Production of Documents. Obtain authoritative and scholarly materials to educate yourself and the court on each of the child's or parent's particular therapies and medical treatments. Research your state and local court evidentiary rules regarding admissibility of this evidence. Obtain all appropriate releases and records from all therapists, service providers, referral entities, and funding sources. Obtain admissible evidence for all billing, invoices, and receipts.
    For each therapy, identify:
    a. the **person** or **organization** who provides the therapy
    b. who **referred** the child to that person or organization
    c. **where** the therapy is received
    d. the **type** of therapy and **methodology** used (for example: behavior therapy using ABA—applied behavior analysis method)
    e. the **frequency** and **duration** of therapy (for example: three times per week, one hour each time)
    f. the **length of time** therapy is **expected to continue** (for example: for the entire school year, for six weeks after the cast is removed, indefinitely, for six months)
    g. **cost** of the therapy
    h. **how** this cost is **paid** (private pay, insurance, funding program)
    i. amount of **uncovered cost** of this therapy
    j. **incidental costs** of this therapy—transportation, caregiver, supplies, meals, equipment
    k. **who takes** the child to the therapy

    Obtain similar information for all ongoing medical treatments of the child or parent.

32. What are the **expectations** regarding **future therapies, medications, and medical treatments**? Ask about this subject through interrogatories and/or depositions. Follow up with Request for Production of Documents. Obtain authoritative and scholarly materials to educate yourself and the court on the future therapies and medications relative to the child's or parent's particular condition. Research your state and local court evidentiary rules regarding admissibility of this evidence. Obtain all appropriate releases.
33. Is the child or parent on a **waiting list** for any therapy, program, school, or funding? Ask about this subject through interrogatories and/or depositions. Follow up with Request for Production of Documents. Obtain all appropriate releases.
34. Itemize all **direct and indirect costs** resulting from the child's or parent's special needs, including therapy, medical treatments, doctors, other practitioners, medications, supplements, equipment, supplies, caregiver training, special nutritional requirements, special clothing and personal care item requirements, home modifications, vehicle modifications, modifications at school or work, nonparental caregiver costs, transportation, and any other costs. Ask about this subject through interrogatories and/or depositions. Follow up with Request for Production of Documents. Obtain all appropriate releases. Obtain admissible evidence for all billing, invoices, and receipts.
35. Laundry list of items the discovery file should contain:
    - **Medical** reports, test results, diagnoses
    - Evaluations
    - Treatment plans
    - Therapy plans
    - Medication plans
    - Child's or parent's **safety plans** for home, school, work, and away
    - Medical **bills**
    - Documentation of all **costs**—see checklist 1
    - **IEPs** (Individual Education Plans) and **504 Plans** current and previous (IEPs and 504 Plans are discussed in footnote 1.)
    - **Information** on every treating **professional**—see checklist 1
    - Copies of **articles** or **book excerpts** providing basic information on child's or parent's particular **condition**
    - Detailed therapy and treatment **schedule**
    - Detailed daily schedule

    Ask about these subjects through interrogatories and/or depositions. Follow up with Request for Production of Documents. Obtain all appropriate releases. Obtain admissible evidence for all reports, documents, billing, invoices, and receipts.

7. TEMPORARY ORDERS—DO YOU NEED TO FILE A PDL MOTION (INTERIM ORDER)?

In addition to the standard reasons for filing a PDL Motion (Motion for Orders Pendente Lite), the following situations might be appropriate for PDL Motions in *divorce cases involving special needs children:*

1. Is a PDL Order necessary to **prevent** the child from **losing** medical treatment, therapy, medication, or any other item currently received?
2. Is a PDL Order necessary to **compel one parent to cooperate** with the child's medical treatment, therapy, medication, or any other item?
3. Is **financial contribution** necessary for the child's special needs, and to **wait** until a final hearing would **cause** the child **harm**?

4. Is an interim order resolving **physical custody**, **visitation**, or **legal custody** issues necessary for the child's special needs, and to **wait** until a final hearing would **cause** the child **harm**?
5. Is an interim order resolving maintenance, payment of household bills, or other **financial matters** necessary for the child's special needs, and to **wait** until a final hearing would **cause** the child **harm**?
6. Is an interim order to **maintain status quo** or to **make changes** regarding any other topic necessary for the child's special needs, and to **wait** until a final hearing would **cause** the child **harm**?

8. CHILD SUPPORT—SPECIAL CONSIDERATIONS REGARDING CHILD SUPPORT

In addition to the standard child support considerations, the following items should be considered when determining the amount of child support needed in a *divorce involving a special needs child:*

1. Costs of therapy
2. Doctor bills, uncovered amounts and co-pays
3. Bills of other practitioners, uncovered amounts and co-pays
4. Medications, uncovered medications and co-pays
5. Cost of supplements
6. Cost of equipment
7. Expenditures for supplies
8. Expenses of caregiver training
9. Extra cost of special nutritional requirements
10. Extra cost of special clothing and personal care item requirements
11. Cost of home modifications
12. Cost of vehicle modifications
13. Cost of modifications at school
14. Nonparental caregiver costs
15. Transportation expenses
16. Any other costs

You can use this checklist as a starting point for evaluating the appropriate amount of spousal support needed for a parent with special needs.

9. CUSTODY—SPECIAL CONSIDERATIONS REGARDING CUSTODY

In addition to the standard custody considerations, the following items should be considered when determining the physical and legal custody of the *special needs child in a divorce:*

1. Who has been the **primary caregiver**?
2. To whom is the child **bonded**?
3. What has been each **parent's response** to the child's special needs?
4. How **supportive** and **cooperative** has each parent been of the child's special needs and treatment?
5. What are the **daily schedules** of each parent?
6. What **training** has each parent had regarding the child's special needs?

7. How **involved** is each parent in the child's daily care; transportation to doctors, therapists, and treatments; medication administration; home therapy and modifications; administrative aspects of the child's special needs, such as making appointments, researching options available for the child, determining a course of treatment or action plan?
8. How has each parent's **life changed** since the child was diagnosed?
9. How will the various custody alternatives **affect the child's** schedule, comfort, treatments, therapies, medication administration?
10. What do the child's **therapists and medical professionals suggest** as the custody arrangement that would be in the child's best interests?
11. **What does the child want?**

Having special needs should not automatically preclude a parent from having custody. The attorneys and judge should go through a mental exercise similar to these 11 questions when evaluating appropriate custody arrangements.

10. VISITATION—SPECIAL CONSIDERATIONS REGARDING VISITATION

In addition to the standard visitation considerations, the following items should be considered when determining the visitation of the special needs child in a divorce:

1. **How likely** is the noncustodial parent to **follow through** on the child's **medication, treatments**, and **appointments** during their periods of visitation?
2. **How likely** is the noncustodial parent to **follow through** on the child's **daily care** during their periods of visitation?
3. **How likely** is the noncustodial parent to **follow through** on maintaining the **consistency** of the child's schedule and routines during their periods of visitation?
4. **Where** will the visitation occur? Will this setting be **appropriate** for the child's condition? Will the child be **comfortable** and **safe** there? Will it be an appropriate **environment** for the child?
5. How will the various visitation alternatives **affect the child's** schedule, comfort, treatments, therapies, medication administration?
6. What do the child's **therapists and medical professionals suggest** as the visitation arrangement that would be in the child's best interests?
7. **What does the child want?**

Having special needs should not automatically preclude a parent from having visitation. The attorneys and judge should go through a mental exercise similar to these seven questions when evaluating appropriate visitation arrangements.

11. SUPPORT SYSTEMS FOR THE SPECIAL NEEDS CHILD—HELP FOR THE SPECIAL NEEDS CHILD DURING AND AFTER DIVORCE

The following entities can be helpful and supportive to a special needs *child whose parents are going through divorce:*

1. Child's **doctors** and medical professionals
2. Child's **therapists**
3. **Other children** in therapy/treatment with child
4. **School counselor**

5. **Clergy**
6. Books and materials for child's particular special needs
7. **Counselor** recommended by child's treating professionals
8. **Classmates**
9. **Divorce support groups** for children
10. **Child's existing circle** of friends, neighbors, and family

12. PROPERTY DISTRIBUTION—SPECIAL CONSIDERATIONS REGARDING PROPERTY DISTRIBUTION, INCLUDING RETIREMENT ACCOUNTS

In addition to the usual considerations, the following subjects should be considered when determining property distribution, including retirement accounts *during divorce involving special needs children:*

1. Who is the primary **breadwinner**?
2. Who is the primary **caregiver**?
3. How is the **actual daily care** of the child and management of the administrative aspects of her condition apportioned between the parents?
4. Who actually **spends the time** with the child, taking him to therapy, treatments, and appointments, and doing therapy with the child?
5. How have the **schedules and jobs/careers** of each parent been affected by the child's special needs?
6. What was the **job/career picture** of each parent **prior** to the child's special needs?
7. What is the **job/career picture** of each parent **now**?
8. What is the **anticipated future job/career picture** of each parent?
9. What was the **retirement account/pension situation** of each parent **prior** to the child's special needs?
10. What is the **retirement account/pension situation** of each parent now?
11. What is the **anticipated future retirement account/pension situation** of each parent?
12. How has each parent been **affected financially** by the child's special needs?
13. If one of the parents will be required to be **unemployed or underemployed** due to the child's special needs, **how much** money do they **need** from the other parent to meet their needs?
14. How much is the other parent **able to contribute** to the unemployed or underemployed caregiver parent?
15. Is it appropriate to consider the **future impact** on the **retirement account/pension** of the unemployed or underemployed caregiver spouse?
16. Is it appropriate to have the **other parent contribute** amounts after the divorce to a **retirement account/pension** of the unemployed or underemployed caregiver spouse?

13. COUNSELING—SPECIAL ISSUES FOR COUNSELING

In addition to the usual considerations, the following subjects should be considered as issues for counseling during or following divorce involving special needs children:

Parents

1. **Guilt** of the parents over the divorce
2. **Anger** at the other parent over the **divorce**

3. **Anger** at the other parent for the **child's condition** of having special needs
4. **Resentment** toward the non-caregiver parent for **walking away** from the situation
5. **Resentment** toward the caregiver spouse over **disagreements** about in-home or residential (institutional) care of the child
6. **Fear** and **worry** about the future—financial, child's prognosis
7. **Hopelessness** and **despair** over their future
8. **Self-pity** and **disappointment** over how their lives have changed, contrary to expectations

Special Needs Children

1. **Guilt** of the special needs child, feeling she caused the divorce
2. **Anger** at the parents for getting divorced
3. **Resentment** of children toward the non-caregiver parent
4. **Fear** of the **unknown**, of the future
5. **Adjustment** to the new routines, new home environments, new spouses or significant others of parent(s)
6. **Transitions, predictability**
7. **Fear** that the caregiver parent will **abandon** them or **institutionalize** them
8. **Fear** that if caregiver parent becomes involved with a **boyfriend** or **girlfriend** that the caregiver parent may **leave the child behind**, especially if non-caregiver parent became involved with a boyfriend or girlfriend during the divorce
9. Wanting to **punish** parent they feel is at **fault**

Siblings of Special Needs Children

1. **Blaming** the special needs child, feeling she caused the divorce
2. **Guilt** about **blaming** the special needs child, feeling she caused the divorce
3. **Anger** at the parents for getting divorced
4. **Resentment** toward the special needs child
5. **Envy** of the extra time spent on the care of the special needs child
6. **Fear** of the **unknown**, of the future
7. **Adjustment** to the new routines, new home environments, new spouses or significant others of parent(s)
8. **Transitions, predictability**
9. **Fear** that the caregiver parent will **abandon** them
10. **Fear** that if caregiver parent becomes involved with a **boyfriend** or **girlfriend** that the caregiver parent may **leave the child behind**, especially if non-caregiver parent became involved with a boyfriend or girlfriend during the divorce
11. Wanting to **punish** parent they feel is at **fault**

Glossary

504 Plan—a legally binding and enforceable document identifying the disability that qualifies the child for reasonable accommodation such as taking necessary medication or having longer test-taking time, and providing a detailed plan for such reasonable accommodation. Does not involve specialized instruction, as in an Individualized Educational Plan (IEP). Not as involved as an IEP. *See also* Individualized Educational Plan.

abuse, alcohol—continued excessive or compulsive use of alcoholic drinks.

abuse, child—to treat a child in such a way as to cause injury or damage.

abuse, drug—continued excessive or compulsive use of legal or illegal drugs.

addiction—compulsive physiological need for and use of a habit-forming substance characterized by well-defined physiological symptoms upon withdrawal.

ADHD/ADD—a catchall term referring to a problem that interferes with a person's ability to maintain attention and stay focused on meaningful tasks, control his impulses, and regulate his activity level.

adjustment disorder—defined in *The Merck Manual* as "[a]n acute response to environmental stress by an adolescent with a basically good adaptive capacity; symptoms abate as stress diminishes."

Affidavit for Dissolution—a written statement of facts that is made under oath and notarized, that stipulates all the facts necessary for a divorce to be granted without the necessity of a formal hearing.

AIDS/HIV (acquired immune deficiency syndrome)—disease of the human immune system caused by infection with HIV (human immunodeficiency virus); commonly transmitted in infected blood, especially during illicit intravenous drug use and in bodily secretions during sexual intercourse.

alcohol abuse—continued excessive or compulsive use of alcoholic drinks.

alimony—spousal support, also known as maintenance.

allergies—extreme or pathological reaction (sneezing, difficulty breathing, a chain of skin rashes) to substances, situations, or physical states that are without comparable effect on the average individual.

Answer—the response to a Petition.

Asperger's syndrome—a developmental disorder resembling autism characterized by impaired social interaction, restricted interests, and repetitive patterns of behavior, yet with normal language and cognitive development.

assets—property of value. This can include the house, real estate, vehicles, retirement accounts, bank accounts, household furnishings, cash, and other items of value.

asthma—chronic lung disorder marked by recurrent episodes of airway obstruction; presents as labored breathing with wheezing, coughing, and a sense of chest constriction, often triggered by hyperreactivity to certain stimuli such as allergens or significant sudden change in air temperature.

attention deficit disorder—*See* ADHD/ADD.

attention deficit hyperactivity disorder—*See* ADHD/ADD.

autism—considered a lifelong neurological disability; usually appears during the first two or three years of life and severely impairs sensory processing, communication (both verbal and nonverbal), socialization, problem solving, and development.

behavioral problems—found frequently in children with learning disorders; include difficulty with impulse control, discipline problems, withdrawal, avoidance, shyness, excessive fears, and aggressiveness.

bipolar disorder—an illness involving extreme mood swings that affect the person's perceptions, emotions, and behavior.

blindness and visual impairment—lack of or deficiency in sight.

cancer—a malignant tumor of potentially unlimited growth that expands locally by means of invasion and systemically through metastasis.

celiac disease—a chronic hereditary intestinal disorder consisting of the inability to absorb the gliadin portion of gluten, which triggers an immune response that damages the intestinal mucosa.

cerebral palsy—a disability resulting from damage to the brain before, during, or shortly after birth; the disability is manifested outwardly by muscular incoordination and speech disturbances.

child abuse—to treat a child in such a way as to cause injury or damage.

child custody—physical custody relates to where the child lives; legal custody refers to decision-making responsibility of the parent or parents.

childhood schizophrenia—disorder characterized by withdrawal, flattened affect (lack of facial expression), apathy, thought disorder (blocking and perseveration), ideas of reference, hallucinations, delusions, and complaints of thought control.

child support—money one parent pays to the other parent to help meet the financial needs of a minor child.

chronic illness—suffering from a disease or ailment of long duration or frequent recurrence, often marked by slowly progressing seriousness.

cognitive problems—problems in thinking, reasoning, and problem solving.

conduct disorder—defined in *The Merck Manual* as "[a] recurrent or persistent pattern of behavior that includes aggression toward people and animals, destruction of property, deceitfulness or theft, and serious violation of rules."

Crohn's disease—chronic ileitis that usually involves the distal portion of the ileum and spreads to the colon; it is characterized by diarrhea, cramping, appetite loss, weight loss, local abscesses, and scarring.

custody—*See* child custody.

cystic fibrosis—a hereditary disease involving functional disorder of the exocrine glands and presenting as faulty digestion from deficiency of pancreatic enzymes, breathing difficulty from accumulation of mucus in the airways, and excessive loss of salt in the sweat.

deafness and hearing impairment—lacking or deficient in the sense of hearing.

Decree of Dissolution—divorce decree. The written order by the judge that grants the divorce and handles the various issues raised in the case.

depression—a mood disorder marked by sadness, inactivity, difficulty thinking, and concentrating, significant increase or decrease in appetite, significant increase or decrease in time spent sleeping, feelings of hopelessness, and sometimes suicidal thoughts or suicide attempts.

developmental disorders—a group of severe conditions caused by mental and/or physical impairments. These delays/impairments may include communication development, physical/motor development, cognitive development, social/emotional development, and/or adaptive/self-help development.

diabetes—a disorder of carbohydrate metabolism caused by a combination of heredity and environmental factors. Usually involves insufficient secretion or utilization of insulin, excessive urine production, excessive amounts of sugar in the blood and urine, thirst, hunger, and weight loss.

diagnosis—the identification of a disease or disorder from its signs and symptoms.

disability—the inability to pursue an occupation, or the impairment in daily activities and/or education because of physical or mental impairment. *See also* specific disabilities in glossary.

discovery—things lawyers do to get information on a lawsuit. Some types of discovery are depositions, interrogatories, requests for production of documents, requests for admissions, and subpoena duces tecum.

dissolution of marriage—the end of a marriage, also known as divorce.

divorce—the end of a marriage, also known as dissolution of marriage.

Down syndrome—a congenital chromosomal condition that affects the development of the brain and the body and causes mental retardation.

drug abuse—continued excessive or compulsive use of legal or illegal drugs.

drug addiction—compulsive physiological need for and use of a drug, legal or illegal, characterized by well-defined physiological symptoms upon withdrawal.

dyslexia—a disorder or difficulty with the use and understanding of language. This can affect all aspects of the use of language: listening, speaking, reading, writing, and spelling.

eating disorders—any of several psychological disorders, such as anorexia nervosa or bulimia, characterized by serious disturbances of eating behavior.

emancipation—the age at which the child becomes a legal adult and the parents are no longer legally responsible for her care.

emotional disturbance—a condition that continues over a long period of time and at such a level that it affects a child's academic performance and/or social relationships and is characterized by inability to learn without known intellectual, sensory, or health causes; inability to maintain social relationships with peers and/or teachers; inappropriate behavior or feelings; general pervasive unhappy or depressed mood; and/or tendency for personal or social problems to result in physical symptoms or fear.

epilepsy—various disorders marked by abnormal brain electrical activity and typically manifested by sudden brief episodes of altered or diminish consciousness, involuntary movements, or convulsions.

evidence—testimony and items that are relevant to the case, and offered by the attorneys for acceptance by the court to prove or disprove allegations in the case. These may include the usual divorce case evidence, such as bank records and employment records. In a special needs case, they may also include individualized educational plans (IEPs), medical records, school records, therapy records, and treatment plans.

fetal alcohol syndrome—a collection of symptoms caused by the mother's chronic alcohol consumption during pregnancy. The symptoms include mental retardation, growth retardation, facial abnormalities, and developmental delays.

fragile X syndrome—a collection of symptoms caused by an abnormality of the X chromosome. The symptoms include facial abnormalities and mental retardation as well as impairment in communication, behavior, social skills, and motor skills.

guardian ad litem—the lawyer appointed by the court to represent the children when the court feels it is necessary. It may be necessary because people have raised credible issues of child abuse, neglect, abandonment, drug or alcohol abuse, or special needs. It may also be necessary when the parents are so contentious with each other that the court feels the children's needs are not being properly addressed by the parents.

headache—pain in the head.

hearing impairment—permanent or fluctuating impairment in hearing; includes but is not limited to deafness.

heart disorders and disease—an abnormal condition of the heart or of the heart and circulation.

HIV/AIDS (acquired immune deficiency syndrome)—disease of the human immune system caused by infection with HIV (human immunodeficiency virus); commonly transmitted in infected blood especially during illicit intravenous drug use and in bodily secretions during sexual intercourse.

Hodgkin's disease—a malignant lymphoma marked by the presence of Reed-Sternberg cells and characterized by progressive enlargement of lymph nodes, spleen, and liver and by progressive anemia.

Individualized Educational Plan (IEP)—a legally binding and enforceable document identifying the disability that qualifies the child for special education and related services, and specifically stating the impact of the child's disability on the educational setting, itemizing the number of minutes per week the child will receive of special services, and clearly delineating measurable goals. An IEP is designed to be used in cases that require specialized instruction, not just reasonable accommodation. It is more involved than a 504 Plan. *See also* 504 Plan.

Individuals with Disabilities Education Act of 2004—Federal law mandating that all children with disabilities have available to them free and appropriate public education, which education provides the special education and related services necessary and is designed to meet the children's unique needs and prepare them for employment and independent living.

institutional care—the care of children, or ill or disabled people in what have, historically, been large, isolated hospital-like establishments. The modern trend has been toward smaller, community-based institutions.

interrogatories—type of discovery used by lawyers to obtain information in a case. Written questions that must be answered in writing under oath, within a certain number of days.

kidney disease—an abnormal condition of the kidneys/renal system.

language disabilities—difficulty in communication skills, articulation, oral-motor skills, and the physical act of communicating a verbal message. *See also* speech and language.

learning disabilities—any of various disorders that interfere with a person's ability to learn, resulting in impaired verbal language function, impaired reasoning, or impaired academic skills. Sometimes thought to be caused by difficulties in processing and integrating information; also called *learning disorders.*

legal custody—decision-making authority regarding the major issues concerning the child, such as medical care, religion, and education.

leukemia—an acute or chronic disease characterized by abnormal increase in the white blood cell count in bodily tissues with or without corresponding increase of those in the circulating blood.

liver disease—disorder or disease in the very large vascular glandular organ, the liver.

lymphomas—usually malignant tumors of lymphoid tissue.

maintenance—spousal support, also known as alimony.

medication—a substance used to cure disease or relieve pain.

mental disorder; mental illness—a mental or bodily condition marked by a sufficient disorganization of personality, mind, and emotions; results in serious impairment of normal psychological function.

mental retardation—characterized by significantly below-average intellectual functioning, with an IQ of 70 or less, as well as resulting impairments in the ability to adapt.

migraine headache—recurrent and usually unilateral severe headache, often accompanied by nausea and vomiting.

multiple disabilities—having more than one disability.

multiple sclerosis (MS)—a demyelinating disease marked by hardened tissue in the brain or spinal cord, usually associated with partial or complete paralysis and with a jerking muscle tremor.

muscular disorders—disorders involving or relating to muscles.

myelomas—a primary tumor of bone marrow, usually involving several different bones at the same time.

neuromuscular disorders—disorders and anomalies of the nerves and muscles.

non-Hodgkin's lymphoma—various malignant lymphomas that are not classified as Hodgkin's disease but do have malignant cells; this condition is characterized by enlarged lymph nodes, fever, night sweats, fatigue, and weight loss.

obesity—excessive accumulation and storage of fat in the body. In an adult, obesity is typically defined as having a body mass index of 30 or greater.

occupational therapy—therapy that includes valuation, assessment, treatment, and consultation. It involves the use of physical activity to maximize and maintain the potential of individuals who are limited by injury, illness, impairment, learning disability, developmental disability, or mental illness.

oppositional defiant disorder (ODD)—disorder that has similar features to conduct disorder because it involves negative, angry, and defiant behavior toward authority figures. ODD does not have a persistent pattern of behavior.

orthopedic impairment—a deformity, disorder, or injury of the skeleton and associated structures.

other health impairment—having a condition or conditions that adversely affect a child's academic performance and/or social relationships due to chronic or acute health problems, including but not limited to asthma, attention deficit disorder, attention deficit hyperactivity disorder, diabetes, epilepsy, heart condition, hemophilia, lead poisoning, leukemia, nephritis, rheumatic fever, and/or sickle-cell anemia.

pervasive developmental disorder (PDD)—similar to autism, often confused with autism. PDD is a less severe disorder than autism. It involves impairment in social interaction, communication, and behavior and usually has some sensory involvement.

physical custody—refers to where the child lives.

physical therapy—therapy designed to improve the patient's physical abilities through activities designed to improve muscle control and motor coordination.

posttraumatic stress disorder (PTSD)—*See* PTSD.

pregnancy—containing a developing embryo, fetus, or unborn offspring within the body.

psychiatric issues—dealing with cases of mental disorder.

psychological issues—relating to the mind, especially in its affective or cognitive functions.

PTSD (posttraumatic stress disorder)—disorder that can occur after major traumatic events even in otherwise stable children and adolescents.

respite care—child care that makes it possible for the primary caregiver parent to run errands and attend to other necessary functions and activities that are not possible while caring for the special needs child.

screening—*See* diagnosis.

seizures—convulsions, sensory disturbances or loss of consciousness resulting from abnormal electrical discharges in the brain.

sensory integration disorder—impairment at a neurological level in the way the brain perceives and processes sensory information. This disorder may cause impairment in emotions, attention, movement, relationships, or adaptive responses.

sexual abuse—to treat a person in a sexual manner in such a way as to cause injury or damage.

sexual assault—illegal sexual contact that usually involves force upon a person without their consent or is inflicted upon a person who is incapable of giving consent.

sexually transmitted diseases (STDs)—various diseases or infections that can be transmitted by direct sexual contact. Syphilis, chlamydia, genital herpes, and gonorrhea are chiefly spread through sexual means. Some STDs, such as hepatitis B and AIDS, can be spread through nonsexual means.

sickle-cell anemia—a chronic anemia characterized by destruction of red blood cells and episodic blocking of blood vessels by the adherence of sickle cells. Sickle cells are abnormal red blood cells of a crescent shape.

special needs—one or more chronic or acute physical, developmental, behavioral, or emotional condition that requires health and/or related services of a type or amount greater than that needed by children generally.

special needs child—a child who has one or more chronic or acute physical, developmental, behavioral, or emotional condition that requires health and/or related services of a type or amount greater than that needed by children generally.

special needs coordinator—a person who serves as a facilitator to the process of special needs being properly addressed in divorce cases.

speech/language impairment—difficulty in communication skills, articulation, oral-motor skills, and the physical act of communicating a verbal message.

spina bifida—a neural tube defect marked by congenital defect of the spinal column, usually with hernial protrusion of the meninges and sometimes the spinal cord.

spousal support—money paid by a person to his or her former spouse, for the support of that former spouse. *Also known as* alimony or maintenance.

stress—a physical, chemical, or emotional factor that causes bodily or mental tension and may be a factor in disease causation.

substance abuse disorder—compulsive physiological need for and use of a habit-forming substance, legal or illegal, characterized by well-defined physiological symptoms upon withdrawal.

suicide—taking one's own life voluntarily and intentionally.

TBI (traumatic brain injury)—occurs when a sudden physical assault on the head causes damage to the brain.

terminally ill child—a child who is in the final stages of a fatal disease, near death.

therapy—therapeutic treatment of a bodily, mental, or behavioral disorder.

trauma—an injury to living tissue caused by an outside force.

traumatic brain injury—*See* TBI.

treatment—to care for by medical or surgical means.

visual impairment—impairment to the vision, including but not limited to blindness.

Index